The Java™
Virtual Machine
Specification

Second Edition

The Java™ Series

Lisa Friendly, Series Editor

Tim Lindholm, Technical Editor

Please see our web site (http://www.awl.com /cseng/javaseries) for more information on these titles.

Ken Arnold and James Gosling, *The Java™ Programming Language, Second Edition*
ISBN 0-201-31006-6

Mary Campione and Kathy Walrath, *The Java™ Tutorial, Second Edition: Object-Oriented Programming for the Internet* (Book/CD)
ISBN 0-201-31007-4

Mary Campione, Kathy Walrath, Alison Huml, and the Tutorial Team, *The Java™ Tutorial Continued: The Rest of the JDK™* (Book/CD)
ISBN 0-201-48558-3

Patrick Chan, *The Java™ Developers Almanac 1999*
ISBN 0-201-43298-6

Patrick Chan and Rosanna Lee, *The Java™ Class Libraries, Second Edition, Volume 2: java.applet, java.awt, java.beans*
ISBN 0-201-31003-1

Patrick Chan, Rosanna Lee, and Doug Kramer, *The Java™ Class Libraries, Second Edition, Volume 1: java.io, java.lang, java.math, java.net, java.text, java.util*
ISBN 0-201-31002-3

Patrick Chan, Rosanna Lee, and Doug Kramer, *The Java™ Class Libraries, Second Edition, Volume 1: 1.2 Supplement*
ISBN 0-201-48552-4

James Gosling, Bill Joy, and Guy Steele, *The Java™ Language Specification*
ISBN 0-201-63451-1

James Gosling, Frank Yellin, and The Java Team, *The Java™ Application Programming Interface, Volume 1: Core Packages*
ISBN 0-201-63453-8

James Gosling, Frank Yellin, and The Java Team, *The Java™ Application Programming Interface, Volume 2: Window Toolkit and Applets*
ISBN 0-201-63459-7

Graham Hamilton, Rick Cattell, and Maydene Fisher, *JDBC™ Database Access with Java™: A Tutorial and Annotated Reference*
ISBN 0-201-30995-5

Jonni Kanerva, *The Java™ FAQ*
ISBN 0-201-63456-2

Doug Lea, *Concurrent Programming in Java™: Design Principles and Patterns*
ISBN 0-201-69581-2

Tim Lindholm and Frank Yellin, *The Java™ Virtual Machine Specification*
ISBN 0-201-63452-X

Henry Sowizral, Kevin Rushforth, and Michael Deering, *The Java™ 3D API Specification*
ISBN 0-201-32576-4

The Java™
Virtual Machine
Specification

Second Edition

Tim Lindholm
Frank Yellin

ADDISON-WESLEY

An imprint of Addison Wesley Longman, Inc.

Reading, Massachusetts • Harlow, England • Menlo Park, California
Berkeley, California • Don Mills, Ontario • Sydney
Bonn • Amsterdam • Tokyo • Mexico City

Library of Congress Cataloging-in-Publication Data

Lindholm, Tim
    The Java virtual machine specification / Tim Lindholm, Frank
  Yellin. -- 2nd ed.
      p.   cm.
    Includes bibliographical references and index.
    ISBN 0-201-43294-3
    1. Java (Computer program language) 2. Internet (Computer
  network) 3. Virtual computer systems.   I. Yellin, Frank.
  II. Title.
  QA76.73.J38L56 1999
  005.13'3--dc21   99-18470
                                          CIP

Text printed on recycled and acid-free paper

1 2 3 4 5 6 7 8 9 -MA- 03 02 01 00 99
First printing, April 1999

Contents

Preface

T HE Java™ virtual machine specification has been written to fully document the design of the Java virtual machine. It is essential for compiler writers who wish to target the Java virtual machine and for programmers who want to implement a compatible Java virtual machine. It is also a definitive source for anyone who wants to know exactly how the Java programming language is implemented.

The Java virtual machine is an abstract machine. References to the *Java virtual machine* throughout this specification refer to this abstract machine rather than to Sun's or any other specific implementation. This book serves as documentation for a concrete implementation of the Java virtual machine only as a blueprint documents a house. An implementation of the Java virtual machine (known as a runtime interpreter) must embody this specification, but is constrained by it only where absolutely necessary.

The Java virtual machine specified here will support the Java programming language specified in *The Java™ Language Specification* (Addison-Wesley, 1996). It is compatible with the Java platform implemented by Sun's JDK™ releases 1.0.2 and 1.1 and the Java® 2 platform implemented by Sun's Java® 2 SDK, Standard Edition, v1.2 (formerly known as JDK release 1.2).

We intend that this specification should sufficiently document the Java virtual machine to make possible compatible clean-room implementations. If you are considering constructing your own Java virtual machine implementation, feel free to contact us to obtain assistance to ensure the 100% compatibility of your implementation.

Send comments on this specification or questions about implementing the Java virtual machine to our electronic mail address: jvm@java.sun.com. To learn the latest about the Java 2 platform, or to download the latest Java 2 SDK release, visit our World Wide Web site at http://java.sun.com. For updated information about the Java Series, including errata for *The Java™ Virtual Machine Specification*, and previews of forthcoming books, visit http://java.sun.com/Series.

The virtual machine that evolved into the Java virtual machine was originally designed by James Gosling in 1992 to support the Oak programming language. The evolution into its present form occurred through the direct and indirect efforts of many people and spanned Sun's Green project, FirstPerson, Inc., the LiveOak project, the Java Products Group, JavaSoft, and today, Sun's Java Software. The authors are grateful to the many contributors and supporters.

This book began as internal project documentation. Kathy Walrath edited that early draft, helping to give the world its first look at the internals of the Java programming language. It was then converted to HTML by Mary Campione and was made available on our Web site before being expanded into book form.

The creation of *The Java*™ *Virtual Machine Specification* owes much to the support of the Java Products Group led by General Manager Ruth Hennigar, to the efforts of series editor Lisa Friendly, and to editor Mike Hendrickson and his group at Addison-Wesley. The many criticisms and suggestions received from reviewers of early online drafts, as well as drafts of the printed book, improved its quality immensely. We owe special thanks to Richard Tuck for his careful review of the manuscript and to the authors of *The Java*™ *Language Specification*, Addison-Wesley, 1996, for allowing us to quote extensively from that book. Particular thanks to Bill Joy whose comments, reviews, and guidance have contributed greatly to the completeness and accuracy of this book.

Notes on the Second Edition

The second edition of *The Java*™ *Virtual Machine Specification* brings the specification of the Java virtual machine up to date with the Java® 2 platform, v1.2. It also includes many corrections and clarifications that update the presentation of the specification without changing the logical specification itself. We have attempted to correct typos and errata (hopefully without introducing new ones) and to add more detail to the specification where it was vague or ambiguous. In particular, we corrected a number of inconsistencies between the first edition of *The Java*™ *Virtual Machine Specification* and *The Java*™ *Language Specification*.

We thank the many readers who combed through the first edition of this book and brought problems to our attention. Several individuals and groups deserve special thanks for pointing out problems or contributing directly to the new material:

Carla Schroer and her teams of compatibility testers in Cupertino, California, and Novosibirsk, Russia (with special thanks to Leonid Arbouzov and Alexei

Kaigorodov), painstakingly wrote compatibility tests for each testable assertion in the first edition. In the process they uncovered many places where the original specification was unclear or incomplete.

Jeroen Vermeulen, Janice Shepherd, Peter Bertelsen, Roly Perera, Joe Darcy, and Sandra Loosemore have all contributed comments and feedback that have improved this edition.

Marilyn Rash and Hilary Selby Polk of Addison Wesley Longman helped us to improve the readability and layout of this edition at the same time as we were incorporating all the technical changes.

Special thanks go to Gilad Bracha, who has brought a new level of rigor to the presentation and has been a major contributor to much of the new material, especially chapters 4 and 5 and the new "Appendix: Summary of Clarifications and Amendments." His dedication to "computational theology" and his commitment to resolving inconsistencies between *The Java*™ *Virtual Machine Specification* and *The Java*™ *Language Specification* have benefited this book tremendously.

Tim Lindholm
Frank Yellin
Java Software, Sun Microsystems, Inc.

References

IEEE Standard for Binary Floating-Point Arithmetic, ANSI/IEEE Std. 754-1985. Available from Global Engineering Documents, 15 Inverness Way East, Englewood, Colorado 80112-5704 USA, +1 800 854 7179.

Hoare, C.A.R. *Hints on Programming Language Design*. Stanford University Computer Science Department Technical Report No CS-73-403, December 1973. Reprinted in Sigact/Sigplan Symposium on Principles of Programming Languages. Association for Computing Machinery, New York, October 1973.

Unicode Consortium, The. *The Unicode Standard: Worldwide Character Encoding*, Version 1.0, Volume 1, ISBN 0-201-56788-1, and Volume 2, ISBN 0-201-60845-6. Updates and additions necessary to bring the Unicode Standard up to version 1.1 may be found at http://www.unicode.org.

Unicode Consortium, The. *The Unicode Standard, Version 2.0*, ISBN 0-201-48345-9. Updates and additions necessary to bring the Unicode Standard up to version 2.1 may be found at http://www.unicode.org.

CHAPTER 1

Introduction

1.1 A Bit of History

THE Java™ programming language is a general-purpose object-oriented concurrent language. Its syntax is similar to C and C++, but it omits many of the features that make C and C++ complex, confusing, and unsafe. The Java platform was initially developed to address the problems of building software for networked consumer devices. It was designed to support multiple host architectures and to allow secure delivery of software components. To meet these requirements, compiled code had to survive transport across networks, operate on any client, and assure the client that it was safe to run.

The popularization of the World Wide Web made these attributes much more interesting. The Internet demonstrated how media-rich content could be made accessible in simple ways. Web browsers such as Mosaic enabled millions of people to roam the Net and made Web surfing part of popular culture. At last there was a medium where what you saw and heard was essentially the same whether you were using a Mac, PC, or UNIX machine, and whether you were connected to a high-speed network or a slow modem.

Web enthusiasts soon discovered that the content supported by the Web's HTML document format was too limited. HTML extensions, such as forms, only highlighted those limitations, while making it clear that no browser could include all the features users wanted. Extensibility was the answer.

Sun's HotJava™ browser showcases the interesting properties of the Java programming language and platform by making it possible to embed programs inside HTML pages. These programs are transparently downloaded into the HotJava browser along with the HTML pages in which they appear. Before being accepted by the browser, the programs are carefully checked to make sure they are safe.

Like HTML pages, compiled programs are network- and host-independent. The programs behave the same way regardless of where they come from or what kind of machine they are being loaded into and run on.

A Web browser incorporating the Java or Java 2 platform is no longer limited to a predetermined set of capabilities. Visitors to Web pages incorporating dynamic content can be assured that their machines cannot be damaged by that content. Programmers can write a program once, and it will run on any machine supplying a Java or Java 2 runtime environment.

1.2 The Java Virtual Machine

The Java virtual machine is the cornerstone of the Java and Java 2 platforms. It is the component of the technology responsible for its hardware- and operating system-independence, the small size of its compiled code, and its ability to protect users from malicious programs.

The Java virtual machine is an abstract computing machine. Like a real computing machine, it has an instruction set and manipulates various memory areas at run time. It is reasonably common to implement a programming language using a virtual machine; the best-known virtual machine may be the P-Code machine of UCSD Pascal.

The first prototype implementation of the Java virtual machine, done at Sun Microsystems, Inc., emulated the Java virtual machine instruction set in software hosted by a handheld device that resembled a contemporary Personal Digital Assistant (PDA). Sun's current Java virtual machine implementations, components of its Java® 2 SDK and Java® 2 Runtime Environment products, emulate the Java virtual machine on Win32 and Solaris™ hosts in much more sophisticated ways. However, the Java virtual machine does not assume any particular implementation technology, host hardware, or host operating system. It is not inherently interpreted, but can just as well be implemented by compiling its instruction set to that of a silicon CPU. It may also be implemented in microcode or directly in silicon.

The Java virtual machine knows nothing of the Java programming language, only of a particular binary format, the `class` file format. A `class` file contains Java virtual machine instructions (or *bytecodes*) and a symbol table, as well as other ancillary information.

For the sake of security, the Java virtual machine imposes strong format and structural constraints on the code in a `class` file. However, any language with functionality that can be expressed in terms of a valid `class` file can be hosted by the Java virtual machine. Attracted by a generally available, machine-independent platform, implementors of other languages are turning to the Java virtual machine as a delivery vehicle for their languages.

1.3 Summary of Chapters

The rest of this book is structured as follows:

- Chapter 2 gives an overview of Java programming language concepts and terminology necessary for the rest of the book.

- Chapter 3 gives an overview of the Java virtual machine architecture.

- Chapter 4 specifies the `class` file format, the hardware- and operating system-independent binary format used to represent compiled classes and interfaces.

- Chapter 5 specifies the start-up of the Java virtual machine and the loading, linking, and initialization of classes and interfaces.

- Chapter 6 specifies the instruction set of the Java virtual machine, presenting the instructions in alphabetical order of opcode mnemonics.

- Chapter 7 introduces compilation of code written in the Java programming language into the instruction set of the Java virtual machine.

- Chapter 8 describes Java virtual machine threads and their interaction with memory.

- Chapter 9 gives a table of Java virtual machine opcode mnemonics indexed by opcode value.

1.4 Notation

Throughout this book we refer to classes and interfaces drawn from the Java and Java 2 platforms. Whenever we refer to a class or interface using a single identifier *N*, the intended reference is to the class or interface `java.lang.`*N*. We use the fully qualified name for classes from packages other than `java.lang`.

    Whenever we refer to a class or interface that is declared in the package `java` or any of its subpackages, the intended reference is to that class or interface as loaded by the bootstrap class loader (§5.3.1). Whenever we refer to a subpackage of a package named `java`, the intended reference is to that subpackage as determined by the bootstrap class loader.

The use of fonts in this book is as follows:

- A `fixed width` font is used for code examples written in the Java programming language, Java virtual machine data types, exceptions, and errors.

- *Italic* is used for Java virtual machine "assembly language," its opcodes and operands, as well as items in the Java virtual machine's runtime data areas. It is also used to introduce new terms and simply for emphasis.

CHAPTER 2

Java Programming Language Concepts

THE Java virtual machine was designed to support the Java programming language. Some concepts and vocabulary from the Java programming language are thus useful when attempting to understand the virtual machine. This chapter gives an overview intended to support the specification of the Java virtual machine, but is not itself a part of that specification.

The content of this chapter has been condensed from the first edition of *The Java*™ *Language Specification*, by James Gosling, Bill Joy, and Guy Steele.[1] Readers familiar with the Java programming language, but not with *The Java*™ *Language Specification*, should at least skim this chapter for the terminology it introduces. Any discrepancies between this chapter and *The Java*™ *Language Specification* should be resolved in favor of *The Java*™ *Language Specification*.

This chapter does not attempt to provide an introduction to the Java programming language. For such an introduction, see *The Java*™ *Programming Language, Second Edition*, by Ken Arnold and James Gosling.

2.1 Unicode

Programs written in the Java programming language supported by JDK release 1.1.7 and the Java 2 platform, v1.2 use the *Unicode* character encoding, version 2.1, as specified in *The Unicode Standard, Version 2.0*, ISBN 0-201-48345-9, and the

---

[1] Including updates for JDK release 1.1 and the Java 2 platform, v1.2, published at `http://java.sun.com`.

update information for Version 2.1 of the Unicode Standard available at `http://www.unicode.org`. Programs written in the Java programming language used version 2.0.14 of the Unicode Standard in JDK releases 1.1 through 1.1.6 and used version 1.1.5 of the Unicode Standard in JDK release 1.0.

Except for comments, identifiers (§2.2), and the contents of character and string literals (§2.3), all input elements in a program written in the Java programming language are formed from only *ASCII* characters. ASCII (ANSI X3.4) is the American Standard Code for Information Interchange. The first 128 characters of the Unicode character encoding are the ASCII characters.

2.2 Identifiers

An *identifier* is an unlimited-length sequence of Unicode *letters* and *digits*, the first of which must be a letter. Letters and digits may be drawn from the entire Unicode character set, which supports most writing scripts in use in the world today. This allows programmers to use identifiers in their programs that are written in their native languages.

The method (§2.10) `Character.isJavaLetter` returns `true` when passed a Unicode character that is considered to be a letter in an identifier. The method `Character.isJavaLetterOrDigit` returns `true` when passed a Unicode character that is considered to be a letter or digit in an identifier.

Two identifiers are the same only if they have the same Unicode character for each letter or digit; identifiers that have the same external appearance may still be different. An identifier must not be the same as a boolean literal (§2.3), the null literal (§2.3), or a keyword in the Java programming language.

2.3 Literals

A *literal* is the source code representation of a value of a primitive type (§2.4.1), the `String` type (§2.4.8), or the null type (§2.4). String literals and, more generally, strings that are the values of constant expressions are "interned" so as to share unique instances, using the method `String.intern`.

The null type has one value, the null reference, denoted by the literal `null`. The `boolean` type has two values, denoted by the literals `true` and `false`.

2.4 Types and Values

The Java programming language is *strongly typed*, which means that every variable and every expression has a type that is known at compile time. Types limit the values that a variable (§2.5) can hold or that an expression can produce, limit the operations supported on those values, and determine the meaning of those operations. Strong typing helps detect errors at compile time.

The types of the Java programming language are divided into two categories: *primitive types* (§2.4.1) and *reference types* (§2.4.6). There is also a special *null type*, the type of the expression null, which has no name. The null reference is the only possible value of an expression of null type and can always be converted to any reference type. In practice, the programmer can ignore the null type and just pretend that null is a special literal that can be of any reference type.

Corresponding to the primitive types and reference types, there are two categories of data values that can be stored in variables, passed as arguments, returned by methods, and operated upon: *primitive values* (§2.4.1) and *reference values* (§2.4.6).

2.4.1 Primitive Types and Values

A *primitive type* is a type that is predefined by the Java programming language and named by a reserved keyword. *Primitive values* do not share state with other primitive values. A variable whose type is a primitive type always holds a primitive value of that type.[2]

The primitive types are the boolean type and the *numeric types*. The numeric types are the *integral types* and the *floating-point types*.

The integral types are byte, short, int, and long, whose values are 8-bit, 16-bit, 32-bit, and 64-bit signed two's-complement integers, respectively, and char, whose values are 16-bit unsigned integers representing Unicode characters (§2.1).

The floating-point types are float and double, which are conceptually associated with the 32-bit single-precision and 64-bit double-precision IEEE 754 values and operations as specified in *IEEE Standard for Binary Floating-Point Arithmetic*, ANSI/IEEE Standard 754-1985 (IEEE, New York).

The boolean type has the truth values true and false.

---

[2] Note that a local variable is not initialized on its creation and is considered to hold a value only once it is assigned (§2.5.1).

2.4.2 Operators on Integral Values

The Java programming language provides a number of operators that act on integral values, including numerical comparison, arithmetic operators, increment and decrement, bitwise logical and shift operators, and numeric cast (§2.6.9).

Operands of certain unary and binary operators are subject to numeric promotion (§2.6.10).

The built-in integer operators do not indicate (positive or negative) overflow in any way; they wrap around on overflow. The only integer operators that can throw an exception are the integer divide and integer remainder operators, which can throw an `ArithmeticException` if the right-hand operand is zero.

Any value of any integral type may be cast to or from any numeric type. There are no casts between integral types and the type `boolean`.

2.4.3 Floating-Point Types, Value Sets, and Values

The IEEE 754 standard includes not only positive and negative sign-magnitude numbers, but also positive and negative zeros, positive and negative *infinities*, and a special *Not-a-Number* value (hereafter abbreviated as "NaN"). The NaN value is used to represent the result of certain invalid operations such as dividing zero by zero.

Every implementation of the Java programming language is required to support two standard sets of floating-point values, called the *float value set* and the *double value set*. In addition, an implementation of the Java programming language may support either or both of two extended-exponent floating-point value sets, called the *float-extended-exponent value set* and the *double-extended-exponent value set*. These extended-exponent value sets may, under certain circumstances, be used instead of the standard value sets to represent the values of expressions of type `float` or `double`.

The finite nonzero values of any floating-point value set can all be expressed in the form $s \cdot m \cdot 2^{(e - N + 1)}$, where s is +1 or −1, m is a positive integer less than 2^N, and e is an integer between $Emin = -(2^{K-1}-2)$ and $Emax = 2^{K-1}-1$, inclusive, and where N and K are parameters that depend on the value set. Some values can be represented in this form in more than one way; for example, supposing that a value v in a value set might be represented in this form using certain values for s, m, and e, then if it happened that m was even and e was less than 2^{K-1}, one could halve m and increase e by 1 to produce a second representation for the same value v. A representation in this form is called *normalized* if $m \geq 2^{N-1}$; otherwise the representation is said to be *denormalized*. If a value in a value set cannot be represented in such a way that $m \geq 2^{N-1}$, then the value is said to be a *denormalized value*, because it has no normalized representation.

The constraints on the parameters N and K (and on the derived parameters *Emin* and *Emax*) for the two required and two optional floating-point value sets are summarized in Table 2.1.

Table 2.1   Floating-point value set parameters

Parameter	float	float-extended-exponent	double	double-extended-exponent
N	24	24	53	53
K	8	≥ 11	11	≥ 15
Emax	+127	$\geq +1023$	+1023	$\geq +16383$
Emin	−126	≤ -1022	−1022	≤ -16382

Where one or both extended-exponent value sets are supported by an implementation, then for each supported extended-exponent value set there is a specific implementation-dependent constant K, whose value is constrained by Table 2.1; this value K in turn dictates the values for *Emin* and *Emax*.

Each of the four value sets includes not only the finite nonzero values that are ascribed to it above, but also the five values positive zero, negative zero, positive infinity, negative infinity, and NaN.

Note that the constraints in Table 2.1 are designed so that every element of the float value set is necessarily also an element of the float-extended-exponent value set, the double value set, and the double-extended-exponent value set. Likewise, each element of the double value set is necessarily also an element of the double-extended-exponent value set. Each extended-exponent value set has a larger range of exponent values than the corresponding standard value set, but does not have more precision.

The elements of the float value set are exactly the values that can be represented using the single floating-point format defined in the IEEE 754 standard, except that there is only one NaN value (IEEE 754 specifies $2^{24} - 2$ distinct NaN values). The elements of the double value set are exactly the values that can be represented using the double floating-point format defined in the IEEE 754 standard, except that there is only one NaN value (IEEE 754 specifies $2^{53} - 2$ distinct NaN values). Note, however, that the elements of the float-extended-exponent and double-extended-exponent value sets defined here do *not* correspond to the values that can be represented using IEEE 754 single extended and double extended formats, respectively.

The float, float-extended-exponent, double, and double-extended-exponent value sets are not types. It is always correct for an implementation of the Java programming language to use an element of the float value set to represent a value of type `float`; however, it may be permissible in certain regions of code for an implementation to use an element of the float-extended-exponent value set instead. Similarly, it is always correct for an implementation to use an element of the double value set to represent a value of type `double`; however, it may be permissible in certain regions of code for an implementation to use an element of the double-extended-exponent value set instead.

Except for NaN, floating-point values are *ordered*; arranged from smallest to largest, they are negative infinity, negative finite nonzero values, positive and negative zero, positive finite nonzero values, and positive infinity.

On comparison, positive zero and negative zero are equal; thus the result of the expression $0.0 == -0.0$ is `true` and the result of $0.0 > -0.0$ is `false`. But other operations can distinguish positive and negative zero; for example, $1.0/0.0$ has the value positive infinity, while the value of $1.0/-0.0$ is negative infinity.

NaN is *unordered*, so the numerical comparison operators <, <=, >, and >= return `false` if either or both operands are NaN. The equality operator == returns `false` if either operand is NaN, and the inequality operator != returns `true` if either operand is NaN. In particular, x != x is `true` if and only if x is NaN, and (x<y) == !(x>=y) will be `false` if x or y is NaN.

Any value of a floating-point type may be cast to or from any numeric type. There are no casts between floating-point types and the type `boolean`.

2.4.4 Operators on Floating-Point Values

The Java programming language provides a number of operators that act on floating-point values, including numerical comparison, arithmetic operators, increment and decrement, and numeric cast (§2.6.9).

If at least one of the operands to a binary operator is of floating-point type, then the operation is a floating-point operation, even if the other operand is integral. Operands of certain unary and binary operators are subject to numeric promotion (§2.6.10).

The values returned by operators on floating-point numbers are those specified by IEEE 754. In particular, the Java programming language requires support of IEEE 754 *denormalized* floating-point numbers and *gradual underflow*, which make it easier to prove desirable properties of particular numerical algorithms.

The Java programming language requires that floating-point arithmetic behave as if every floating-point operator rounded its floating-point result to the result precision. *Inexact* results must be rounded to the representable value nearest to the infinitely precise result; if the two nearest representable values are equally near, the one having zero as its least significant bit is chosen. This is the IEEE 754 standard's default rounding mode known as *round to nearest* mode.

When converting a floating-point value to an integer, *round towards zero* mode is used (§2.6.3). Round towards zero mode acts as though the number were truncated, discarding the significand bits. Round towards zero mode chooses as its result the format's value closest to and no greater in magnitude than the infinitely precise result.

The floating-point operators of the Java programming language produce no exceptions (§2.16). An operation that overflows produces a signed infinity; an operation that underflows produces a denormalized value or a signed zero; and an operation that has no mathematically definite result produces NaN. All numeric operations (except for numeric comparison) with NaN as an operand produce NaN as a result.

Any value of any floating-point type may be cast (§2.6.9) to or from any numeric type. There are no casts between floating-point types and the type `boolean`.

2.4.5 Operators on `boolean` Values

The boolean operators include relational operators and logical operators. Only `boolean` expressions can be used in control flow statements and as the first operand of the conditional operator `?:`. An integral value x can be converted to a value of type `boolean`, following the C language convention that any nonzero value is `true`, by the expression `x!=0`. An object reference `obj` can be converted to a value of type `boolean`, following the C language convention that any reference other than `null` is `true`, by the expression `obj!=null`.

There are no casts between the type `boolean` and any other type.

2.4.6 Reference Types, Objects, and Reference Values

There are three kinds of reference types: the *class types* (§2.8), the *interface types* (§2.13), and the *array types* (§2.15). An *object* is a dynamically created class instance or an array. The reference values (often just *references*) are *pointers* to these objects and a special null reference, which refers to no object.

A class instance is explicitly created by a *class instance creation expression*, or by invoking the `newInstance` method of class `Class`. An array is explicitly created by an *array creation expression*. An object is created in the heap and is garbage-collected after there are no more references to it. Objects cannot be reclaimed or freed by explicit language directives.

There may be many references to the same object. Most objects have state, stored in the fields of objects that are instances of classes or in the variables that are the components of an array object. If two variables contain references to the same object, the state of the object can be modified using one variable's reference to the object, and then the altered state can be observed through the other variable's reference.

Each object has an associated *lock* (§2.19, §8.13) that is used by `synchronized` methods and by the `synchronized` statement to provide control over concurrent access to state by multiple threads (§2.19, §8.12).

Reference types form a hierarchy. Each class type is a subclass of another class type, except for the class `Object` (§2.4.7), which is the superclass (§2.8.3) of all other class and array types. All objects, including arrays, support the methods of class `Object`. String literals (§2.3) are references to instances of class `String` (§2.4.8).

2.4.7 The Class `Object`

The standard class `Object` is the superclass (§2.8.3) of all other classes. A variable of type `Object` can hold a reference to any object, whether it is an instance of a class or an array. All class and array types inherit the methods of class `Object`.

2.4.8 The Class `String`

Instances of class `String` represent sequences of Unicode characters (§2.1). A `String` object has a constant, unchanging value. String literals (§2.3) are references to instances of class `String`.

2.4.9 Operators on Objects

The operators on objects include field access, method invocation, cast, string concatenation, comparison for equality, `instanceof`, and the conditional operator `?:`.

2.5 Variables

A *variable* is a storage location. It has an associated type, sometimes called its *compile-time type*, that is either a primitive type (§2.4.1) or a reference type (§2.4.6). A variable always contains a value that is assignment compatible (§2.6.7) with its type. A variable of a primitive type always holds a value of that exact primitive type. A variable of reference type can hold either a null reference or a reference to any object whose class is assignment compatible (§2.6.7) with the type of the variable.

Compatibility of the value of a variable with its type is guaranteed by the design of the language because default values (§2.5.1) are compatible and all assignments to a variable are checked, at compile time, for assignment compatibility. There are seven kinds of variables:

1. A *class variable* is a field of a class type declared using the keyword `static` (§2.9.1) within a class declaration, or with or without the keyword `static` in an interface declaration. Class variables are created when the class or interface is loaded (§2.17.2) and are initialized on creation to default values (§2.5.1). The class variable effectively ceases to exist when its class or interface is unloaded (§2.17.8).

2. An *instance variable* is a field declared within a class declaration without using the keyword `static` (§2.9.1). If a class *T* has a field *a* that is an instance variable, then a new instance variable *a* is created and initialized to a default value (§2.5.1) as part of each newly created object of class *T* or of any class that is a subclass of *T*. The instance variable effectively ceases to exist when the object of which it is a field is no longer referenced, after any necessary finalization of the object (§2.17.7) has been completed.

3. *Array components* are unnamed variables that are created and initialized to default values (§2.5.1) whenever a new object that is an array is created (§2.17.6). The array components effectively cease to exist when the array is no longer referenced.

4. *Method parameters* name argument values passed to a method. For every parameter declared in a method declaration, a new parameter variable is created each time that method is invoked. The new variable is initialized with the corresponding argument value from the method invocation. The method parameter effectively ceases to exist when the execution of the body of the method is complete.

5. *Constructor parameters* name argument values passed to a constructor. For every parameter declared in a constructor declaration, a new parameter variable is created each time a class instance creation expression or explicit constructor invocation is evaluated. The new variable is initialized with the corresponding argument value from the creation expression or constructor invocation. The constructor parameter effectively ceases to exist when the execution of the body of the constructor is complete.

6. An *exception-handler parameter* variable is created each time an exception is caught by a `catch` clause of a `try` statement (§2.16.2). The new variable is initialized with the actual object associated with the exception (§2.16.3). The exception-handler parameter effectively ceases to exist when execution of the block associated with the `catch` clause (§2.16.2) is complete.

7. *Local variables* are declared by local variable declaration statements. Whenever the flow of control enters a block or a `for` statement, a new variable is created for each local variable declared in a local variable declaration statement immediately contained within that block or `for` statement. The local variable is not initialized, however, until the local variable declaration statement that declares it is executed. The local variable effectively ceases to exist when the execution of the block or `for` statement is complete.

2.5.1 Initial Values of Variables

Every variable in a program must have a value before it is used:

- Each class variable, instance variable, and array component is initialized with a *default value* when it is created:

  - For type `byte`, the default value is zero, that is, the value of `(byte)0`.

  - For type `short`, the default value is zero, that is, the value of `(short)0`.

  - For type `int`, the default value is zero, that is, `0`.

  - For type `long`, the default value is zero, that is, `0L`.

  - For type `float`, the default value is positive zero, that is, `0.0f`.

  - For type `double`, the default value is positive zero, that is, `0.0`.

  - For type `char`, the default value is the null character, that is, `'\u0000'`.

  - For type `boolean`, the default value is `false`.

- For all reference types (§2.4.6), the default value is null (§2.3).

- Each method parameter (§2.5) is initialized to the corresponding argument value provided by the invoker of the method.

- Each constructor parameter (§2.5) is initialized to the corresponding argument value provided by an object creation expression or explicit constructor invocation.

- An exception-handler parameter (§2.16.2) is initialized to the thrown object representing the exception (§2.16.3).

- A local variable must be explicitly given a value, by either initialization or assignment, before it is used.

2.5.2 Variables Have Types, Objects Have Classes

Every object belongs to some particular class. This is the class that was mentioned in the class instance creation expression that produced the object, or the class whose class object was used to invoke the newInstance method to produce the object. This class is called *the* class of the object. An object is said to be an *instance* of its class and of all superclasses of its class. Sometimes the class of an object is called its "runtime type," but "class" is the more accurate term.

(Sometimes a variable or expression is said to have a "runtime type," but that is an abuse of terminology; it refers to the class of the object referred to by the value of the variable or expression at run time, assuming that the value is not null. Properly speaking, type is a compile-time notion. A variable or expression has a type; an object or array has no type, but belongs to a class.)

The type of a variable is always declared, and the type of an expression can be deduced at compile time. The type limits the possible values that the variable can hold or the expression can produce at run time. If a runtime value is a reference that is not null, it refers to an object or array that has a class (not a type), and that class will necessarily be compatible with the compile-time type.

Even though a variable or expression may have a compile-time type that is an interface type, there are no instances of interfaces (§2.13). A variable or expression whose type is an interface type can reference any object whose class implements that interface.

Every array also has a class. The classes for arrays have strange names that are not valid identifiers; for example, the class for an array of int components has the name "[I".

2.6 Conversions and Promotions

A *conversion* from type S to type T allows an expression of type S to be treated at compile time as if it were of type T instead. In some cases this will require a corresponding action at run time to check the validity of the conversion or to translate the runtime value of the expression into a form appropriate for the new type T.

Numeric promotions are conversions that change an operand of a numeric operation to a wider type, or both operands of a numeric operation to a common type, so that an operation can be performed.

In the Java programming language, there are six broad kinds of conversions:

- Identity conversions
- Widening primitive conversions
- Narrowing primitive conversions
- Widening reference conversions
- Narrowing reference conversions
- String conversions

There are five *conversion contexts* in which conversion expressions can occur. Each context allows conversions in some of the above-named categories but not others. The conversion contexts are:

- Assignment conversion (§2.6.7), which converts the type of an expression to the type of a specified variable. The conversions permitted for assignment are limited in such a way that assignment conversion never causes an exception.

- Method invocation conversion (§2.6.8), which is applied to each argument in a method or constructor invocation, and, except in one case, performs the same conversions that assignment conversion does. Method invocation conversion never causes an exception.

- Casting conversion (§2.6.9), which converts the type of an expression to a type explicitly specified by a cast operator. It is more inclusive than assignment or method invocation conversion, allowing any specific conversion other than a string conversion, but certain casts to a reference type may cause an exception at run time.

- String conversion, which allows any type to be converted to type `String` (§2.4.8).

- Numeric promotion, which brings the operands of a numeric operator to a common type so that an operation can be performed.

String conversion only applies to operands of the binary + and += operators when one of the arguments is a `String`; it will not be covered further.

2.6.1 Identity Conversions

A conversion from a type to that same type is permitted for any type.

2.6.2 Widening Primitive Conversions

The following conversions on primitive types are called the *widening primitive conversions*:

- `byte` to `short`, `int`, `long`, `float`, or `double`

- `short` to `int`, `long`, `float`, or `double`

- `char` to `int`, `long`, `float`, or `double`

- `int` to `long`, `float`, or `double`

- `long` to `float` or `double`

- `float` to `double`

Widening conversions do not lose information about the sign or order of magnitude of a numeric value. Conversions widening from an integral type to another integral type do not lose any information at all; the numeric value is preserved exactly. Conversions widening from `float` to `double` in `strictfp` expressions (§2.18) also preserve the numeric value exactly; however, such conversions that are not `strictfp` may lose information about the overall magnitude of the converted value.

Conversion of an `int` or a `long` value to `float`, or of a `long` value to `double`, may lose precision, that is, the result may lose some of the least significant bits of the value; the resulting floating-point value is a correctly rounded version of the integer value, using IEEE 754 round to nearest mode (§2.4.4).

According to this rule, a widening conversion of a signed integer value to an integral type simply sign-extends the two's-complement representation of the integer value to fill the wider format. A widening conversion of a value of type char to an integral type zero-extends the representation of the character value to fill the wider format.

Despite the fact that loss of precision may occur, widening conversions among primitive types never result in a runtime exception (§2.16).

2.6.3 Narrowing Primitive Conversions

The following conversions on primitive types are called *narrowing primitive conversions*:

- byte to char

- short to byte or char

- char to byte or short

- int to byte, short, or char

- long to byte, short, char, or int

- float to byte, short, char, int, or long

- double to byte, short, char, int, long, or float

Narrowing conversions may lose information about the sign or order of magnitude, or both, of a numeric value (for example, narrowing an int value 32763 to type byte produces the value -5). Narrowing conversions may also lose precision.

A narrowing conversion of a signed integer to an integral type simply discards all but the *n* lowest-order bits, where *n* is the number of bits used to represent the type. This may cause the resulting value to have a different sign from the input value.

A narrowing conversion of a character to an integral type likewise simply discards all but the *n* lowest bits, where *n* is the number of bits used to represent the type. This may cause the resulting value to be a negative number, even though characters represent 16-bit unsigned integer values.

In a narrowing conversion of a floating-point number to an integral type, if the floating-point number is NaN, the result of the conversion is 0 of the appropriate type. If the floating-point number is too large to be represented by the integral type or is positive infinity, the result is the largest representable value of the integral type. If the floating-point number is too small to be represented or is negative infinity, the result is the smallest representable value of the integral type. Otherwise, the result is the floating-point number rounded towards zero to an integer value using IEEE 754 round towards zero mode (§2.4.4)

A narrowing conversion from `double` to `float` behaves in accordance with IEEE 754. The result is correctly rounded using IEEE 754 round to nearest mode (§2.4.4). A value too small to be represented as a `float` is converted to a positive or negative zero; a value too large to be represented as a `float` is converted to a positive or negative infinity. A `double` NaN is always converted to a `float` NaN.

Despite the fact that overflow, underflow, or loss of precision may occur, narrowing conversions among primitive types never result in a runtime exception.

2.6.4 Widening Reference Conversions

Widening reference conversions never require a special action at run time and therefore never throw an exception at run time. Because they do not affect the Java virtual machine, they will not be considered further.

2.6.5 Narrowing Reference Conversions

The following permitted conversions are called the *narrowing reference conversions*:

- From any class type S to any class type T, provided that S is a superclass of T. (An important special case is that there is a narrowing conversion from the class type `Object` to any other class type.)

- From any class type S to any interface type K, provided that S is not `final` and does not implement K. (An important special case is that there is a narrowing conversion from the class type `Object` to any interface type.)

- From type `Object` to any array type.

- From type `Object` to any interface type.

- From any interface type J to any class type T that is not `final`.

- From any interface type J to any class type T that is `final`, provided that T implements J.

- From any interface type J to any interface type K, provided that J is not a subinterface of K and there is no method name m such that J and K both declare a method named m with the same signature but different return types.

- From any array type *SC*[] to any array type *TC*[], provided that *SC* and *TC* are reference types and there is a permitted narrowing conversion from *SC* to *TC*.

Such conversions require a test at run time to find out whether the actual reference value is a legitimate value of the new type. If it is not, the Java virtual machine throws a ClassCastException.

2.6.6 Value Set Conversion

Value set conversion is the process of mapping a floating-point value from one value set (§2.4.3) to another without changing its type.

For each operation in an expression that is not FP-strict (§2.18), value set conversion allows an implementation of the Java programming language to choose between two options:

- If the value is an element of the float-extended-exponent value set, then the implementation may map the value to the nearest element of the float value set. This conversion may result in overflow (in which case the value is replaced by an infinity of the same sign) or underflow (in which case the value may lose precision because it is replaced by a denormalized number or zero of the same sign).

- If the value is an element of the double-extended-exponent value set, then the implementation may map the value to the nearest element of the double value set. This conversion may result in overflow (in which case the value is replaced by an infinity of the same sign) or underflow (in which case the value may lose precision because it is replaced by a denormalized number or zero of the same sign).

Within an FP-strict expression, value set conversion does not provide any choices; every implementation must behave in the same way:

- If the value is of type float and is not an element of the float value set, then the implementation must map the value to the nearest element of the float value set. This conversion may result in overflow or underflow.

- If the value is of type double and is not an element of the double value set, then the implementation must map the value to the nearest element of the double value set. This conversion may result in overflow or underflow.

Within an FP-strict expression, mapping values from the float-extended-exponent value set or double-extended-exponent value set is necessary only when a method is called whose declaration is not FP-strict and the implementation has chosen to represent the result of the method call as an element of an extended-exponent value set.

Whether in FP-strict code or code that is not FP-strict, value set conversion always leaves unchanged any value whose type is neither `float` nor `double`.

2.6.7 Assignment Conversion

Assignment conversion occurs when the value of an expression is assigned to a variable: the type of the expression must be converted to the type of the variable. Assignment contexts allow the use of an identity conversion (§2.6.1), a widening primitive conversion (§2.6.2), or a widening reference conversion (§2.6.4). In addition, a narrowing primitive conversion (§2.6.3) may be used if all of the following conditions are satisfied:

- The expression is a constant expression of type `int`.

- The type of the variable is `byte`, `short`, or `char`.

- The value of the expression is representable in the type of the variable.

If the type of the expression can be converted to the type of a variable by assignment conversion, we say the expression (or its value) is *assignable* to the variable or, equivalently, that the type of the expression is *assignment compatible* with the type of the variable.

If the type of the variable is `float` or `double`, then value set conversion (§2.6.6) is applied after the type conversion:

- If the value is of type `float` and is an element of the float-extended-exponent value set, then the implementation must map the value to the nearest element of the float value set. This conversion may result in overflow or underflow.

- If the value is of type `double` and is an element of the double-extended-exponent value set, then the implementation must map the value to the nearest element of the double value set. This conversion may result in overflow or underflow.

An assignment conversion never causes an exception. A value of primitive type must not be assigned to a variable of reference type. A value of reference type must not be assigned to a variable of primitive type. A value of type `boolean` can be assigned only to a variable of type `boolean`. A value of the null type may be assigned to a variable of any reference type.

Assignment of a value of compile-time reference type *S* (source) to a variable of compile-time reference type *T* (target) is permitted:

- If *S* is a class type:

  - If *T* is a class type, then *S* must be the same class as *T*, or *S* must be a subclass of *T*.

  - If *T* is an interface type, then *S* must implement interface *T*.

- If *S* is an interface type:

  - If *T* is a class type, then *T* must be `Object`.

  - If *T* is an interface type, then *T* must be the same interface as *S*, or *T* must be a superinterface of *S*.

- If *S* is an array type *SC*[], that is, an array of components of type *SC*:

  - If *T* is a class type, then *T* must be `Object`.

  - If *T* is an interface type, then *T* must be either `Cloneable` or `java.io.Serializable`.

  - If *T* is an array type *TC*[], that is, an array of components of type *TC*, then either

    - *TC* and *SC* must be the same primitive type, or

    - *TC* and *SC* are both reference types and type *SC* is assignable to *TC*.

2.6.8 Method Invocation Conversion

Method invocation conversion is applied to each argument value in a method or constructor invocation: the type of the argument expression must be converted to the type of the corresponding parameter. Method invocation contexts allow the use of an identity conversion (§2.6.1), a widening primitive conversion (§2.6.2), or a widening reference conversion (§2.6.4). Method invocation conversions specifically do not include the implicit narrowing of integer constants that is part of assignment conversion (§2.6.7).

If the type of an argument expression is either `float` or `double`, then value set conversion (§2.6.6) is applied after the type conversion:

- If an argument value of type `float` is an element of the float-extended-exponent value set, then the implementation must map the value to the nearest element of the float value set. This conversion may result in overflow or underflow.

- If an argument value of type `double` is an element of the double-extended-exponent value set, then the implementation must map the value to the nearest element of the double value set. This conversion may result in overflow or underflow.

2.6.9 Casting Conversion

Casting conversions are more powerful than assignment or method invocation conversions applied to the operand of a cast operator: the type of the operand expression must be converted to the type explicitly named by the cast operator. Casting contexts allow the use of an identity conversion (§2.6.1), a widening primitive conversion (§2.6.2), a narrowing primitive conversion (§2.6.3), a widening reference conversion (§2.6.4), or a narrowing reference conversion (§2.6.5). Thus, casting conversions are more inclusive than assignment or method invocation conversions: a cast can do any permitted conversion other than a string conversion.

Value set conversion (§2.6.6) is applied after the type conversion.

Casting can convert a value of any numeric type to any other numeric type. A value of type `boolean` cannot be cast to another type. A value of reference type cannot be cast to a value of primitive type.

Some casts can be proven incorrect at compile time and result in a compile-time error. Otherwise, either the cast can be proven correct at compile time, or a runtime validity check is required. (See *The Java*™ *Language Specification* for details.) If the value at run time is a null reference, then the cast is allowed. If the check at run time fails, a `ClassCastException` is thrown.

2.6.10 Numeric Promotion

Numeric promotion is applied to the operands of an arithmetic operator. Numeric promotion contexts allow the use of an identity conversion (§2.6.1) or a widening primitive conversion (§2.6.2).

Numeric promotions are used to convert the operands of a numeric operator to a common type where an operation can be performed. The two kinds of numeric promotion are *unary numeric promotion* and *binary numeric promotion*. The analogous conversions in C are called "the usual unary conversions" and "the usual binary conversions." Numeric promotion is not a general feature of the Java programming language, but rather a property of specific built-in operators.

An operator that applies unary numeric promotion to a single operand of numeric type converts an operand of type `byte`, `short`, or `char` to `int` by a widening primitive conversion, and otherwise leaves the operand alone. Value set conversion (§2.6.6) is then applied. The operands of the shift operators are promoted independently using unary numeric promotions.

When an operator applies binary numeric promotion to a pair of numeric operands, the following rules apply, in order, using widening primitive conversion to convert operands as necessary:

- If either operand is of type `double`, the other is converted to `double`.

- Otherwise, if either operand is of type `float`, the other is converted to `float`.

- Otherwise, if either operand is of type `long`, the other is converted to `long`.

- Otherwise, both operands are converted to type `int`.

After type conversion, if any, value set conversion is applied to each operand.

2.7 Names and Packages

Names are used to refer to entities declared in a program. A declared entity is a package, type, member (field or method) of a type, parameter, or local variable. Programs are organized sets of *packages*.

2.7.1 Simple Names and Qualified Names

A *simple name* is a single identifier (§2.2). *Qualified names* (§2.7.4) provide access to members of packages and reference types. A qualified name consists of a name, a "." token, and an identifier.

Not all identifiers are part of a name. Identifiers are also used in declarations, where the identifier determines the name by which an entity will be known, in field access expressions and method invocation expressions, and in statement labels and `break` and `continue` statements that refer to statement labels.

2.7.2 Packages

A package consists of a number of compilation units and has a hierarchical name. Packages are independently developed, and each package has its own set of names, which helps to prevent name conflicts. Each Java virtual machine implementation determines how packages, compilation units, and subpackages are created and stored; which top-level package names are in scope in a particular compilation; and which packages are accessible. Packages may be stored in a local file system, in a distributed file system, or in some form of database.

A package name component or class name might contain a character that cannot legally appear in a host file system's ordinary directory or file name: for instance, a Unicode character on a system that allows only ASCII characters in file names.

A Java virtual machine implementation must support at least one unnamed package; it may support more than one but is not required to do so. Which compilation units are in each unnamed package is determined by the host system. Unnamed packages are provided principally for convenience when developing small or temporary applications or when just beginning development.

An `import` declaration allows a type declared in another package to be known by a simple name rather than by the fully qualified name (§2.7.5) of the type. An import declaration affects only the type declarations of a single compilation unit. A compilation unit automatically imports each of the `public` type names declared in the predefined package `java.lang`.

2.7.3 Members

Packages and reference types have *members*. The members of a package (§2.7.2) are subpackages and all the class (§2.8) and interface (§2.13) types declared in all the compilation units of the package. The members of a reference type are fields (§2.9), methods (§2.10), and nested classes and interfaces.

2.7.3.1 The Members of a Package

In general, the subpackages of a package are determined by the host system. However, the standard package `java` always has the subpackages `lang`, `util`, `io`, and `net`. No two distinct members of the same package may have the same simple name (§2.7.1), but members of different packages may have the same simple name.

2.7.3.2 The Members of a Class Type

The members of a class type (§2.8) are fields (§2.9), methods (§2.10), and nested classes and interfaces. These include members inherited from its direct superclass (§2.8.3), if it has one, members inherited from any direct superinterfaces (§2.13.2), and any members declared in the body of the class. There is no restriction against a field and a method of a class type having the same simple name.

A class type may have two or more methods with the same simple name if they have different numbers of parameters or different parameter types in at least one parameter position. Such a method member name is said to be *overloaded*. A class type may contain a declaration for a method with the same name and the same signature as a method that would otherwise be inherited from a superclass or superinterface. In this case, the method of the superclass or superinterface is not inherited. If the method not inherited is `abstract`, the new declaration is said to *implement* the method; if it is not `abstract`, the new declaration is said to *override* it.

2.7.3.3 The Members of an Interface Type

The members of an interface type (§2.13) are fields, methods, and nested classes and interfaces. The members of an interface are the members inherited from any direct superinterfaces (§2.13.2) and members declared in the body of the interface.

2.7.3.4 The Members of an Array Type

The members of an array type (§2.15) are the members inherited from its superclass, the class `Object` (§2.4.7), and the field `length`, which is a constant (`final`) field of every array.

2.7.4 Qualified Names and Access Control

Qualified names (§2.7.1) are a means of access to members of packages and reference types; related means of access include field access expressions and method invocation expressions. All three are syntactically similar in that a "." token appears, preceded by some indication of a package, type, or expression having a type and followed by an identifier that names a member of the package or type. These are collectively known as constructs for *qualified access*.

The Java programming language provides mechanisms for limiting qualified access, to prevent users of a package or class from depending on unnecessary details of the implementation of that package or class. Access control also applies to constructors.

Whether a package is accessible is determined by the host system.

A class or interface may be declared `public`, in which case it may be accessed, using a qualified name, by any class or interface that can access the package in which it is declared. A class or interface that is not declared `public` may be accessed from, and only from, anywhere in the package in which it is declared.

Every field or method of an interface must be `public`. Every member of a `public` interface is implicitly `public`, whether or not the keyword `public` appears in its declaration. It follows that a member of an interface is accessible if and only if the interface itself is accessible.

A field, method, or constructor of a class may be declared using at most one of the `public`, `private`, or `protected` keywords. A `public` member may be accessed by any class or interface. A `private` member may be accessed only from within the class that contains its declaration. A member that is not declared `public`, `protected`, or `private` is said to have *default access* and may be accessed from, and only from, anywhere in the package in which it is declared.

A `protected` member of an object may be accessed only by code responsible for the implementation of that object. To be precise, a `protected` member may be accessed from anywhere in the package in which it is declared and, in addition, it may be accessed from within any declaration of a subclass of the class type that contains its declaration, provided that certain restrictions are obeyed.

2.7.5 Fully Qualified Names

Every package, class, interface, array type, and primitive type has a fully qualified name. It follows that every type except the null type has a fully qualified name.

- The fully qualified name of a primitive type is the keyword for that primitive type, namely, `boolean`, `char`, `byte`, `short`, `int`, `long`, `float`, or `double`.

- The fully qualified name of a named package that is not a subpackage of a named package is its simple name.

- The fully qualified name of a named package that is a subpackage of another named package consists of the fully qualified name of the containing package followed by "." followed by the simple (member) name of the subpackage.

- The fully qualified name of a class or interface that is declared in an unnamed package is the simple name of the class or interface.

- The fully qualified name of a class or interface that is declared in a named package consists of the fully qualified name of the package followed by "." followed by the simple name of the class or interface.

- The fully qualified name of an array type consists of the fully qualified name of the component type of the array type followed by "[]".

2.8 Classes

A *class declaration* specifies a new reference type and provides its implementation. Each class is implemented as an extension or subclass of a single existing class. A class may also implement one or more interfaces.

The body of a class declares members (fields and methods), static initializers, and constructors.

2.8.1 Class Names

If a class is declared in a named package with the fully qualified name *P*, then the class has the fully qualified name *P.Identifier*. If the class is in an unnamed package, then the class has the fully qualified name *Identifier*.

Two classes are the *same class* (and therefore the *same type*) if they are loaded by the same class loader (§2.17.2) and they have the same fully qualified name (§2.7.5).

2.8.2 Class Modifiers

A class declaration may include *class modifiers*. A class may be declared `public`, as discussed in §2.7.4.

An `abstract` class is a class that is incomplete, or considered incomplete. Only `abstract` classes may have `abstract` methods (§2.10.3), that is, methods that are declared but not yet implemented.

A class can be declared `final` if its definition is complete and no subclasses are desired or required. Because a `final` class never has any subclasses, the methods of a `final` class cannot be overridden in a subclass. A class cannot be both `final` and `abstract`, because the implementation of such a class could never be completed.

A class can be declared `strictfp` to indicate that all expressions in the methods of the class are FP-strict (§2.18), whether or not the methods themselves are declared FP-strict.

A class is declared `public` to make its type available to packages other than the one in which it is declared. A `public` class is accessible from other packages, using either its fully qualified name or a shorter name created by an `import` declaration (§2.7.2), whenever the host permits access to its package. If a class lacks the `public` modifier, access to the class declaration is limited to the package in which it is declared.

2.8.3 Superclasses and Subclasses

The optional `extends` clause in a class declaration specifies the *direct superclass* of the current class, the class from whose implementation the implementation of the current class is derived. A class is said to be a *direct subclass* of the class it `extends`. Only the class `Object` (§2.4.7) has no direct superclass. If the `extends` clause is omitted from a class declaration, then the superclass of the new class is `Object`.

The *subclass* relationship is the transitive closure of the direct subclass relationship. A class *A* is a subclass of a class *C* if *A* is a direct subclass of *C*, or if there is a direct subclass *B* of *C* and class *A* is a subclass of *B*. Class *A* is said to be a *superclass* of class *C* whenever *C* is a subclass of *A*.

2.8.4 The Class Members

The members of a class type include all of the following:

- Members inherited from its direct superclass (§2.8.3), except in class `Object`, which has no direct superclass.

- Members inherited from any direct superinterfaces (§2.13.2).

- Members declared in the body of the class.

Members of a superclass that are declared `private` are not inherited by subclasses of that class. Members of a class that are not declared `private`, `protected`, or `public` are not inherited by subclasses declared in a package other than the one in which the class is declared. Constructors (§2.12) and static initializers (§2.11) are not members and therefore are not inherited.

2.9 Fields

The variables of a class type are its *fields*. Class (`static`) variables exist once per class. Instance variables exist once per instance of the class. Fields may include initializers and may be modified using various modifier keywords.

If the class declares a field with a certain name, then the declaration of that field is said to *hide* any and all accessible declarations of fields with the same name in the superclasses and superinterfaces of the class. A class inherits from its direct superclass and direct superinterfaces all the fields of the superclass and superinterfaces that are accessible to code in the class and are not hidden by a declaration in the class. A hidden field can be accessed by using a qualified name (if it is `static`) or by using a field access expression that contains a cast to a superclass type or the keyword `super`.

A value stored in a field of type `float` is always an element of the float value set (§2.4.3); similarly, a value stored in a field of type `double` is always an element of the double value set. It is not permitted for a field of type `float` to contain an element of the float-extended-exponent value set that is not also an element of the float value set, nor for a field of type `double` to contain an element of the double-extended-exponent value set that is not also an element of the double value set.

2.9.1 Field Modifiers

Fields may be declared `public`, `protected`, or `private`, as discussed in §2.7.4.

If a field is declared `static`, there exists exactly one incarnation of the field, no matter how many instances (possibly zero) of the class may eventually be created. A `static` field, sometimes called a *class variable*, is incarnated when the class is initialized (§2.17.4).

A field that is not declared `static` is called an *instance variable*. Whenever a new instance of a class is created, a new variable associated with that instance is created for every instance variable declared in that class or in any of its superclasses.

A field can be declared `final`, in which case its declarator must include a variable initializer (§2.9.2). Both class and instance variables (`static` and non-`static` fields) may be declared `final`. Once a `final` field has been initialized, it always contains the same value. If a `final` field holds a reference to an object, then the state of the object may be changed by operations on the object, but the field will always refer to the same object.

Variables may be marked `transient` to indicate that they are not part of the persistent state of an object. The `transient` attribute can be used by an implementation to support special system services. *The Java*™ *Language Specification* does not yet specify details of such services.

The Java programming language allows threads that access shared variables to keep private working copies of the variables; this allows a more efficient implementation of multiple threads (§2.19). These working copies need to be reconciled with the master copies in the shared main memory only at prescribed synchronization points, namely, when objects are locked or unlocked (§2.19). As a rule, to make sure that shared variables are consistently and reliably updated, a thread should ensure that it has exclusive access to such variables by obtaining a lock that conventionally enforces mutual exclusion for those shared variables.

Alternatively, a field may be declared `volatile`, in which case a thread must reconcile its working copy of the field with the master copy every time it accesses the variable. Moreover, operations on the master copies of one or more volatile variables on behalf of a thread are performed by the main memory in exactly the order that the thread requested. A `final` field cannot also be declared `volatile`.

2.9.2 Initialization of Fields

If a field declaration contains a variable initializer, then it has the semantics of an assignment to the declared variable, and:

- If the declaration is for a class variable (that is, a `static` field), then the variable initializer is evaluated and the assignment performed exactly once, when the class is initialized (§2.17.4).

- If the declaration is for an instance variable (that is, a field that is not `static`), then the variable initializer is evaluated and the assignment performed each time an instance of the class is created.

2.10 Methods

A *method* declares executable code that can be invoked, passing a fixed number of values as arguments. Every method declaration belongs to some class. A class inherits from its direct superclass (§2.8.3) and any direct superinterfaces (§2.13.2) all the accessible methods of the superclass and superinterfaces, with one exception: if a name is declared as a method in the new class, then no method with the same signature (§2.10.2) is inherited. Instead, the newly declared method is said to *override* any such method declaration. An overriding method must not conflict with the definition that it overrides, for instance, by having a different return type. Overridden methods of the superclass can be accessed using a method invocation expression involving the `super` keyword.

2.10.1 Formal Parameters

The *formal parameters* of a method, if any, are specified by a list of comma-separated parameter specifiers. Each parameter specifier consists of a type and an identifier that specifies the name of the parameter. When the method is invoked, the values of the actual argument expressions initialize newly created parameter variables (§2.5), each of the declared type, before execution of the body of the method.

A method parameter of type `float` always contains an element of the float value set (§2.4.3); similarly, a method parameter of type `double` always contains an element of the double value set. It is not permitted for a method parameter of type `float` to contain an element of the float-extended-exponent value set that is not also an element of the float value set, nor for a method parameter of type `double` to contain an element of the double-extended-exponent value set that is not also an element of the double value set.

Where an actual argument expression corresponding to a parameter variable is not FP-strict (§2.18), evaluation of that actual argument expression is permitted to use values drawn from the appropriate extended-exponent value sets. Prior to being stored in the parameter variable, the result of such an expression is mapped to the nearest value in the corresponding standard value set by method invocation conversion (§2.6.8).

2.10.2 Method Signature

The *signature* of a method consists of the name of the method and the number and type of formal parameters (§2.10.1) of the method. A class may not declare two methods with the same signature.

2.10.3 Method Modifiers

The access modifiers `public`, `protected`, and `private` are discussed in Section 2.7.4.

An `abstract` method declaration introduces the method as a member, providing its signature (§2.10.2), return type, and `throws` clause (if any), but does not provide an implementation. The declaration of an `abstract` method *m* must appear within an abstract class (call it *A*). Every subclass of *A* that is not itself abstract must provide an implementation for *m*. A method declared abstract cannot also be declared to be private, static, final, native, strictfp, or synchronized.

A method that is declared static is called a *class method*. A class method is always invoked without reference to a particular object. A class method may refer to other fields and methods of the class by simple name only if they are class methods and class (static) variables.

A method that is not declared static is an *instance method*. An instance method is always invoked with respect to an object, which becomes the current object to which the keywords this and super refer during execution of the method body.

A method can be declared final to prevent subclasses from overriding or hiding it. A private method and all methods declared in a final class (§2.8.2) are implicitly final, because it is impossible to override them. If a method is final or implicitly final, a compiler or a runtime code generator can safely "inline" the body of a final method, replacing an invocation of the method with the code in its body.

A synchronized method will acquire a monitor lock (§2.19) before it executes. For a class (static) method, the lock associated with the class object for the method's class is used. For an instance method, the lock associated with this (the object for which the method is invoked) is used. The same per-object lock is used by the synchronized statement.

A method can be declared strictfp to indicate that all expressions in the method are FP-strict (§2.18).

A method can be declared native to indicate that it is implemented in platform-dependent code, typically written in another programming language such as C, C++, or assembly language. A method may not be declared to be both native and strictfp.

2.11 Static Initializers

Any *static initializers* declared in a class are executed when the class is initialized (§2.17.4) and, together with any field initializers (§2.9.2) for class variables, may be used to initialize the class variables of the class (§2.17.4).

The static initializers and class variable initializers are executed in textual order. They may not refer to class variables declared in the class whose declarations appear textually after the use, even though these class variables are in scope.

This restriction is designed to catch, at compile time, most circular or otherwise malformed initializations.

2.12 Constructors

A *constructor* is used in the creation of an object that is an instance of a class. The constructor declaration looks like a method declaration that has no result type. Constructors are invoked by class instance creation expressions (§2.17.6), by the conversions and concatenations caused by the string concatenation operator +, and by explicit constructor invocations from other constructors; they are never invoked by method invocation expressions.

Constructor declarations are not members. They are never inherited and therefore are not subject to hiding or overriding.

If a constructor body does not begin with an explicit constructor invocation and the constructor being declared is not part of the primordial class `Object`, then the constructor body is implicitly assumed by the compiler to begin with a superclass constructor invocation "`super();`", an invocation of the constructor of the direct superclass that takes no arguments.

If a class declares no constructors then a *default constructor*, which takes no arguments, is automatically provided. If the class being declared is `Object`, then the default constructor has an empty body. Otherwise, the default constructor takes no arguments and simply invokes the superclass constructor with no arguments. If the class is declared `public`, then the default constructor is implicitly given the access modifier `public`. Otherwise, the default constructor has the default access implied by no access modifier (§2.7.4).

A class can be designed to prevent code outside the class declaration from creating instances of the class by declaring at least one constructor, in order to prevent the creation of an implicit constructor, and declaring all constructors to be `private`.

2.12.1 Constructor Modifiers

Access to constructors is governed by the access modifiers `public`, `protected`, and `private` (§2.7.4).

A constructor cannot be `abstract`, `static`, `final`, `native`, or `synchronized`. A constructor cannot be declared to be `strictfp`. This difference in the definitions for method modifiers (§2.10.3) and constructor modifiers is an intentional language design choice; it effectively ensures that a constructor is FP-strict (§2.18) if and only if its class is FP-strict, so to speak.

2.13 Interfaces

An *interface* is a reference type whose members are constants and `abstract` methods. This type has no implementation, but otherwise unrelated classes can implement it by providing implementations for its `abstract` methods. Programs can use interfaces to make it unnecessary for related classes to share a common `abstract` superclass or to add methods to `Object`.

An interface may be declared to be a *direct extension* of one or more other interfaces, meaning that it implicitly specifies all the `abstract` methods and constants of the interfaces it extends, except for any constants that it may hide, and perhaps adds newly declared members of its own.

A class may be declared to *directly implement* one or more interfaces, meaning that any instance of the class implements all the `abstract` methods specified by that interface. A class necessarily implements all the interfaces that its direct superclasses and direct superinterfaces do. This (multiple) interface inheritance allows objects to support (multiple) common behaviors without sharing any implementation.

A variable whose declared type is an interface type may have as its value a reference to an object that is an instance of any class that is declared to implement the specified interface. It is not sufficient that the class happens to implement all the `abstract` methods of the interface; the class or one of its superclasses must actually be declared to implement the interface, or else the class is not considered to implement the interface.

2.13.1 Interface Modifiers

An interface declaration may be preceded by the interface modifiers `public`, `strictfp`, and `abstract`. The access modifier `public` is discussed in (§2.7.4). Every interface is implicitly `abstract`. All members of interfaces are implicitly `public`.

An interface cannot be `final`, because the implementation of such a class could never be completed.

2.13.2 Superinterfaces

If an `extends` clause is provided, then the interface being declared extends each of the other named interfaces and therefore inherits the methods and constants of each of the other named interfaces. Any class that `implements` the declared interface is also considered to implement all the interfaces that this interface extends and that are accessible to the class.

The `implements` clause in a class declaration lists the names of interfaces that are *direct superinterfaces* of the class being declared. All interfaces in the current package are accessible. Interfaces in other packages are accessible if the host system permits access to the package and the interface is declared `public`.

An interface type K is a *superinterface* of class type C if K is a direct super-interface of C; or if C has a direct superinterface J that has K as a superinterface; or if K is a superinterface of the direct superclass of C. A class is said to *implement* all its superinterfaces.

There is no analogue of the class `Object` for interfaces; that is, while every class is an extension of class `Object`, there is no single interface of which all interfaces are extensions.

2.13.3 Interface Members

The members of an interface are those members inherited from direct superinterfaces and those members declared in the interface. The interface inherits, from the interfaces it extends, all members of those interfaces, except for fields with the same names as fields it declares. Interface members are either fields or methods.

2.13.3.1 Interface (Constant) Fields

Every field declaration in the body of an interface is implicitly `static` and `final`. Interfaces do not have instance variables. Every field declaration in an interface is itself implicitly `public`. A constant declaration in an interface must not include either of the modifiers `transient` or `volatile`.

Every field in the body of an interface must have an initialization expression, which need not be a constant expression. The variable initializer is evaluated and the assignment performed exactly once, when the interface is initialized (§2.17.4).

2.13.3.2 Interface (Abstract) Methods

Every method declaration in the body of an interface is implicitly `abstract` and implicitly `public`.

A method declared in the body of an interface must not be declared `static`, because `static` methods cannot be `abstract`.

A method declared in the body of an interface must not be declared `native`, `strictfp`, or `synchronized`, because those keywords describe implementation properties rather than interface properties; however, a method declared in an interface may be implemented by a method that is declared `native`, `strictfp`, or `synchronized` in a class that implements the interface. A method declared in the body of an interface must not be declared `final`; however, one may be implemented by a method that is declared `final` in a class that implements the interface.

2.13.4 Overriding, Inheritance, and Overloading in Interfaces

If the interface declares a method, then the declaration of that method is said to *override* any and all methods with the same signature in the superinterfaces of the interface that would otherwise be accessible to code in this interface.

An interface inherits from its direct superinterfaces all methods of the superinterfaces that are not overridden by a method declared in the interface.

If two methods of an interface (whether both are declared in the same interface, or both are inherited by an interface, or one is declared and one is inherited) have the same name but different signatures, then the method name is said to be *overloaded*.

2.14 Nested Classes and Interfaces

JDK release 1.1 added *nested classes and interfaces* to the Java programming language. Nested classes and interfaces are sometimes referred to as *inner classes and interfaces*, which are one sort of nested classes and interfaces. However, nested classes and interfaces also encompass nested top-level classes and interfaces, which are not inner classes or interfaces.

A full specification of nested classes and interfaces will be published in the second edition of *The Java™ Language Specification*. Until then, interested persons should refer to the Inner Classes Specification, which may be found at `http://java.sun.com/products/jdk/1.1/docs/guide/innerclasses/spec/innerclasses.doc.html`.

2.15 Arrays

Arrays are objects, are dynamically created, and may be assigned to variables of type `Object` (§2.4.7). All methods on arrays are inherited from class `Object` except the `clone` method, which arrays override. All arrays implement the interfaces `Cloneable` and `java.io.Serializable`.

An array object contains a number of variables. That number may be zero, in which case the array is said to be *empty*. The variables contained in an array have no names; instead they are referenced by array access expressions that use non-negative integer index values. These variables are called the *components* of the array. If an array has *n* components, we say *n* is the *length* of the array.

An array of zero components is not the same as the null reference (§2.4).

An array component of type `float` is always an element of the float value set (§2.4.3); similarly, a component of type `double` is always an element of the double value set. A component of type `float` may not be an element of the float-extended-exponent value set unless it is also an element of the float value set. A component of type `double` may not be an element of the double-extended-exponent value set unless it is also an element of the double value set.

2.15.1 Array Types

All the components of an array have the same type, called the *component type* of the array. If the component type of an array is *T*, then the type of the array itself is written *T*[].

The component type of an array may itself be an array type. The components of such an array may contain references to subarrays. If, starting from any array type, one considers its component type, and then (if that is also an array type) the component type of that type, and so on, eventually one must reach a component type that is not an array type; this is called the *element type* of the original array, and the components at this level of the data structure are called the *elements* of the original array.

There are three situations in which an element of an array can be an array: if the element type is of type `Object` (§2.4.7), `Cloneable`, or `java.io.Serializable`, then some or all of the elements may be arrays, because every array object can be assigned to a variable of one of those types.

In the Java programming language, unlike in C, an array of `char` is not a `String` (§2.4.7), and neither a `String` nor an array of `char` is terminated by `'\u0000'` (the NUL-character). A `String` object is immutable (its value never changes), while an array of `char` has mutable elements.

The element type of an array may be any type, whether primitive or reference. In particular, arrays with an interface type as the component type are supported; the elements of such an array may have as their value a null reference or instances of any class type that implements the interface. Arrays with an `abstract` class type as the component type are supported; the elements of such an array may have as their value a null reference or instances of any subclass of this `abstract` class that is not itself `abstract`.

2.15.2 Array Variables

A variable of array type holds a reference to an object. Declaring a variable of array type does not create an array object or allocate any space for array components. It creates only the variable itself, which can contain a reference to an array.

Because an array's length is not part of its type, a single variable of array type may contain references to arrays of different lengths. Once an array object is created, its length never changes. To make an array variable refer to an array of different length, a reference to a different array must be assigned to the variable.

If an array variable v has type $A[]$, where A is a reference type, then v can hold a reference to any array type $B[]$, provided B can be assigned to A (§2.6.7).

2.15.3 Array Creation

An array is created by an *array creation expression* or an *array initializer*.

2.15.4 Array Access

A component of an array is accessed using an *array access expression*. Arrays may be indexed by `int` values; `short`, `byte`, or `char` values may also be used as they are subjected to unary numeric promotion (§2.6.10) and become `int` values.

All arrays are 0-origin. An array with length n can be indexed by the integers 0 through $n - 1$. All array accesses are checked at run time; an attempt to use an index that is less than zero or greater than or equal to the length of the array causes an `ArrayIndexOutOfBoundsException` to be thrown.

2.16 Exceptions

When a program violates the semantic constraints of the Java programming language, the Java virtual machine signals this error to the program as an *exception*. An example of such a violation is an attempt to index outside the bounds of an array. The Java programming language specifies that an exception will be thrown when semantic constraints are violated and will cause a nonlocal transfer of control from the point where the exception occurred to a point that can be specified by the programmer. An exception is said to be *thrown* from the point where it occurred and is said to be *caught* at the point to which control is transferred. A method invocation that completes because an exception causes transfer of control to a point outside the method is said to *complete abruptly*.

Programs can also throw exceptions explicitly, using `throw` statements. This provides an alternative to the old-fashioned style of handling error conditions by returning distinguished error values, such as the integer value -1, where a negative value would not normally be expected.

Every exception is represented by an instance of the class `Throwable` or one of its subclasses; such an object can be used to carry information from the point at which an exception occurs to the handler that catches it. Handlers are established by `catch` clauses of `try` statements. During the process of throwing an exception, the Java virtual machine abruptly completes, one by one, any expressions, statements, method and constructor invocations, static initializers, and field initialization expressions that have begun but not completed execution in the current thread. This process continues until a handler is found that indicates that it handles the thrown exception by naming the class of the exception or a superclass of the class of the exception. If no such handler is found, then the method `uncaughtException` is invoked for the `ThreadGroup` that is the parent of the current thread.

In the Java programming language the exception mechanism is integrated with the synchronization model (§2.19) so that locks are properly released as `synchronized` statements and so that invocations of `synchronized` methods complete abruptly.

The specific exceptions covered in this section are that subset of the predefined exceptions that can be thrown directly by the operation of the Java virtual machine. Additional exceptions can be thrown by class library or user code; these exceptions are not covered here. See *The Java*™ *Language Specification* for information on all predefined exceptions.

2.16.1   The Causes of Exceptions

An exception is thrown for one of three reasons:

1. An abnormal execution condition was synchronously detected by the Java virtual machine. These exceptions are not thrown at an arbitrary point in the program, but rather at a point where they are specified as a possible result of an expression evaluation or statement execution, such as:

   • When an operation violates the normal semantics of the Java programming language, for example indexing outside the bounds of an array.

   • When an error occurs in loading or linking part of the program.

   • When some limit on a resource is exceeded, for example when too much memory is used.

2. A `throw` statement was executed.

3. An asynchronous exception occurred because:

   • The `stop` method of class `Thread` or `ThreadGroup` was invoked, or

   • An internal error occurred in the virtual machine implementation.

Exceptions are represented by instances of the class `Throwable` and instances of its subclasses. These classes are, collectively, the *exception classes*.

2.16.2 Handling an Exception

When an exception is thrown, control is transferred from the code that caused the exception to the nearest dynamically enclosing `catch` clause of a `try` statement that handles the exception.

A statement or expression is *dynamically enclosed* by a `catch` clause if it appears within the `try` block of the `try` statement of which the `catch` clause is a part, or if the caller of the statement or expression is dynamically enclosed by the `catch` clause.

The *caller* of a statement or expression depends on where it occurs:

• If within a method, then the caller is the method invocation expression that was executed to cause the method to be invoked.

• If within a constructor or the initializer for an instance variable, then the caller is the class instance creation expression or the method invocation of `newInstance` that was executed to cause an object to be created.

- If within a static initializer or an initializer for a `static` variable, then the caller is the expression that used the class or interface so as to cause it to be initialized.

Whether a particular `catch` clause *handles* an exception is determined by comparing the class of the object that was thrown to the declared type of the parameter of the `catch` clause. The `catch` clause handles the exception if the type of its parameter is the class of the exception or a superclass of the class of the exception. Equivalently, a `catch` clause will catch any exception object that is an `instanceof` the declared parameter type.

The control transfer that occurs when an exception is thrown causes abrupt completion of expressions and statements until a `catch` clause is encountered that can handle the exception; execution then continues by executing the block of that `catch` clause. The code that caused the exception is never resumed.

If no `catch` clause handling an exception can be found, then the current thread (the thread that encountered the exception) is terminated, but only after all `finally` clauses have been executed and the method `uncaughtException` has been invoked for the `ThreadGroup` that is the parent of the current thread.

In situations where it is desirable to ensure that one block of code is always executed after another, even if that other block of code completes abruptly, a `try` statement with a `finally` clause may be used. If a `try` or `catch` block in a `try-finally` or `try-catch-finally` statement completes abruptly, then the `finally` clause is executed during propagation of the exception, even if no matching `catch` clause is ultimately found. If a `finally` clause is executed because of abrupt completion of a `try` block and the `finally` clause itself completes abruptly, then the reason for the abrupt completion of the `try` block is discarded and the new reason for abrupt completion is propagated from there.

Most exceptions occur synchronously as a result of an action by the thread in which they occur and at a point in the program that is specified to possibly result in such an exception. An asynchronous exception is, by contrast, an exception that can potentially occur at any point in the execution of a program.

Asynchronous exceptions are rare. They occur only as a result of:

- An invocation of the `stop` method of class `Thread` or `ThreadGroup`.

- An internal error in the Java virtual machine implementation.

A `stop` method may be invoked by one thread to affect another thread or all the threads in a specified thread group. It is asynchronous because it may occur at any point in the execution of the other thread or threads. An internal error is considered asynchronous so that it may be handled using the same mechanism that handles the stop method, as will now be described.

The Java programming language permits a small but bounded amount of execution to occur before an asynchronous exception is thrown. This delay is permitted to allow optimized code to detect and throw these exceptions at points where it is practical to handle them while obeying the semantics of the language.

A simple implementation might poll for asynchronous exceptions at the point of each control transfer instruction. Since a program has a finite size, this provides a bound on the total delay in detecting an asynchronous exception. Since no asynchronous exception will occur between control transfers, the code generator has some flexibility to reorder computation between control transfers for greater performance.

All exceptions in the Java programming language are *precise*: when the transfer of control takes place, all effects of the statements executed and expressions evaluated before the point from which the exception is thrown must appear to have taken place. No expressions, statements, or parts thereof that occur after the point from which the exception is thrown may appear to have been evaluated. If optimized code has speculatively executed some of the expressions or statements which follow the point at which the exception occurs, such code must be prepared to hide this speculative execution from the user-visible state of the program.

2.16.3 The Exception Hierarchy

The possible exceptions in a program are organized in a hierarchy of classes, rooted at class Throwable, a direct subclass of Object. The classes Exception and Error are direct subclasses of Throwable. The class RuntimeException is a direct subclass of Exception.

Programs can use the preexisting exception classes in throw statements, or define additional exception classes as subclasses of Throwable or of any of its subclasses, as appropriate. To take advantage of compile-time checking for exception handlers, it is typical to define most new exception classes as checked exception classes, specifically as subclasses of Exception that are not subclasses of RuntimeException.

2.16.4 The Classes Exception and RuntimeException

The class Exception is the superclass of all the standard exceptions that ordinary programs may wish to recover from.

The class `RuntimeException` is a subclass of class `Exception`. The subclasses of `RuntimeException` are unchecked exception classes. The package `java.lang` defines the following standard unchecked runtime exceptions:

- `ArithmeticException`: An exceptional arithmetic situation has arisen, such as an integer division or integer remainder operation with a zero divisor.

- `ArrayStoreException`: An attempt has been made to store into an array component a value whose class is not assignment compatible with the component type of the array.

- `ClassCastException`: An attempt has been made to cast a reference to an object to an inappropriate type.

- `IllegalMonitorStateException`: A thread has attempted to wait on or notify other threads waiting on an object that it has not locked.

- `IndexOutOfBoundsException`: Either an index of some sort (such as to an array, a string, or a vector) or a subrange, specified either by two index values or by an index and a length, was out of range.

- `NegativeArraySizeException`: An attempt was made to create an array with a negative length.

- `NullPointerException`: An attempt was made to use a null reference in a case where an object reference was required.

- `SecurityException`: A security violation was detected.

The class `Error` and its standard subclasses are exceptions from which ordinary programs are not ordinarily expected to recover. The class `Error` is a separate subclass of `Throwable`, distinct from `Exception` in the class hierarchy, in order to allow programs to use the idiom

```
} catch (Exception e) {
```

to catch all exceptions from which recovery may be possible without catching errors from which recovery is typically not possible. Package `java.lang` defines all the error classes described here.

The Java virtual machine throws an object that is an instance of a subclass of `LinkageError` when a loading (§2.17.2), linking (§2.17.3), or initialization (§2.17.4) error occurs.

- The loading process is described in (§2.17.2). The errors `ClassFormat-Error`, `ClassCircularityError`, `NoClassDefFoundError`, and `UnsupportedClassVersionError` are described there.

- The linking process is described in (§2.17.3). The linking errors `NoSuch-FieldError`, `NoSuchMethodError`, `InstantiationError`, and `Illegal-AccessError` are described there.

- The class verification process is described in (§2.17.3). The verification failure error `VerifyError` is described there.

- The class initialization process is described in (§2.17.4). A virtual machine will throw the error `ExceptionInInitializerError` if execution of a static initializer or of an initializer for a `static` field (§2.11) results in an exception that is not an `Error` or a subclass of `Error`.

A `LinkageError` may also be thrown at run time:

- An `AbstractMethodError` is thrown at run time if an `abstract` method is invoked.

- An `UnsatisfiedLinkError` is thrown at run time if the Java virtual machine cannot find an appropriate definition of a method declared to be `native`.

A Java virtual machine implementation throws an object that is an instance of a subclass of the class `VirtualMachineError` when an internal error or resource limitation prevents it from implementing the semantics of the Java programming language. This specification defines the following virtual machine errors:

- `InternalError`: An internal error has occurred in the Java virtual machine implementation because of a fault in the software implementing the virtual machine, a fault in the underlying host system software, or a fault in the hardware. This error is delivered asynchronously when it is detected and may occur at any point in a program.

- `OutOfMemoryError`: The Java virtual machine implementation has run out of either virtual or physical memory, and the automatic storage manager was unable to reclaim enough memory to satisfy an object creation request.

- `StackOverflowError`: The Java virtual machine implementation has run out of stack space for a thread, typically because the thread is doing an unbounded number of recursive invocations as a result of a fault in the executing program.

- `UnknownError`: An exception or error has occurred, but the Java virtual machine implementation is unable to report the actual exception or error.

2.17 Execution

This section specifies activities that occur during execution of a program. It is organized around the life cycle of the Java virtual machine and of the classes, interfaces, and objects that form a program. It specifies the detailed procedures used in starting up the virtual machine (§2.17.1), class and interface type loading (§2.17.2), linking (§2.17.3), and initialization (§2.17.4). It then specifies the procedures for creation of new class instances (§2.17.6). It concludes by describing the unloading of classes (§2.17.8) and the procedure followed when a virtual machine exits (§2.17.9).

2.17.1 Virtual Machine Start-up

The Java virtual machine starts execution by invoking the method `main` of some specified class and passing it a single argument, which is an array of strings. This causes the specified class to be loaded (§2.17.2), linked (§2.17.3) to other types that it uses, and initialized (§2.17.4). The method `main` must be declared `public`, `static`, and `void`.

The manner in which the initial class is specified to the Java virtual machine is beyond the scope of this specification, but it is typical, in host environments that use command lines, for the fully qualified name of the class to be specified as a command-line argument and for subsequent command-line arguments to be used as strings to be provided as the argument to the method `main`. For example, using Sun's Java 2 SDK for Solaris, the command line

```
java Terminator Hasta la vista Baby!
```

will start a Java virtual machine by invoking the method `main` of class `Terminator` (a class in an unnamed package) and passing it an array containing the four strings `"Hasta"`, `"la"`, `"vista"`, and `"Baby!"`.

We now outline the steps the virtual machine may take to execute `Terminator`, as an example of the loading, linking, and initialization processes that are described further in later sections.

The initial attempt to execute the method `main` of class `Terminator` discovers that the class `Terminator` is not loaded—that is, the virtual machine does not currently contain a binary representation for this class. The virtual machine then uses a `ClassLoader` (§2.17.2) to attempt to find such a binary representation. If this process fails, an error is thrown. This loading process is described further in (§2.17.2).

After `Terminator` is loaded, it must be initialized before `main` can be invoked, and a type (class or interface) must always be linked before it is initialized. Linking (§2.17.3) involves verification, preparation, and (optionally) resolution.

Verification (§2.17.3) checks that the loaded representation of `Terminator` is well formed, with a proper symbol table. Verification also checks that the code that implements `Terminator` obeys the semantic requirements of the Java virtual machine. If a problem is detected during verification, an error is thrown.

Preparation (§2.17.3) involves allocation of static storage and any data structures that are used internally by the virtual machine, such as method tables.

Resolution (§2.17.3) is the process of checking symbolic references from class `Terminator` to other classes and interfaces, by loading the other classes and interfaces that are mentioned and checking that the references are correct.

The resolution step is optional at the time of initial linkage. An implementation may resolve a symbolic reference from a class or interface that is being linked very early, even to the point of resolving all symbolic references from the classes and interfaces that are further referenced, recursively. (This resolution may result in errors from further loading and linking steps.) This implementation choice represents one extreme and is similar to the kind of static linkage that has been done for many years in simple implementations of the C language.

An implementation may instead choose to resolve a symbolic reference only when it is actually used; consistent use of this strategy for all symbolic references would represent the "laziest" form of resolution. In this case, if `Terminator` had several symbolic references to another class, the references might be resolved one at a time or perhaps not at all, if these references were never used during execution of the program.

The only requirement regarding when resolution is performed is that any errors detected during resolution must be thrown at a point in the program where some action is taken by the program that might, directly or indirectly, require linkage to the class or interface involved in the error. In the "static" example implementation choice described earlier, loading and linking errors could occur before the program is executed if they involved a class or interface mentioned in the class `Terminator` or any of the further, recursively referenced classes and interfaces. In a system that implemented the "laziest" resolution, these errors would be thrown only when a symbolic reference was used.

In our running example, the virtual machine is still trying to execute the method `main` of class `Terminator`. This is permitted only if the class has been initialized (§2.17.4).

Initialization consists of execution of any class variable initializers and static initializers of the class `Terminator`, in textual order. But before `Terminator` can be initialized, its direct superclass must be initialized, as well as the direct superclass of its direct superclass, and so on, recursively. In the simplest case, `Terminator` has `Object` as its implicit direct superclass; if class `Object` has not yet been initialized, then it must be initialized before `Terminator` is initialized.

If class `Terminator` has another class `Super` as its superclass, then `Super` must be initialized before `Terminator`. This requires loading, verifying, and preparing `Super`, if this has not already been done, and, depending on the implementation, may also involve resolving the symbolic references from `Super` and so on, recursively.

Initialization may thus cause loading, linking, and initialization errors, including such errors involving other types.

Finally, after completion of the initialization for class `Terminator` (during which other consequential loading, linking, and initializing may have occurred), the method `main` of `Terminator` is invoked.

2.17.2 Loading

Loading refers to the process of finding the binary form of a class or interface type with a particular name, perhaps by computing it on the fly, but more typically by retrieving a binary representation previously computed from source code by a compiler and constructing, from that binary form, a `Class` object to represent the class or interface. The binary format of a class or interface is normally the `class` file format (see Chapter 4, "The `class` File Format").

The loading process is implemented by the class `ClassLoader` and its subclasses. Different subclasses of `ClassLoader` may implement different loading policies. In particular, a class loader may cache binary representations of classes and interfaces, prefetch them based on expected usage, or load a group of related classes together. These activities may not be completely transparent to a running application if, for example, a newly compiled version of a class is not found because an older version is cached by a class loader. It is the responsibility of a class loader, however, to reflect loading errors only at points in the program where they could have arisen without prefetching or group loading.

If an error occurs during class loading, then an instance of one of the following subclasses of class `LinkageError` will be thrown at any point in the program that (directly or indirectly) uses the type:

- `ClassFormatError`: The binary data that purports to specify a requested compiled class or interface is malformed.

- `UnsupportedClassVersionError`: A class or interface could not be loaded because it is represented using an unsupported version of the `class` file format.[3]

- `ClassCircularityError`: A class or interface could not be loaded because it would be its own superclass or superinterface (§2.13.2).

- `NoClassDefFoundError`: No definition for a requested class or interface could be found by the relevant class loader.

2.17.3 Linking: Verification, Preparation, and Resolution

Linking is the process of taking a binary form of a class or interface type and combining it into the runtime state of the Java virtual machine, so that it can be executed. A class or interface type is always loaded before it is linked. Three different activities are involved in linking: verification, preparation, and resolution of symbolic references.

The Java programming language allows an implementation flexibility as to when linking activities (and, because of recursion, loading) take place, provided that the semantics of the language are respected, that a class or interface is completely verified and prepared before it is initialized, and that errors detected during linkage are thrown at a point in the program where some action is taken by the program that might require linkage to the class or interface involved in the error.

For example, an implementation may choose to resolve each symbolic reference in a class or interface individually, only when it is used (lazy or late resolution), or to resolve them all at once, for example, while the class is being verified (static resolution). This means that the resolution process may continue, in some implementations, after a class or interface has been initialized.

Verification ensures that the binary representation of a class or interface is structurally correct. For example, it checks that every instruction has a valid oper-

---

[3] `UnsupportedClassVersionError`, a subclass of `ClassFormatError`, was introduced in the Java 2 platform, v1.2, to enable easy identification of a `ClassFormatError` caused by an attempt to load a class represented using an unsupported version of the `class` file format.

ation code; that every branch instruction branches to the start of some other instruction, rather than into the middle of an instruction; that every method is provided with a structurally correct signature; and that every instruction obeys the type discipline of the Java programming language.

If an error occurs during verification, then an instance of the following subclass of class `LinkageError` will be thrown at the point in the program that caused the class to be verified:

- `VerifyError`: The binary definition for a class or interface failed to pass a set of required checks to verify that it cannot violate the integrity of the Java virtual machine.

Preparation involves creating the static fields for a class or interface and initializing such fields to the standard default values (§2.5.1). This does not require the execution of any Java virtual machine code; explicit initializers for static fields are executed as part of initialization (§2.17.4), not preparation.

Implementations of the Java virtual machine may precompute additional data structures at preparation time in order to make later operations on a class or interface more efficient. One particularly useful data structure is a "method table" or other data structure that allows any method to be invoked on instances of a class without requiring a search of superclasses at invocation time.

The binary representation of a class or interface references other classes and interfaces and their fields, methods, and constructors symbolically, using the fully qualified names (§2.7.5) of the other classes and interfaces. For fields and methods these symbolic references include the name of the class or interface type that declares the field or method, as well as the name of the field or method itself, together with appropriate type information.

Before a symbolic reference can be used it must undergo *resolution*, wherein a symbolic reference is validated and, typically, replaced with a direct reference that can be more efficiently processed if the reference is used repeatedly.

If an error occurs during resolution, then an instance of one of the following subclasses of class `IncompatibleClassChangeError`, or of some other subclass, or of `IncompatibleClassChangeError` itself (which is a subclass of the class `LinkageError`) may be thrown at any point in the program that uses a symbolic reference to the type:

- `IllegalAccessError`: A symbolic reference has been encountered that specifies a use or assignment of a field, or invocation of a method, or creation of an instance of a class to which the code containing the reference does not have access because the field or method was declared `private`, `protected`, or default access (not `public`), or because the class was not declared `public`. This can occur, for example, if a field that is originally declared `public` is changed to be `private` after another class that refers to the field has been compiled.

- `InstantiationError`: A symbolic reference has been encountered that is used in a class instance creation expression, but an instance cannot be created because the reference turns out to refer to an interface or to an `abstract` class. This can occur, for example, if a class that is originally not `abstract` is changed to be `abstract` after another class that refers to the class in question has been compiled.

- `NoSuchFieldError`: A symbolic reference has been encountered that refers to a specific field of a specific class or interface, but the class or interface does not declare a field of that name. This can occur, for example, if a field declaration was deleted from a class after another class that refers to the field was compiled.

- `NoSuchMethodError`: A symbolic reference has been encountered that refers to a specific method of a specific class or interface, but the class or interface does not declare a method of that name and signature. This can occur, for example, if a method declaration was deleted from a class after another class that refers to the method was compiled.

2.17.4 Initialization

Initialization of a class consists of executing its static initializers (§2.11) and the initializers for static fields (§2.9.2) declared in the class. Initialization of an interface consists of executing the initializers for fields declared in the interface (§2.13.3.1).

Before a class or interface is initialized, its direct superclass must be initialized, but interfaces implemented by the class need not be initialized. Similarly, the superinterfaces of an interface need not be initialized before the interface is initialized.

A class or interface type T will be *initialized* immediately before one of the following occurs:

- T is a class and an instance of T is created.

- T is a class and a static method of T is invoked.

- A nonconstant static field of *T* is used or assigned. A constant field is one that is (explicitly or implicitly) both `final` and `static`, and that is initialized with the value of a compile-time constant expression. A reference to such a field must be resolved at compile time to a copy of the compile-time constant value, so uses of such a field never cause initialization.

Invocation of certain methods in library classes (§3.12) also causes class or interface initialization. See the Java 2 platform's class library specifications (for example, class `Class` and package `java.lang.reflect`) for details.

The intent here is that a type have a set of initializers that put it in a consistent state and that this state be the first state that is observed by other classes. The static initializers and class variable initializers are executed in textual order and may not refer to class variables declared in the class whose declarations appear textually after the use, even though these class variables are in scope. This restriction is designed to detect, at compile time, most circular or otherwise malformed initializations.

Before a class or interface is initialized its superclass is initialized, if it has not previously been initialized.

2.17.5 Detailed Initialization Procedure

Initialization of a class or interface requires careful synchronization, since some other thread may be trying to initialize the same class or interface at the same time. There is also the possibility that initialization of a class or interface may be requested recursively as part of the initialization of that class or interface; for example, a variable initializer in class *A* might invoke a method of an unrelated class *B*, which might in turn invoke a method of class *A*. The implementation of the Java virtual machine is responsible for taking care of synchronization and recursive initialization by using the following procedure. It assumes that the `Class` object has already been verified and prepared and that the `Class` object contains state that can indicate one of four situations:

- This `Class` object is verified and prepared but not initialized.

- This `Class` object is being initialized by some particular thread *T*.

- This `Class` object is fully initialized and ready for use.

- This `Class` object is in an erroneous state, perhaps because the verification step failed or because initialization was attempted and failed.

The procedure for initializing a class or interface is then as follows:

1. Synchronize on the `Class` object that represents the class or interface to be initialized. This involves waiting until the current thread can obtain the lock for that object (§8.13).

2. If initialization by some other thread is in progress for the class or interface, then `wait` on this `Class` object (which temporarily releases the lock). When the current thread awakens from the `wait`, repeat this step.

3. If initialization is in progress for the class or interface by the current thread, then this must be a recursive request for initialization. Release the lock on the `Class` object and complete normally.

4. If the class or interface has already been initialized, then no further action is required. Release the lock on the `Class` object and complete normally.

5. If the `Class` object is in an erroneous state, then initialization is not possible. Release the lock on the `Class` object and throw a `NoClassDefFoundError`.

6. Otherwise, record the fact that initialization of the `Class` object is now in progress by the current thread and release the lock on the `Class` object.

7. Next, if the `Class` object represents a class rather than an interface, and the direct superclass of this class has not yet been initialized, then recursively perform this entire procedure for the uninitialized superclass. If the initialization of the direct superclass completes abruptly because of a thrown exception, then lock this `Class` object, label it erroneous, notify all waiting threads, release the lock, and complete abruptly, throwing the same exception that resulted from the initializing the superclass.

8. Next, execute either the class variable initializers and static initializers of the class or the field initializers of the interface, in textual order, as though they were a single block, except that `final static` variables and fields of interfaces whose values are compile-time constants are initialized first.

9. If the execution of the initializers completes normally, then lock this `Class` object, label it fully initialized, notify all waiting threads, release the lock, and complete this procedure normally.

10. Otherwise, the initializers must have completed abruptly by throwing some exception E. If the class of E is not `Error` or one of its subclasses, then create a new instance of the class `ExceptionInInitializerError`, with E as the

argument, and use this object in place of *E* in the following step. But if a new instance of `ExceptionInInitializerError` cannot be created because an `OutOfMemoryError` occurs, then instead use an `OutOfMemoryError` object in place of *E* in the following step.

11. Lock the `Class` object, label it erroneous, notify all waiting threads, release the lock, and complete this procedure abruptly with reason *E* or its replacement as determined in the previous step.

In some early implementations of the Java virtual machine, an exception during class initialization was ignored rather than allowing it to cause an `ExceptionInInitializerError` as described here.

2.17.6 Creation of New Class Instances

A new class instance is explicitly created when one of the following situations occurs:

- Evaluation of a class instance creation expression creates a new instance of the class whose name appears in the expression.

- Invocation of the `newInstance` method of class `Class` creates a new instance of the class represented by the `Class` object for which the method was invoked.

A new class instance may be implicitly created in the following situations:

- Loading of a class or interface that contains a `String` literal may create a new `String` object (§2.4.8) to represent that literal. This may not occur if the a `String` object has already been created to represent a previous occurrence of that literal, or if the `String.intern` method has been invoked on a `String` object representing the same string as the literal.

- Execution of a string concatenation operator that is not part of a constant expression sometimes creates a new `String` object to represent the result. String concatenation operators may also create temporary wrapper objects for a value of a primitive type (§2.4.1).

Each of these situations identifies a particular constructor to be called with specified arguments (possibly none) as part of the class instance creation process.

Whenever a new class instance is created, memory space is allocated for it with room for all the instance variables declared in the class type and all the instance variables declared in each superclass of the class type, including all the instance variables that may be hidden. If there is not sufficient space available to allocate memory for the object, then creation of the class instance completes abruptly with an `OutOfMemoryError`. Otherwise, all the instance variables in the new object, including those declared in superclasses, are initialized to their default values (§2.5.1).

Just before a reference to the newly created object is returned as the result, the indicated constructor is processed to initialize the new object using the following procedure:

1. Assign the arguments for the constructor to newly created parameter variables for this constructor invocation.

2. If this constructor begins with an explicit constructor invocation of another constructor in the same class (using `this`), then evaluate the arguments and process that constructor invocation recursively using these same five steps. If that constructor invocation completes abruptly, then this procedure completes abruptly for the same reason. Otherwise, continue with step 5.

3. If this constructor does not begin with an explicit constructor invocation of another constructor in the same class (using `this`) and is in a class other than `Object`, then this constructor will begin with an explicit or implicit invocation of a superclass constructor (using `super`). Evaluate the arguments and process that superclass constructor invocation recursively using these same five steps. If that constructor invocation completes abruptly, then this procedure completes abruptly for the same reason. Otherwise, continue with step 4.

4. Execute the instance variable initializers for this class, assigning their values to the corresponding instance variables, in the left-to-right order in which they appear textually in the source code for the class. If execution of any of these initializers results in an exception, then no further initializers are processed and this procedure completes abruptly with that same exception. Otherwise, continue with step 5. (In some early implementations, the compiler incorrectly omitted the code to initialize a field if the field initializer expression was a constant expression whose value was equal to the default initialization value for its type. This was a bug.)

5. Execute the rest of the body of this constructor. If that execution completes abruptly, then this procedure completes abruptly for the same reason. Otherwise, this procedure completes normally.

Unlike C++, the Java programming language does not specify altered rules for method dispatch during the creation of a new class instance. If methods are invoked that are overridden in subclasses in the object being initialized, then these overriding methods are used, even before the new object is completely created.

2.17.7 Finalization of Class Instances

The class `Object` has a `protected` method called `finalize`; this method can be overridden by other classes. The particular definition of `finalize` that can be invoked for an object is called the *finalizer* of that object. Before the storage for an object is reclaimed by the garbage collector, the Java virtual machine will invoke the finalizer of that object.

Finalizers provide a chance to free up resources (such as file descriptors or operating system graphics contexts) that cannot be freed automatically by an automatic storage manager. In such situations, simply reclaiming the memory used by an object would not guarantee that the resources it held would be reclaimed.

The Java programming language does not specify how soon a finalizer will be invoked, except to say that it will happen before the storage for the object is reused. Nor does the language specify which thread will invoke the finalizer for any given object. If an uncaught exception is thrown during the finalization, the exception is ignored and finalization of that object terminates.

The `finalize` method declared in class `Object` takes no action. However, the fact that class `Object` declares a `finalize` method means that the `finalize` method for any class can always invoke the `finalize` method for its superclass, which is usually good practice. (Unlike constructors, finalizers do not automatically invoke the finalizer for the superclass; such an invocation must be coded explicitly.)

For efficiency, an implementation may keep track of classes that do not override the `finalize` method of class `Object` or that override it in a trivial way, such as

```
protected void finalize() { super.finalize(); }
```

We encourage implementations to treat such objects as having a finalizer that is not overridden and to finalize them more efficiently.

The `finalize` method may be invoked explicitly, just like any other method. However, doing so does not have any effect on the object's eventual automatic finalization.

The Java virtual machine imposes no ordering on `finalize` method calls. Finalizers may be called in any order or even concurrently.

As an example, if a circularly linked group of unfinalized objects becomes unreachable, then all the objects may become finalizable together. Eventually, the finalizers for these objects may be invoked in any order or even concurrently using multiple threads. If the automatic storage manager later finds that the objects are unreachable, then their storage can be reclaimed.

2.17.8 Unloading of Classes and Interfaces

A class or interface may be unloaded if and only if its class loader is unreachable. The bootstrap class loader is always reachable; as a result, system classes may never be unloaded.

2.17.9 Virtual Machine Exit

The Java virtual machine terminates all its activity and exits when one of two things happens:

- All the threads that are not daemon threads (§2.19) terminate.

- Some thread invokes the `exit` method of class `Runtime` or class `System`, and the exit operation is permitted by the security manager.

A program can specify that all finalizers that have not been automatically invoked are to be run before the virtual machine exits. This is done by invoking the method `runFinalizersOnExit` of the class `System` with the argument `true`.[4] By default finalizers are not run on exit. Once running finalizers on exit has been enabled it may be disabled by invoking `runFinalizersOnExit` with the argument `false`. An invocation of the `runFinalizersOnExit` method is permitted only if the caller is allowed to `exit` and is otherwise rejected by the security manager.

2.18 FP-strict Expressions

If the type of an expression is `float` or `double`, then there is a question as to what value set (§2.4.3) the value of the expression may be drawn from. This is governed

---

[4] The method `runFinalizersOnExit` was first implemented in JDK release 1.1 but has been deprecated in the Java 2 platform, v1.2.

by the rules of value set conversion (§2.6.6); these rules in turn depend on whether or not the expression is *FP-strict*.

Every compile-time constant expression is FP-strict. If an expression is not a compile-time constant expression, then consider all the class declarations, interface declarations, and method declarations that contain the expression. If *any* such declaration bears the `strictfp` modifier, then the expression is FP-strict.

It follows that an expression is not FP-strict if and only if it is not a compile-time constant expression *and* it does not appear within any declaration that has the `strictfp` modifier.

Within an FP-strict expression, all intermediate values must be elements of the float value set or the double value set, implying that the results of all FP-strict expressions must be those predicted by IEEE 754 arithmetic on operands represented using single and double formats. Within an expression that is not FP-strict, some leeway is granted for an implementation to use an extended exponent range to represent intermediate results; the net effect, roughly speaking, is that a calculation might produce "the correct answer" in situations where exclusive use of the float value set or double value set might result in overflow or underflow.

2.19 Threads

While most of the preceding discussion is concerned only with the behavior of code as executed by a single thread, the Java virtual machine can support many threads of execution at once. These threads independently execute code that operates on values and objects residing in a shared main memory. Threads may be supported by having many hardware processors, by time-slicing a single hardware processor, or by time-slicing many hardware processors.

Any thread may be marked as a *daemon thread*. When code running in some thread creates a new `Thread` object, that new thread is initially marked as a daemon thread if and only if the creating thread is a daemon thread. A program can change whether or not a particular thread is a daemon thread by calling the `setDaemon` method in class `Thread`. The Java virtual machine initially starts up with a single nondaemon thread, which typically calls the method `main` of some class. The virtual machine may also create other daemon threads for internal purposes. The Java virtual machine exits when all nondaemon threads have terminated (§2.17.9).

By providing mechanisms for *synchronizing* the concurrent activity of threads, the Java programming language supports the coding of programs that, though concurrent, still exhibit deterministic behavior. To synchronize threads the language uses *monitors*, a mechanism for allowing one thread at a time to execute a region of code. The behavior of monitors is explained in terms of *locks*. There is a lock associated with each object.

The `synchronized` statement performs two special actions relevant only to multithreaded operation:

1. After computing a reference to an object but before executing its body, it locks a lock associated with the object.

2. After execution of the body has completed, either normally or abruptly, it unlocks that same lock. As a convenience, a method may be declared `synchronized`; such a method behaves as if its body were contained in a `synchronized` statement.

The methods `wait`, `notify`, and `notifyAll` of class `Object` support an efficient transfer of control from one thread to another. Rather than simply "spinning" (repeatedly locking and unlocking an object to see whether some internal state has changed), which consumes computational effort, a thread can suspend itself using `wait` until such time as another thread awakens it using `notify` or `notifyAll`. This is especially appropriate in situations where threads have a producer–consumer relationship (actively cooperating on a common goal) rather than a mutual exclusion relationship (trying to avoid conflicts while sharing a common resource).

As a thread executes code, it carries out a sequence of actions. A thread may *use* the value of a variable or *assign* it a new value. (Other actions include arithmetic operations, conditional tests, and method invocations, but these do not involve variables directly.) If two or more concurrent threads act on a shared variable, there is a possibility that the actions on the variable will produce timing-dependent results. This dependence on timing is inherent in concurrent programming and produces one of the few situations where the result of a program is not determined solely by *The Java™ Language Specification*.

Each thread has a working memory, in which it may keep copies of the values of variables from the main memory that are shared between all threads. To access a shared variable, a thread usually first obtains a lock and flushes its working memory. This guarantees that shared values will thereafter be loaded from the shared main memory to the working memory of the thread. By unlocking a lock, a thread guarantees that the values held by the thread in its working memory will be written back to the main memory.

The interaction of threads with the main memory, and thus with each other, may be explained in terms of certain low-level actions. There are rules about the order in which these actions may occur. These rules impose constraints on any implementation of the Java programming language. A programmer may rely on the rules to predict the possible behaviors of a concurrent program. The rules do, however, intentionally give the implementor certain freedoms. The intent is to permit certain standard hardware and software techniques that can greatly improve the speed and efficiency of concurrent code.

Briefly put, the important consequences of the rules are the following:

- Proper use of synchronization constructs will allow reliable transmission of values or sets of values from one thread to another through shared variables.

- When a thread uses the value of a variable, the value it obtains is in fact a value stored into the variable by that thread or by some other thread. This is true even if the program does not contain code for proper synchronization. For example, if two threads store references to different objects into the same reference value, the variable will subsequently contain a reference to one object or the other, not a reference to some other object or a corrupted reference value. (There is a special exception for `long` and `double` values; see §8.4.)

- In the absence of explicit synchronization, an implementation is free to update the main memory in an order that may be surprising. Therefore, the programmer who prefers to avoid surprises should use explicit synchronization.

The details of the interaction of threads with the main memory, and thus with each other, are discussed in detail in Chapter 8, "Threads and Locks."

CHAPTER 3

The Structure of the Java Virtual Machine

THIS book specifies an abstract machine. It does not document any particular implementation of the Java virtual machine, including Sun Microsystems'.

To implement the Java virtual machine correctly, you need only be able to read the `class` file format and correctly perform the operations specified therein. Implementation details that are not part of the Java virtual machine's specification would unnecessarily constrain the creativity of implementors. For example, the memory layout of runtime data areas, the garbage-collection algorithm used, and any internal optimization of the Java virtual machine instructions (for example, translating them into machine code) are left to the discretion of the implementor.

3.1 The `class` File Format

Compiled code to be executed by the Java virtual machine is represented using a hardware- and operating system-independent binary format, typically (but not necessarily) stored in a file, known as the `class` file format. The `class` file format precisely defines the representation of a class or interface, including details such as byte ordering that might be taken for granted in a platform-specific object file format.

Chapter 4, "The `class` File Format," covers the `class` file format in detail.

3.2 Data Types

Like the Java programming language, the Java virtual machine operates on two kinds of types: *primitive types* and *reference types*. There are, correspondingly, two kinds of values that can be stored in variables, passed as arguments, returned by methods, and operated upon: *primitive values* and *reference values.*

The Java virtual machine expects that nearly all type checking is done prior to run time, typically by a compiler, and does not have to be done by the Java virtual machine itself. Values of primitive types need not be tagged or otherwise be inspectable to determine their types at run time, or to be distinguished from values of reference types. Instead, the instruction set of the Java virtual machine distinguishes its operand types using instructions intended to operate on values of specific types. For instance, *iadd*, *ladd*, *fadd*, and *dadd* are all Java virtual machine instructions that add two numeric values and produce numeric results, but each is specialized for its operand type: `int`, `long`, `float`, and `double`, respectively. For a summary of type support in the Java virtual machine instruction set, see §3.11.1.

The Java virtual machine contains explicit support for objects. An object is either a dynamically allocated class instance or an array. A reference to an object is considered to have Java virtual machine type `reference`. Values of type `reference` can be thought of as pointers to objects. More than one reference to an object may exist. Objects are always operated on, passed, and tested via values of type `reference`.

3.3 Primitive Types and Values

The primitive data types supported by the Java virtual machine are the *numeric types*, the `boolean` type (§3.3.4),[1] and the `returnAddress` type (§3.3.3). The numeric types consist of the *integral types* (§3.3.1) and the *floating-point types* (§3.3.2). The integral types are:

- `byte`, whose values are 8-bit signed two's-complement integers

- `short`, whose values are 16-bit signed two's-complement integers

- `int`, whose values are 32-bit signed two's-complement integers

- `long`, whose values are 64-bit signed two's-complement integers

- `char`, whose values are 16-bit unsigned integers representing Unicode characters (§2.1)

---

[1] The first edition of *The Java™ Virtual Machine Specification* did not consider `boolean` to be a Java virtual machine type. However, `boolean` values do have limited support in the Java virtual machine. This second edition clarifies the issue by treating `boolean` as a type.

The floating-point types are:

- `float`, whose values are elements of the float value set or, where supported, the float-extended-exponent value set

- `double`, whose values are elements of the double value set or, where supported, the double-extended-exponent value set

The values of the `boolean` type encode the truth values `true` and `false`.

The values of the `returnAddress` type are pointers to the opcodes of Java virtual machine instructions. Of the primitive types only the `returnAddress` type is not directly associated with a Java programming language type.

3.3.1 Integral Types and Values

The values of the integral types of the Java virtual machine are the same as those for the integral types of the Java programming language (§2.4.1):

- For `byte`, from −128 to 127 (-2^7 to 2^7-1), inclusive

- For `short`, from −32768 to 32767 (-2^{15} to $2^{15}-1$), inclusive

- For `int`, from −2147483648 to 2147483647 (-2^{31} to $2^{31}-1$), inclusive

- For `long`, from −9223372036854775808 to 9223372036854775807 (-2^{63} to $2^{63}-1$), inclusive

- For `char`, from 0 to 65535 inclusive

3.3.2 Floating-Point Types, Value Sets, and Values

The floating-point types are `float` and `double`, which are conceptually associated with the 32-bit single-precision and 64-bit double-precision format IEEE 754 values and operations as specified in *IEEE Standard for Binary Floating-Point Arithmetic*, ANSI/IEEE Std. 754-1985 (IEEE, New York).

The IEEE 754 standard includes not only positive and negative sign-magnitude numbers, but also positive and negative zeros, positive and negative *infinities*, and a special *Not-a-Number value* (hereafter abbreviated as "NaN"). The NaN value is used to represent the result of certain invalid operations such as dividing zero by zero.

Every implementation of the Java virtual machine is required to support two standard sets of floating-point values, called the *float value set* and the *double value set.* In addition, an implementation of the Java virtual machine may, at its option, support either or both of two extended-exponent floating-point value sets, called the *float-extended-exponent value set* and the *double-extended-exponent value set*. These extended-exponent value sets may, under certain circumstances, be used instead of the standard value sets to represent the values of type float or double.

The finite nonzero values of any floating-point value set can all be expressed in the form $s \cdot m \cdot 2^{(e - N + 1)}$, where s is +1 or −1, m is a positive integer less than 2^N, and e is an integer between $Emin = -(2^{K-1} - 2)$ and $Emax = 2^{K-1} - 1$, inclusive, and where N and K are parameters that depend on the value set. Some values can be represented in this form in more than one way; for example, supposing that a value v in a value set might be represented in this form using certain values for s, m, and e, then if it happened that m were even and e were less than 2^{K-1}, one could halve m and increase e by 1 to produce a second representation for the same value v. A representation in this form is called *normalized* if $m \geq 2^{N-1}$; otherwise the representation is said to be *denormalized*. If a value in a value set cannot be represented in such a way that $m \geq 2^{N-1}$, then the value is said to be a *denormalized value*, because it has no normalized representation.

The constraints on the parameters N and K (and on the derived parameters *Emin* and *Emax*) for the two required and two optional floating-point value sets are summarized in Table 3.1.

Table 3.1   Floating-point value set parameters

Parameter	float	float-extended-exponent	double	double-extended-exponent
N	24	24	53	53
K	8	≥ 11	11	≥ 15
Emax	+127	$\geq +1023$	+1023	$\geq +16383$
Emin	−126	≤ -1022	−1022	≤ -16382

Where one or both extended-exponent value sets are supported by an implementation, then for each supported extended-exponent value set there is a specific implementation-dependent constant K, whose value is constrained by Table 3.1; this value K in turn dictates the values for *Emin* and *Emax*.

Each of the four value sets includes not only the finite nonzero values that are ascribed to it above, but also the five values positive zero, negative zero, positive infinity, negative infinity, and NaN.

Note that the constraints in Table 3.1 are designed so that every element of the float value set is necessarily also an element of the float-extended-exponent value set, the double value set, and the double-extended-exponent value set. Likewise, each element of the double value set is necessarily also an element of the double-extended-exponent value set. Each extended-exponent value set has a larger range of exponent values than the corresponding standard value set, but does not have more precision.

The elements of the float value set are exactly the values that can be represented using the single floating-point format defined in the IEEE 754 standard, except that there is only one NaN value (IEEE 754 specifies $2^{24} - 2$ distinct NaN values). The elements of the double value set are exactly the values that can be represented using the double floating-point format defined in the IEEE 754 standard, except that there is only one NaN value (IEEE 754 specifies $2^{53} - 2$ distinct NaN values). Note, however, that the elements of the float-extended-exponent and double-extended-exponent value sets defined here do *not* correspond to the values that be represented using IEEE 754 single extended and double extended formats, respectively. This specification does not mandate a specific representation for the values of the floating-point value sets except where floating-point values must be represented in the `class` file format (§4.4.4, §4.4.5).

The float, float-extended-exponent, double, and double-extended-exponent value sets are not types. It is always correct for an implementation of the Java virtual machine to use an element of the float value set to represent a value of type `float`; however, it may be permissible in certain contexts for an implementation to use an element of the float-extended-exponent value set instead. Similarly, it is always correct for an implementation to use an element of the double value set to represent a value of type `double`; however, it may be permissible in certain contexts for an implementation to use an element of the double-extended-exponent value set instead.

Except for NaNs, values of the floating-point value sets are *ordered*. When arranged from smallest to largest, they are negative infinity, negative finite values, positive and negative zero, positive finite values, and positive infinity.

Floating-point positive zero and floating-point negative zero compare as equal, but there are other operations that can distinguish them; for example, dividing `1.0` by `0.0` produces positive infinity, but dividing `1.0` by `-0.0` produces negative infinity.

NaNs are *unordered*, so numerical comparisons and tests for numerical equality have the value `false` if either or both of their operands are NaN. In particular, a test for numerical equality of a value against itself has the value `false` if and only if the value is NaN. A test for numerical inequality has the value `true` if either operand is NaN.

3.3.3 The `returnAddress` Type and Values

The `returnAddress` type is used by the Java virtual machine's *jsr*, *ret*, and *jsr_w* instructions. The values of the `returnAddress` type are pointers to the opcodes of Java virtual machine instructions. Unlike the numeric primitive types, the `returnAddress` type does not correspond to any Java programming language type and cannot be modified by the running program.

3.3.4 The `boolean` Type

Although the Java virtual machine defines a `boolean` type, it only provides very limited support for it. There are no Java virtual machine instructions solely dedicated to operations on `boolean` values. Instead, expressions in the Java programming language that operate on `boolean` values are compiled to use values of the Java virtual machine `int` data type.

The Java virtual machine does directly support `boolean` arrays. Its *newarray* instruction enables creation of `boolean` arrays. Arrays of type `boolean` are accessed and modified using the `byte` array instructions *baload* and *bastore*.[2]

The Java virtual machine encodes `boolean` array components using *1* to represent `true` and *0* to represent `false`. Where Java programming language `boolean` values are mapped by compilers to values of Java virtual machine type `int`, the compilers must use the same encoding.

3.4 Reference Types and Values

There are three kinds of `reference` types: class types, array types, and interface types. Their values are references to dynamically created class instances, arrays, or class instances or arrays that implement interfaces, respectively. A `reference` value may also be the special null reference, a reference to no object, which will be denoted here by `null`. The `null` reference initially has no runtime type, but may be cast to any type (§2.4).

---

[2] In Sun's JDK releases 1.0 and 1.1, and the Java 2 SDK, Standard Edition, v1.2, `boolean` arrays in the Java programming language are encoded as Java virtual machine `byte` arrays, using 8 bits per `boolean` element.

The Java virtual machine specification does not mandate a concrete value encoding `null`.

3.5 Runtime Data Areas

The Java virtual machine defines various runtime data areas that are used during execution of a program. Some of these data areas are created on Java virtual machine start-up and are destroyed only when the Java virtual machine exits. Other data areas are per thread. Per-thread data areas are created when a thread is created and destroyed when the thread exits.

3.5.1 The pc Register

The Java virtual machine can support many threads of execution at once (§2.19). Each Java virtual machine thread has its own `pc` (program counter) register. At any point, each Java virtual machine thread is executing the code of a single method, the current method (§3.6) for that thread. If that method is not `native`, the `pc` register contains the address of the Java virtual machine instruction currently being executed. If the method currently being executed by the thread is `native`, the value of the Java virtual machine's `pc` register is undefined. The Java virtual machine's `pc` register is wide enough to hold a `returnAddress` or a native pointer on the specific platform.

3.5.2 Java Virtual Machine Stacks

Each Java virtual machine thread has a private *Java virtual machine stack*, created at the same time as the thread.[3] A Java virtual machine stack stores frames (§3.6). A Java virtual machine stack is analogous to the stack of a conventional language such as C: it holds local variables and partial results, and plays a part in method invocation and return. Because the Java virtual machine stack is never manipulated directly except to push and pop frames, frames may be heap allocated. The memory for a Java virtual machine stack does not need to be contiguous.

The Java virtual machine specification permits Java virtual machine stacks either to be of a fixed size or to dynamically expand and contract as required by the computation. If the Java virtual machine stacks are of a fixed size, the size of each Java virtual machine stack may be chosen independently when that stack is

---

[3] In the first edition of this specification, the Java virtual machine stack was known as the *Java stack*.

created. A Java virtual machine implementation may provide the programmer or the user control over the initial size of Java virtual machine stacks, as well as, in the case of dynamically expanding or contracting Java virtual machine stacks, control over the maximum and minimum sizes.[4]

The following exceptional conditions are associated with Java virtual machine stacks:

- If the computation in a thread requires a larger Java virtual machine stack than is permitted, the Java virtual machine throws a `StackOverflowError`.

- If Java virtual machine stacks can be dynamically expanded, and expansion is attempted but insufficient memory can be made available to effect the expansion, or if insufficient memory can be made available to create the initial Java virtual machine stack for a new thread, the Java virtual machine throws an `OutOfMemoryError`.

3.5.3 Heap

The Java virtual machine has a *heap* that is shared among all Java virtual machine threads. The heap is the runtime data area from which memory for all class instances and arrays is allocated.

The heap is created on virtual machine start-up. Heap storage for objects is reclaimed by an automatic storage management system (known as a *garbage collector*); objects are never explicitly deallocated. The Java virtual machine assumes no particular type of automatic storage management system, and the storage management technique may be chosen according to the implementor's system requirements. The heap may be of a fixed size or may be expanded as required by the computation and may be contracted if a larger heap becomes unnecessary. The memory for the heap does not need to be contiguous.

A Java virtual machine implementation may provide the programmer or the user control over the initial size of the heap, as well as, if the heap can be dynami-

---

[4] In Sun's implementations of the Java virtual machine in JDK releases 1.0.2 and 1.1, and the Java 2 SDK, Standard Edition, v1.2, Java virtual machine stacks are discontiguous and are independently expanded as required by the computation. Those implementations do not free memory allocated for a Java virtual machine stack until the associated thread terminates. Expansion is subject to a size limit for any one stack. The Java virtual machine stack size limit may be set on virtual machine start-up using the "-oss" flag. The Java virtual machine stack size limit can be used to limit memory consumption or to catch runaway recursions.

cally expanded or contracted, control over the maximum and minimum heap size.[5]
The following exceptional condition is associated with the heap:

- If a computation requires more heap than can be made available by the automatic storage management system, the Java virtual machine throws an `OutOfMemoryError`.

3.5.4 Method Area

The Java virtual machine has a *method area* that is shared among all Java virtual machine threads. The method area is analogous to the storage area for compiled code of a conventional language or analogous to the "text" segment in a UNIX process. It stores per-class structures such as the runtime constant pool, field and method data, and the code for methods and constructors, including the special methods (§3.9) used in class and instance initialization and interface type initialization.

The method area is created on virtual machine start-up. Although the method area is logically part of the heap, simple implementations may choose not to either garbage collect or compact it. This version of the Java virtual machine specification does not mandate the location of the method area or the policies used to manage compiled code. The method area may be of a fixed size or may be expanded as required by the computation and may be contracted if a larger method area becomes unnecessary. The memory for the method area does not need to be contiguous.

A Java virtual machine implementation may provide the programmer or the user control over the initial size of the method area, as well as, in the case of a varying-size method area, control over the maximum and minimum method area size.[6]
The following exceptional condition is associated with the method area:

- If memory in the method area cannot be made available to satisfy an allocation request, the Java virtual machine throws an `OutOfMemoryError`.

---

[5] Sun's implementations of the Java virtual machine in JDK releases 1.0.2 and 1.1, and the Java 2 SDK, Standard Edition, v1.2, dynamically expand the heap as required by the computation, but never contract the heap. The initial and maximum sizes may be specified on virtual machine start-up using the "`-ms`" and "`-mx`" flags, respectively.

[6] Sun's implementation of the Java virtual machine in JDK release 1.0.2 dynamically expands the method area as required by the computation, but never contracts the method area. The Java virtual machine implementations in Sun's JDK release 1.1 and the Java 2 SDK, Standard Edition, v1.2 garbage collect the method area. In neither case is user control over the initial, minimum, or maximum size of the method area provided.

3.5.5 Runtime Constant Pool

A *runtime constant pool* is a per-class or per-interface runtime representation of the
`constant_pool` table in a `class` file (§4.4). It contains several kinds of constants,
ranging from numeric literals known at compile time to method and field references
that must be resolved at run time. The runtime constant pool serves a function similar to that of a symbol table for a conventional programming language, although
it contains a wider range of data than a typical symbol table.

Each runtime constant pool is allocated from the Java virtual machine's
method area (§3.5.4). The runtime constant pool for a class or interface is constructed when the class or interface is created (§5.3) by the Java virtual machine.

The following exceptional condition is associated with the construction of the
runtime constant pool for a class or interface:

- When creating a class or interface, if the construction of the runtime constant
  pool requires more memory than can be made available in the method area of
  the Java virtual machine, the Java virtual machine throws an `OutOfMemory-`
  `Error`.

See Chapter 5 for information about the construction of the runtime constant
pool.

3.5.6 Native Method Stacks

An implementation of the Java virtual machine may use conventional stacks, colloquially called "C stacks," to support `native` methods, methods written in a language other than the Java programming language. Native method stacks may also be
used by the implementation of an interpreter for the Java virtual machine's instruction set in a language such as C. Java virtual machine implementations that cannot
load `native` methods and that do not themselves rely on conventional stacks need
not supply native method stacks. If supplied, native method stacks are typically allocated per thread when each thread is created.

The Java virtual machine specification permits native method stacks either to
be of a fixed size or to dynamically expand and contract as required by the computation. If the native method stacks are of a fixed size, the size of each native
method stack may be chosen independently when that stack is created. In any
case, a Java virtual machine implementation may provide the programmer or the
user control over the initial size of the native method stacks. In the case of

varying-size native method stacks, it may also make available control over the maximum and minimum method stack sizes.[7]

The following exceptional conditions are associated with native method stacks:

- If the computation in a thread requires a larger native method stack than is permitted, the Java virtual machine throws a `StackOverflowError`.

- If native method stacks can be dynamically expanded and native method stack expansion is attempted but insufficient memory can be made available, or if insufficient memory can be made available to create the initial native method stack for a new thread, the Java virtual machine throws an `OutOfMemory-Error`.

3.6 Frames

A *frame* is used to store data and partial results, as well as to perform dynamic linking, return values for methods, and dispatch exceptions.

A new frame is created each time a method is invoked. A frame is destroyed when its method invocation completes, whether that completion is normal or abrupt (it throws an uncaught exception). Frames are allocated from the Java virtual machine stack (§3.5.2) of the thread creating the frame. Each frame has its own array of local variables (§3.6.1), its own operand stack (§3.6.2), and a reference to the runtime constant pool (§3.5.5) of the class of the current method.

The sizes of the local variable array and the operand stack are determined at compile time and are supplied along with the code for the method associated with the frame (§4.7.3). Thus the size of the frame data structure depends only on the implementation of the Java virtual machine, and the memory for these structures can be allocated simultaneously on method invocation.

Only one frame, the frame for the executing method, is active at any point in a given thread of control. This frame is referred to as the *current frame*, and its method is known as the *current method*. The class in which the current method is

---

[7] Sun's implementations of the Java virtual machine in JDK releases 1.0.2 and 1.1, and the Java 2 SDK, Standard Edition, v1.2, allocate fixed-size native method stacks of a single size. The size of the native method stacks may be set on virtual machine start-up using the "`-ss`" flag. The native method stack size limit can be used to limit memory consumption or to catch runaway recursions in `native` methods. Sun's implementations do *not* check for native method stack overflow.

defined is the *current class*. Operations on local variables and the operand stack are typically with reference to the current frame.

A frame ceases to be current if its method invokes another method or if its method completes. When a method is invoked, a new frame is created and becomes current when control transfers to the new method. On method return, the current frame passes back the result of its method invocation, if any, to the previous frame. The current frame is then discarded as the previous frame becomes the current one.

Note that a frame created by a thread is local to that thread and cannot be referenced by any other thread.

3.6.1 Local Variables

Each frame (§3.6) contains an array of variables known as its *local variables*. The length of the local variable array of a frame is determined at compile time and supplied in the binary representation of a class or interface along with the code for the method associated with the frame (§4.7.3).

A single local variable can hold a value of type `boolean`, `byte`, `char`, `short`, `int`, `float`, `reference`, or `returnAddress`. A pair of local variables can hold a value of type `long` or `double`.

Local variables are addressed by indexing. The index of the first local variable is zero. An integer is be considered to be an index into the local variable array if and only if that integer is between zero and one less than the size of the local variable array.

A value of type `long` or type `double` occupies two consecutive local variables. Such a value may only be addressed using the lesser index. For example, a value of type `double` stored in the local variable array at index n actually occupies the local variables with indices n and $n+1$; however, the local variable at index $n+1$ cannot be loaded from. It can be stored into. However, doing so invalidates the contents of local variable n.

The Java virtual machine does not require n to be even. In intuitive terms, values of types `double` and `long` need not be 64-bit aligned in the local variables array. Implementors are free to decide the appropriate way to represent such values using the two local variables reserved for the value.

The Java virtual machine uses local variables to pass parameters on method invocation. On class method invocation any parameters are passed in consecutive local variables starting from local variable *0*. On instance method invocation, local variable *0* is always used to pass a reference to the object on which the instance method is being invoked (`this` in the Java programming language). Any parameters are subsequently passed in consecutive local variables starting from local variable *1*.

3.6.2 Operand Stacks

Each frame (§3.6) contains a last-in-first-out (LIFO) stack known as its *operand stack*. The maximum depth of the operand stack of a frame is determined at compile time and is supplied along with the code for the method associated with the frame (§4.7.3).

Where it is clear by context, we will sometimes refer to the operand stack of the current frame as simply the operand stack.

The operand stack is empty when the frame that contains it is created. The Java virtual machine supplies instructions to load constants or values from local variables or fields onto the operand stack. Other Java virtual machine instructions take operands from the operand stack, operate on them, and push the result back onto the operand stack. The operand stack is also used to prepare parameters to be passed to methods and to receive method results.

For example, the *iadd* instruction adds two `int` values together. It requires that the `int` values to be added be the top two values of the operand stack, pushed there by previous instructions. Both of the `int` values are popped from the operand stack. They are added, and their sum is pushed back onto the operand stack. Subcomputations may be nested on the operand stack, resulting in values that can be used by the encompassing computation.

Each entry on the operand stack can hold a value of any Java virtual machine type, including a value of type `long` or type `double`.

Values from the operand stack must be operated upon in ways appropriate to their types. It is not possible, for example, to push two `int` values and subsequently treat them as a `long` or to push two `float` values and subsequently add them with an *iadd* instruction. A small number of Java virtual machine instructions (the *dup* instructions and *swap*) operate on runtime data areas as raw values without regard to their specific types; these instructions are defined in such a way that they cannot be used to modify or break up individual values. These restrictions on operand stack manipulation are enforced through `class` file verification (§4.9).

At any point in time an operand stack has an associated depth, where a value of type `long` or `double` contributes two units to the depth and a value of any other type contributes one unit.

3.6.3 Dynamic Linking

Each frame (§3.6) contains a reference to the runtime constant pool (§3.5.5) for the type of the current method to support *dynamic linking* of the method code. The class file code for a method refers to methods to be invoked and variables to be accessed via symbolic references. Dynamic linking translates these symbolic method references into concrete method references, loading classes as necessary to resolve as-yet-undefined symbols, and translates variable accesses into appropriate offsets in storage structures associated with the runtime location of these variables.

This late binding of the methods and variables makes changes in other classes that a method uses less likely to break this code.

3.6.4 Normal Method Invocation Completion

A method invocation *completes normally* if that invocation does not cause an exception (§2.16, §3.10) to be thrown, either directly from the Java virtual machine or as a result of executing an explicit throw statement. If the invocation of the current method completes normally, then a value may be returned to the invoking method. This occurs when the invoked method executes one of the return instructions (§3.11.8), the choice of which must be appropriate for the type of the value being returned (if any).

The current frame (§3.6) is used in this case to restore the state of the invoker, including its local variables and operand stack, with the program counter of the invoker appropriately incremented to skip past the method invocation instruction. Execution then continues normally in the invoking method's frame with the returned value (if any) pushed onto the operand stack of that frame.

3.6.5 Abrupt Method Invocation Completion

A method invocation *completes abruptly* if execution of a Java virtual machine instruction within the method causes the Java virtual machine to throw an exception (§2.16, §3.10), and that exception is not handled within the method. Execution of an *athrow* instruction also causes an exception to be explicitly thrown and, if the exception is not caught by the current method, results in abrupt method invocation completion. A method invocation that completes abruptly never returns a value to its invoker.

3.6.6 Additional Information

A frame may be extended with additional implementation-specific information, such as debugging information.

3.7 Representation of Objects

The Java virtual machine does not mandate any particular internal structure for objects.[8]

3.8 Floating-Point Arithmetic

The Java virtual machine incorporates a subset of the floating-point arithmetic specified in *IEEE Standard for Binary Floating-Point Arithmetic* (ANSI/IEEE Std. 754-1985, New York).

3.8.1 Java Virtual Machine Floating-Point Arithmetic and IEEE 754

The key differences between the floating-point arithmetic supported by the Java virtual machine and the IEEE 754 standard are:

- The floating-point operations of the Java virtual machine do not throw exceptions, trap, or otherwise signal the IEEE 754 exceptional conditions of invalid operation, division by zero, overflow, underflow, or inexact. The Java virtual machine has no signaling NaN value.

- The Java virtual machine does not support IEEE 754 signaling floating-point comparisons.

- The rounding operations of the Java virtual machine always use IEEE 754 round to nearest mode. Inexact results are rounded to the nearest representable value, with ties going to the value with a zero least-significant bit. This is the IEEE 754 default mode. But Java virtual machine instructions that convert

---

[8] In some of Sun's implementations of the Java virtual machine, a reference to a class instance is a pointer to a *handle* that is itself a pair of pointers: one to a table containing the methods of the object and a pointer to the Class object that represents the type of the object, and the other to the memory allocated from the heap for the object data.

values of floating-point types to values of integral types round toward zero. The Java virtual machine does not give any means to change the floating-point rounding mode.

- The Java virtual machine does not support either the IEEE 754 single extended or double extended format, except insofar as the double and double-extended-exponent value sets may be said to support the single extended format. The float-extended-exponent and double-extended-exponent value sets, which may optionally be supported, do not correspond to the values of the IEEE 754 extended formats: the IEEE 754 extended formats require extended precision as well as extended exponent range.

3.8.2 Floating-Point Modes

Every method has a *floating-point mode*, which is either *FP-strict* or *not FP-strict*. The floating-point mode of a method is determined by the setting of the ACC_STRICT bit of the access_flags item of the method_info structure (§4.6) defining the method. A method for which this bit is set is FP-strict; otherwise, the method is not FP-strict.

Note that this mapping of the ACC_STRICT bit implies that methods in classes compiled by a compiler that predates the Java 2 platform, v1.2, are effectively not FP-strict.

We will refer to an operand stack as having a given floating-point mode when the method whose invocation created the frame containing the operand stack has that floating-point mode. Similarly, we will refer to a Java virtual machine instruction as having a given floating-point mode when the method containing that instruction has that floating-point mode.

If a float-extended-exponent value set is supported (§3.3.2), values of type float on an operand stack that is not FP-strict may range over that value set except where prohibited by value set conversion (§3.8.3). If a double-extended-exponent value set is supported (§3.3.2), values of type double on an operand stack that is not FP-strict may range over that value set except where prohibited by value set conversion.

In all other contexts, whether on the operand stack or elsewhere, and regardless of floating-point mode, floating-point values of type float and double may only range over the float value set and double value set, respectively. In particular, class and instance fields, array elements, local variables, and method parameters may only contain values drawn from the standard value sets.

3.8.3 Value Set Conversion

An implementation of the Java virtual machine that supports an extended floating-point value set is permitted or required, under specified circumstances, to map a value of the associated floating-point type between the extended and the standard value sets. Such a *value set conversion* is not a type conversion, but a mapping between the value sets associated with the same type.

Where value set conversion is indicated, an implementation is permitted to perform one of the following operations on a value:

- If the value is of type `float` and is not an element of the float value set, it maps the value to the nearest element of the float value set.

- If the value is of type `double` and is not an element of the double value set, it maps the value to the nearest element of the double value set.

In addition, where value set conversion is indicated certain operations are required:

- Suppose execution of a Java virtual machine instruction that is not FP-strict causes a value of type `float` to be pushed onto an operand stack that is FP-strict, passed as a parameter, or stored into a local variable, a field, or an element of an array. If the value is not an element of the float value set, it maps the value to the nearest element of the float value set.

- Suppose execution of a Java virtual machine instruction that is not FP-strict causes a value of type `double` to be pushed onto an operand stack that is FP-strict, passed as a parameter, or stored into a local variable, a field, or an element of an array. If the value is not an element of the double value set, it maps the value to the nearest element of the double value set.

Such required value set conversions may occur as a result of passing a parameter of a floating-point type during method invocation, including `native` method invocation; returning a value of a floating-point type from a method that is not FP-strict to a method that is FP-strict; or storing a value of a floating-point type into a local variable, a field, or an array in a method that is not FP-strict.

Not all values from an extended-exponent value set can be mapped exactly to a value in the corresponding standard value set. If a value being mapped is too large to be represented exactly (its exponent is greater than that permitted by the standard value set), it is converted to a (positive or negative) infinity of the corresponding type. If a value being mapped is too small to be represented exactly (its exponent is smaller than that permitted by the standard value set), it is rounded to the nearest of a representable denormalized value or zero of the same sign.

Value set conversion preserves infinities and NaNs and cannot change the sign of the value being converted. Value set conversion has no effect on a value that is not of a floating-point type.

3.9 Specially Named Initialization Methods

At the level of the Java virtual machine, every constructor (§2.12) appears as an *instance initialization method* that has the special name <init>. This name is supplied by a compiler. Because the name <init> is not a valid identifier, it cannot be used directly in a program written in the Java programming language. Instance initialization methods may be invoked only within the Java virtual machine by the *invokespecial* instruction, and they may be invoked only on uninitialized class instances. An instance initialization method takes on the access permissions (§2.7.4) of the constructor from which it was derived.

A class or interface has at most one *class or interface initialization method* and is initialized (§2.17.4) by invoking that method. The initialization method of a class or interface is static and takes no arguments. It has the special name <clinit>. This name is supplied by a compiler. Because the name <clinit> is not a valid identifier, it cannot be used directly in a program written in the Java programming language. Class and interface initialization methods are invoked implicitly by the Java virtual machine; they are never invoked directly from any Java virtual machine instruction, but are invoked only indirectly as part of the class initialization process.

3.10 Exceptions

In the Java programming language, throwing an exception results in an immediate nonlocal transfer of control from the point where the exception was thrown. This transfer of control may abruptly complete, one by one, multiple statements, constructor invocations, static and field initializer evaluations, and method invocations. The process continues until a catch clause (§2.16.2) is found that handles the thrown value. If no such clause can be found, the current thread exits.

In cases where a finally clause (§2.16.2) is used, the finally clause is executed during the propagation of an exception thrown from the associated try block and any associated `catch` block, even if no `catch` clause that handles the thrown exception may be found.

As implemented by the Java virtual machine, each `catch` or `finally` clause of a method is represented by an exception handler. An exception handler specifies the range of offsets into the Java virtual machine code implementing the method for which the exception handler is active, describes the type of exception that the exception handler is able to handle, and specifies the location of the code that is to handle that exception. An exception matches an exception handler if the offset of the instruction that caused the exception is in the range of offsets of the exception handler and the exception type is the same class as or a subclass of the class of exception that the exception handler handles. When an exception is thrown, the Java virtual machine searches for a matching exception handler in the current method. If a matching exception handler is found, the system branches to the exception handling code specified by the matched handler.

If no such exception handler is found in the current method, the current method invocation completes abruptly (§3.6.5). On abrupt completion, the operand stack and local variables of the current method invocation are discarded, and its frame is popped, reinstating the frame of the invoking method. The exception is then rethrown in the context of the invoker's frame and so on, continuing up the method invocation chain. If no suitable exception handler is found before the top of the method invocation chain is reached, the execution of the thread in which the exception was thrown is terminated.

The order in which the exception handlers of a method are searched for a match is important. Within a `class` file the exception handlers for each method are stored in a table (§4.7.3). At run time, when an exception is thrown, the Java virtual machine searches the exception handlers of the current method in the order that they appear in the corresponding exception handler table in the `class` file, starting from the beginning of that table. Because `try` statements are structured, a compiler for the Java programming language can always order the entries of the exception handler table such that, for any thrown exception and any program counter value in that method, the first exception handler that matches the thrown exception corresponds to the innermost matching `catch` or `finally` clause.

Note that the Java virtual machine does not enforce nesting of or any ordering of the exception table entries of a method (§4.9.5). The exception handling semantics of the Java programming language are implemented only through cooperation with the compiler. When `class` files are generated by some other means, the defined search procedure ensures that all Java virtual machines will behave consistently.

More information on the implementation of `catch` and `finally` clauses is given in Chapter 7, "Compiling for the Java Virtual Machine."

3.11   Instruction Set Summary

A Java virtual machine instruction consists of a one-byte *opcode* specifying the operation to be performed, followed by zero or more *operands* supplying arguments or data that are used by the operation. Many instructions have no operands and consist only of an opcode.

Ignoring exceptions, the inner loop of a Java virtual machine interpreter is effectively

```
do {
    fetch an opcode;
    if (operands) fetch operands;
    execute the action for the opcode;
} while (there is more to do);
```

The number and size of the operands are determined by the opcode. If an operand is more than one byte in size, then it is stored in *big-endian* order—high-order byte first. For example, an unsigned 16-bit index into the local variables is stored as two unsigned bytes, *byte1* and *byte2*, such that its value is

$$(byte1 << 8) \mid byte2$$

The bytecode instruction stream is only single-byte aligned. The two exceptions are the *tableswitch* and *lookupswitch* instructions, which are padded to force internal alignment of some of their operands on 4-byte boundaries.

The decision to limit the Java virtual machine opcode to a byte and to forgo data alignment within compiled code reflects a conscious bias in favor of compactness, possibly at the cost of some performance in naive implementations. A one-byte opcode also limits the size of the instruction set. Not assuming data alignment means that immediate data larger than a byte must be constructed from bytes at run time on many machines.

3.11.1   Types and the Java Virtual Machine

Most of the instructions in the Java virtual machine instruction set encode type information about the operations they perform. For instance, the *iload* instruction loads the contents of a local variable, which must be an `int`, onto the operand stack. The *fload* instruction does the same with a `float` value. The two instructions may have identical implementations, but have distinct opcodes.

For the majority of typed instructions, the instruction type is represented explicitly in the opcode mnemonic by a letter: *i* for an `int` operation, *l* for `long`, *s* for `short`, *b* for `byte`, *c* for `char`, *f* for `float`, *d* for `double`, and *a* for `reference`. Some instructions for which the type is unambiguous do not have a type letter in their mnemonic. For instance, *arraylength* always operates on an object that is an array. Some instructions, such as *goto*, an unconditional control transfer, do not operate on typed operands.

Given the Java virtual machine's one-byte opcode size, encoding types into opcodes places pressure on the design of its instruction set. If each typed instruction supported all of the Java virtual machine's runtime data types, there would be more instructions than could be represented in a byte. Instead, the instruction set of the Java virtual machine provides a reduced level of type support for certain operations. In other words, the instruction set is intentionally not orthogonal. Separate instructions can be used to convert between unsupported and supported data types as necessary.

Table 3.2 summarizes the type support in the instruction set of the Java virtual machine. A specific instruction, with type information, is built by replacing the *T* in the instruction template in the opcode column by the letter in the type column. If the type column for some instruction template and type is blank, then no instruction exists supporting that type of operation. For instance, there is a load instruction for type `int`, *iload*, but there is no load instruction for type `byte`.

Note that most instructions in Table 3.2 do not have forms for the integral types `byte`, `char`, and `short`. None have forms for the `boolean` type. Compilers encode loads of literal values of types `byte` and `short` using Java virtual machine instructions that sign-extend those values to values of type `int` at compile time or run time. Loads of literal values of types `boolean` and `char` are encoded using instructions that zero-extend the literal to a value of type `int` at compile time or run time. Likewise, loads from arrays of values of type `boolean`, `byte`, `short`, and `char` are encoded using Java virtual machine instructions that sign-extend or zero-extend the values to values of type `int`. Thus, most operations on values of actual types `boolean`, `byte`, `char`, and `short` are correctly performed by instructions operating on values of computational type `int`.

Table 3.2   Type support in the Java virtual machine instruction set

opcode	byte	short	int	long	float	double	char	reference
Tipush	bipush	sipush						
Tconst			iconst	lconst	fconst	dconst		aconst
Tload			iload	lload	fload	dload		aload
Tstore			istore	lstore	fstore	dstore		astore
Tinc			iinc					
Taload	baload	saload	iaload	laload	faload	daload	caload	aaload
Tastore	bastore	sastore	iastore	lastore	fastore	dastore	castore	aastore
Tadd			iadd	ladd	fadd	dadd		
Tsub			isub	lsub	fsub	dsub		
Tmul			imul	lmul	fmul	dmul		
Tdiv			idiv	ldiv	fdiv	ddiv		
Trem			irem	lrem	frem	drem		
Tneg			ineg	lneg	fneg	dneg		
Tshl			ishl	lshl				
Tshr			ishr	lshr				
Tushr			iushr	lushr				
Tand			iand	land				
Tor			ior	lor				
Txor			ixor	lxor				
i2T	i2b	i2s		i2l	i2f	i2d		
l2T			l2i		l2f	l2d		
f2T			f2i	f2l		f2d		
d2T			d2i	d2l	d2f			
Tcmp				lcmp				
Tcmpl					fcmpl	dcmpl		
Tcmpg					fcmpg	dcmpg		
if_TcmpOP			if_icmpOP					if_acmpOP
Treturn			ireturn	lreturn	freturn	dreturn		areturn

The mapping between Java virtual machine actual types and Java virtual machine computational types is summarized by Table 3.3.

Table 3.3 Java virtual machine actual and computational types

Actual Type	Computational Type	Category
boolean	int	category 1
byte	int	category 1
char	int	category 1
short	int	category 1
int	int	category 1
float	float	category 1
reference	reference	category 1
returnAddress	returnAddress	category 1
long	long	category 2
double	double	category 2

Certain Java virtual machine instructions such as *pop* and *swap* operate on the operand stack without regard to type; however, such instructions are constrained to use only on values of certain categories of computational types, also given in Table 3.3.

The remainder of this chapter summarizes the Java virtual machine instruction set.

3.11.2 Load and Store Instructions

The load and store instructions transfer values between the local variables (§3.6.1) and the operand stack (§3.6.2) of a Java virtual machine frame (§3.6):

- Load a local variable onto the operand stack: *iload, iload_<n>, lload, lload_<n>, fload, fload_<n>, dload, dload_<n>, aload, aload_<n>*.

- Store a value from the operand stack into a local variable: *istore, istore_<n>, lstore, lstore_<n>, fstore, fstore_<n>, dstore, dstore_<n>, astore, astore_<n>*.

- Load a constant onto the operand stack: *bipush, sipush, ldc, ldc_w, ldc2_w, aconst_null, iconst_m1, iconst_<i>, lconst_<l>, fconst_<f>, dconst_<d>*.

- Gain access to more local variables using a wider index, or to a larger immediate operand: *wide*.

Instructions that access fields of objects and elements of arrays (§3.11.5) also transfer data to and from the operand stack.

Instruction mnemonics shown above with trailing letters between angle brackets (for instance, *iload_<n>*) denote families of instructions (with members *iload_0*, *iload_1*, *iload_2*, and *iload_3* in the case of *iload_<n>*). Such families of instructions are specializations of an additional generic instruction (*iload*) that takes one operand. For the specialized instructions, the operand is implicit and does not need to be stored or fetched. The semantics are otherwise the same (*iload_0* means the same thing as *iload* with the operand *0*). The letter between the angle brackets specifies the type of the implicit operand for that family of instructions: for *<n>*, a nonnegative integer; for *<i>*, an int; for *<l>*, a long; for *<f>*, a float; and for *<d>*, a double. Forms for type int are used in many cases to perform operations on values of type byte, char, and short (§3.11.1).

This notation for instruction families is used throughout *The Java*™ *Virtual Machine Specification.*

3.11.3 Arithmetic Instructions

The arithmetic instructions compute a result that is typically a function of two values on the operand stack, pushing the result back on the operand stack. There are two main kinds of arithmetic instructions: those operating on integer values and those operating on floating-point values. Within each of these kinds, the arithmetic instructions are specialized to Java virtual machine numeric types. There is no direct support for integer arithmetic on values of the byte, short, and char types (§3.11.1), or for values of the boolean type; those operations are handled by instructions operating on type int. Integer and floating-point instructions also differ in their behavior on overflow and divide-by-zero. The arithmetic instructions are as follows:

- Add: *iadd, ladd, fadd, dadd.*

- Subtract: *isub, lsub, fsub, dsub.*

- Multiply: *imul, lmul, fmul, dmul.*

- Divide: *idiv, ldiv, fdiv, ddiv.*

- Remainder: *irem, lrem, frem, drem.*

- Negate: *ineg, lneg, fneg, dneg.*

- Shift: *ishl, ishr, iushr, lshl, lshr, lushr.*

- Bitwise OR: *ior, lor*.

- Bitwise AND: *iand, land*.

- Bitwise exclusive OR: *ixor, lxor*.

- Local variable increment: *iinc*.

- Comparison: *dcmpg, dcmpl, fcmpg, fcmpl, lcmp*.

The semantics of the Java programming language operators on integer and floating-point values (§2.4.2, §2.4.4) are directly supported by the semantics of the Java virtual machine instruction set.

The Java virtual machine does not indicate overflow during operations on integer data types. The only integer operations that can throw an exception are the integer divide instructions (*idiv* and *ldiv*) and the integer remainder instructions (*irem* and *lrem*), which throw an `ArithmeticException` if the divisor is zero.

Java virtual machine operations on floating-point numbers behave as specified in IEEE 754. In particular, the Java virtual machine requires full support of IEEE 754 *denormalized* floating-point numbers and *gradual underflow*, which make it easier to prove desirable properties of particular numerical algorithms.

The Java virtual machine requires that floating-point arithmetic behave as if every floating-point operator rounded its floating-point result to the result precision. *Inexact* results must be rounded to the representable value nearest to the infinitely precise result; if the two nearest representable values are equally near, the one having a least significant bit of zero is chosen. This is the IEEE 754 standard's default rounding mode, known as *round to nearest* mode.

The Java virtual machine uses the IEEE 754 *round towards zero* mode when converting a floating-point value to an integer. This results in the number being truncated; any bits of the significand that represent the fractional part of the operand value are discarded. Round towards zero mode chooses as its result the type's value closest to, but no greater in magnitude than, the infinitely precise result.

The Java virtual machine's floating-point operators do not throw runtime exceptions (not to be confused with IEEE 754 floating-point exceptions). An operation that overflows produces a signed infinity, an operation that underflows produces a denormalized value or a signed zero, and an operation that has no mathematically definite result produces NaN. All numeric operations with NaN as an operand produce NaN as a result.

Comparisons on values of type `long` (*lcmp*) perform a signed comparison. Comparisons on values of floating-point types (*dcmpg, dcmpl, fcmpg, fcmpl*) are performed using IEEE 754 nonsignaling comparisons.

3.11.4 Type Conversion Instructions

The type conversion instructions allow conversion between Java virtual machine numeric types. These may be used to implement explicit conversions in user code or to mitigate the lack of orthogonality in the instruction set of the Java virtual machine.

The Java virtual machine directly supports the following widening numeric conversions:

- `int` to `long`, `float`, or `double`

- `long` to `float` or `double`

- `float` to `double`

The widening numeric conversion instructions are *i2l*, *i2f*, *i2d*, *l2f*, *l2d*, and *f2d*. The mnemonics for these opcodes are straightforward given the naming conventions for typed instructions and the punning use of 2 to mean "to." For instance, the *i2d* instruction converts an `int` value to a `double`. Widening numeric conversions do not lose information about the overall magnitude of a numeric value. Indeed, conversions widening from `int` to `long` and `int` to `double` do not lose any information at all; the numeric value is preserved exactly. Conversions widening from `float` to `double` that are FP-strict (§3.8.2) also preserve the numeric value exactly; however, such conversions that are not FP-strict may lose information about the overall magnitude of the converted value.

Conversion of an `int` or a `long` value to `float`, or of a `long` value to `double`, may lose *precision*, that is, may lose some of the least significant bits of the value; the resulting floating-point value is a correctly rounded version of the integer value, using IEEE 754 round to nearest mode.

A widening numeric conversion of an `int` to a `long` simply sign-extends the two's-complement representation of the `int` value to fill the wider format. A widening numeric conversion of a `char` to an integral type zero-extends the representation of the `char` value to fill the wider format.

Despite the fact that loss of precision may occur, widening numeric conversions never cause the Java virtual machine to throw a runtime exception (not to be confused with an IEEE 754 floating-point exception).

Note that widening numeric conversions do not exist from integral types `byte`, `char`, and `short` to type `int`. As noted in §3.11.1, values of type `byte`, `char`, and `short` are internally widened to type `int`, making these conversions implicit.

The Java virtual machine also directly supports the following narrowing numeric conversions:

- `int` to `byte`, `short`, or `char`

- `long` to `int`

- `float` to `int` or `long`

- `double` to `int`, `long`, or `float`

The narrowing numeric conversion instructions are *i2b*, *i2c*, *i2s*, *l2i*, *f2i*, *f2l*, *d2i*, *d2l*, and *d2f*. A narrowing numeric conversion can result in a value of different sign, a different order of magnitude, or both; it may thereby lose precision.

A narrowing numeric conversion of an `int` or `long` to an integral type *T* simply discards all but the *N* lowest-order bits, where *N* is the number of bits used to represent type *T*. This may cause the resulting value not to have the same sign as the input value.

In a narrowing numeric conversion of a floating-point value to an integral type *T*, where *T* is either `int` or `long`, the floating-point value is converted as follows:

- If the floating-point value is NaN, the result of the conversion is an `int` or `long` 0.

- Otherwise, if the floating-point value is not an infinity, the floating-point value is rounded to an integer value *V* using IEEE 754 round towards zero mode. There are two cases:

  - If *T* is `long` and this integer value can be represented as a `long`, then the result is the `long` value *V*.

  - If *T* is of type `int` and this integer value can be represented as an `int`, then the result is the `int` value *V*.

- Otherwise:

  - Either the value must be too small (a negative value of large magnitude or negative infinity), and the result is the smallest representable value of type `int` or `long`.

  - Or the value must be too large (a positive value of large magnitude or positive infinity), and the result is the largest representable value of type `int` or `long`.

A narrowing numeric conversion from `double` to `float` behaves in accordance with IEEE 754. The result is correctly rounded using IEEE 754 round to nearest mode. A value too small to be represented as a `float` is converted to a positive or negative zero of type `float`; a value too large to be represented as a `float` is converted to a positive or negative infinity. A `double` NaN is always converted to a `float` NaN.

Despite the fact that overflow, underflow, or loss of precision may occur, narrowing conversions among numeric types never cause the Java virtual machine to throw a runtime exception (not to be confused with an IEEE 754 floating-point exception).

3.11.5 Object Creation and Manipulation

Although both class instances and arrays are objects, the Java virtual machine creates and manipulates class instances and arrays using distinct sets of instructions:

- Create a new class instance: *new*.

- Create a new array: *newarray, anewarray, multianewarray*.

- Access fields of classes (`static` fields, known as class variables) and fields of class instances (non-`static` fields, known as instance variables): *getfield, putfield, getstatic, putstatic*.

- Load an array component onto the operand stack: *baload, caload, saload, iaload, laload, faload, daload, aaload*.

- Store a value from the operand stack as an array component: *bastore, castore, sastore, iastore, lastore, fastore, dastore, aastore*.

- Get the length of array: *arraylength*.

- Check properties of class instances or arrays: *instanceof, checkcast*.

3.11.6 Operand Stack Management Instructions

A number of instructions are provided for the direct manipulation of the operand stack: *pop, pop2, dup, dup2, dup_x1, dup2_x1, dup_x2, dup2_x2, swap*.

3.11.7 Control Transfer Instructions

The control transfer instructions conditionally or unconditionally cause the Java virtual machine to continue execution with an instruction other than the one following the control transfer instruction. They are:

- Conditional branch: *ifeq, iflt, ifle, ifne, ifgt, ifge, ifnull, ifnonnull, if_icmpeq, if_icmpne, if_icmplt, if_icmpgt, if_icmple, if_icmpge, if_acmpeq, if_acmpne.*

- Compound conditional branch: *tableswitch, lookupswitch.*

- Unconditional branch: *goto, goto_w, jsr, jsr_w, ret.*

The Java virtual machine has distinct sets of instructions that conditionally branch on comparison with data of `int` and `reference` types. It also has distinct conditional branch instructions that test for the null reference and thus is not required to specify a concrete value for `null` (§3.4).

Conditional branches on comparisons between data of types `boolean`, `byte`, `char`, and `short` are performed using `int` comparison instructions (§3.11.1). A conditional branch on a comparison between data of types `long`, `float`, or `double` is initiated using an instruction that compares the data and produces an `int` result of the comparison (§3.11.3). A subsequent `int` comparison instruction tests this result and effects the conditional branch. Because of its emphasis on `int` comparisons, the Java virtual machine provides a rich complement of conditional branch instructions for type `int`.

All `int` conditional control transfer instructions perform signed comparisons.

3.11.8 Method Invocation and Return Instructions

The following four instructions invoke methods:

- *invokevirtual* invokes an instance method of an object, dispatching on the (virtual) type of the object. This is the normal method dispatch in the Java programming language.

- *invokeinterface* invokes a method that is implemented by an interface, searching the methods implemented by the particular runtime object to find the appropriate method.

- *invokespecial* invokes an instance method requiring special handling, whether an instance initialization method (§3.9), a `private` method, or a superclass method.

- *invokestatic* invokes a class (`static`) method in a named class.

The method return instructions, which are distinguished by return type, are *ireturn* (used to return values of type `boolean`, `byte`, `char`, `short`, or `int`), *lreturn*, *freturn*, *dreturn*, and *areturn*. In addition, the *return* instruction is used to return from methods declared to be `void`, instance initialization methods, and class or interface initialization methods.

3.11.9 Throwing Exceptions

An exception is thrown programmatically using the *athrow* instruction. Exceptions can also be thrown by various Java virtual machine instructions if they detect an abnormal condition.

3.11.10 Implementing `finally`

The implementation of the `finally` keyword uses the *jsr*, *jsr_w*, and *ret* instructions. See Section 4.9.6, "Exceptions and `finally`," and Section 7.13, "Compiling `finally`."

3.11.11 Synchronization

The Java virtual machine supports synchronization of both methods and sequences of instructions within a method using a single synchronization construct: the *monitor*.

Method-level synchronization is handled as part of method invocation and return (see Section 3.11.8, "Method Invocation and Return Instructions").

Synchronization of sequences of instructions is typically used to encode the synchronized blocks of the Java programming language. The Java virtual machine supplies the *monitorenter* and *monitorexit* instructions to support such constructs.

Proper implementation of synchronized blocks requires cooperation from a compiler targeting the Java virtual machine. The compiler must ensure that at any method invocation completion a *monitorexit* instruction will have been executed for each *monitorenter* instruction executed since the method invocation. This must be the case whether the method invocation completes normally (§3.6.4) or abruptly (§3.6.5).

The compiler enforces proper pairing of *monitorenter* and *monitorexit* instructions on abrupt method invocation completion by generating exception handlers (§3.10) that will match any exception and whose associated code executes the necessary *monitorexit* instructions (§7.14).

3.12 Class Libraries

The Java virtual machine must provide sufficient support for the implementation of the class libraries of the associated platform. Some of the classes in these libraries cannot be implemented without the cooperation of the Java virtual machine.

Classes that might require special support from the Java virtual machine include those that support:

- Reflection, such as the classes in the package `java.lang.reflect` and the class `Class`.

- Loading and creation of a class or interface. The most obvious example is the class `ClassLoader`.

- Linking and initialization of a class or interface. The example classes cited above fall into this category as well.

- Security, such as the classes in the package `java.security` and other classes such as `SecurityManager`.

- Multithreading, such as the class `Thread`.

- Weak references, such as the classes in the package `java.lang.ref`.[9]

The list above is meant to be illustrative rather than comprehensive. An exhaustive list of these classes or of the functionality they provide is beyond the scope of this book. See the specifications of the Java and Java 2 platform class libraries for details.

3.13 Public Design, Private Implementation

Thus far this book has sketched the public view of the Java virtual machine: the `class` file format and the instruction set. These components are vital to the hardware-, operating system-, and implementation-independence of the Java virtual machine. The implementor may prefer to think of them as a means to securely communicate fragments of programs between hosts each implementing the Java or Java 2 platform, rather than as a blueprint to be followed exactly.

---

[9] Weak references were introduced in the Java 2 platform, v1.2.

It is important to understand where the line between the public design and the private implementation lies. A Java virtual machine implementation must be able to read `class` files and must exactly implement the semantics of the Java virtual machine code therein. One way of doing this is to take this document as a specification and to implement that specification literally. But it is also perfectly feasible and desirable for the implementor to modify or optimize the implementation within the constraints of this specification. So long as the `class` file format can be read and the semantics of its code are maintained, the implementor may implement these semantics in any way. What is "under the hood" is the implementor's business, as long as the correct external interface is carefully maintained.[10]

The implementor can use this flexibility to tailor Java virtual machine implementations for high performance, low memory use, or portability. What makes sense in a given implementation depends on the goals of that implementation. The range of implementation options includes the following:

- Translating Java virtual machine code at load time or during execution into the instruction set of another virtual machine.

- Translating Java virtual machine code at load time or during execution into the native instruction set of the host CPU (sometimes referred to as *just-in-time*, or *JIT*, code generation).

The existence of a precisely defined virtual machine and object file format need not significantly restrict the creativity of the implementor. The Java virtual machine is designed to support many different implementations, providing new and interesting solutions while retaining compatibility between implementations.

---

[10] There are some exceptions: debuggers, profilers, and just-in-time code generators can each require access to elements of the Java virtual machine that are normally considered to be "under the hood." Where appropriate, Sun is working with other Java virtual machine implementors and tools vendors to develop common interfaces to the Java virtual machine for use by such tools, and to promote those interfaces across the industry. Information on publicly available low-level interfaces to the Java virtual machine will be made available at `http://java.sun.com`.

CHAPTER 4

The `class` File Format

THIS chapter describes the Java virtual machine `class` file format. Each `class` file contains the definition of a single class or interface. Although a class or interface need not have an external representation literally contained in a file (for instance, because the class is generated by a class loader), we will colloquially refer to any valid representation of a class or interface as being in the `class` file format.

A `class` file consists of a stream of 8-bit bytes. All 16-bit, 32-bit, and 64-bit quantities are constructed by reading in two, four, and eight consecutive 8-bit bytes, respectively. Multibyte data items are always stored in big-endian order, where the high bytes come first. In the Java and Java 2 platforms, this format is supported by interfaces `java.io.DataInput` and `java.io.DataOutput` and classes such as `java.io.DataInputStream` and `java.io.DataOutputStream`.

This chapter defines its own set of data types representing `class` file data: The types u1, u2, and u4 represent an unsigned one-, two-, or four-byte quantity, respectively. In the Java and Java 2 platforms, these types may be read by methods such as `readUnsignedByte`, `readUnsignedShort`, and `readInt` of the interface `java.io.DataInput`.

This chapter presents the `class` file format using pseudostructures written in a C-like structure notation. To avoid confusion with the fields of classes and class instances, etc., the contents of the structures describing the `class` file format are referred to as *items*. Successive items are stored in the `class` file sequentially, without padding or alignment.

Tables, consisting of zero or more variable-sized items, are used in several `class` file structures. Although we use C-like array syntax to refer to table items, the fact that tables are streams of varying-sized structures means that it is not possible to translate a table index directly to a byte offset into the table.

Where we refer to a data structure as an array, it consists of zero or more contiguous fixed-sized items and can be indexed like an array.

4.1 The `ClassFile` Structure

A class file consists of a single `ClassFile` structure:

```
ClassFile {
    u4 magic;
    u2 minor_version;
    u2 major_version;
    u2 constant_pool_count;
    cp_info constant_pool[constant_pool_count-1];
    u2 access_flags;
    u2 this_class;
    u2 super_class;
    u2 interfaces_count;
    u2 interfaces[interfaces_count];
    u2 fields_count;
    field_info fields[fields_count];
    u2 methods_count;
    method_info methods[methods_count];
    u2 attributes_count;
    attribute_info attributes[attributes_count];
}
```

The items in the `ClassFile` structure are as follows:

magic

> The `magic` item supplies the magic number identifying the `class` file format; it has the value `0xCAFEBABE`.

minor_version, major_version

> The values of the `minor_version` and `major_version` items are the minor and major version numbers of this `class` file. Together, a major and a minor version number determine the version of the class file format. If a `class` file has major version number *M* and minor version number *m*, we denote the version of its `class`

file format as *M.m.* Thus, class file format versions may be ordered lexicographically, for example, 1.5 < 2.0 < 2.1.

A Java virtual machine implementation can support a class file format of version *v* if and only if *v* lies in some contiguous range $Mi.0 \leq v \leq Mj.m$. Only Sun can specify what range of versions a Java virtual machine implementation conforming to a certain release level of the Java platform may support.[1]

constant_pool_count

The value of the constant_pool_count item is equal to the number of entries in the constant_pool table plus one. A constant_pool index is considered valid if it is greater than zero and less than constant_pool_count, with the exception for constants of type long and double noted in §4.4.5.

constant_pool[]

The constant_pool is a table of structures (§4.4) representing various string constants, class and interface names, field names, and other constants that are referred to within the ClassFile structure and its substructures. The format of each constant_pool table entry is indicated by its first "tag" byte.

The constant_pool table is indexed from 1 to constant_pool_count−1.

access_flags

The value of the access_flags item is a mask of flags used to denote access permissions to and properties of this class or interface. The interpretation of each flag, when set, is as shown in Table 4.1.

---

[1] The Java virtual machine implementation of Sun's JDK release 1.0.2 supports class file format versions 45.0 through 45.3 inclusive. Sun's JDK releases 1.1.X can support class file formats of versions in the range 45.0 through 45.65535 inclusive. Implementations of version 1.2 of the Java 2 platform can support class file formats of versions in the range 45.0 through 46.0 inclusive.

Table 4.1   Class access and property modifiers

Flag Name	Value	Interpretation
ACC_PUBLIC	0x0001	Declared public; may be accessed from outside its package.
ACC_FINAL	0x0010	Declared final; no subclasses allowed.
ACC_SUPER	0x0020	Treat superclass methods specially when invoked by the *invokespecial* instruction.
ACC_INTERFACE	0x0200	Is an interface, not a class.
ACC_ABSTRACT	0x0400	Declared abstract; may not be instantiated.

An interface is distinguished by its ACC_INTERFACE flag being set. If its ACC_INTERFACE flag is not set, this class file defines a class, not an interface.

If the ACC_INTERFACE flag of this class file is set, its ACC_ABSTRACT flag must also be set (§2.13.1) and its ACC_PUBLIC flag may be set. Such a class file may not have any of the other flags in Table 4.1 set.

If the ACC_INTERFACE flag of this class file is not set, it may have any of the other flags in Table 4.1 set. However, such a class file cannot have both its ACC_FINAL and ACC_ABSTRACT flags set (§2.8.2).

The setting of the ACC_SUPER flag indicates which of two alternative semantics for its *invokespecial* instruction the Java virtual machine is to express; the ACC_SUPER flag exists for backward compatibility for code compiled by Sun's older compilers for the Java programming language. All new implementations of the Java virtual machine should implement the semantics for *invokespecial* documented in this specification. All new compilers to the instruction set of the Java virtual machine should set the ACC_SUPER flag. Sun's older compilers generated ClassFile flags with ACC_SUPER unset. Sun's older Java virtual machine implementations ignore the flag if it is set.

All bits of the access_flags item not assigned in Table 4.1 are reserved for future use. They should be set to zero in generated class files and should be ignored by Java virtual machine implementations.

this_class

The value of the this_class item must be a valid index into the constant_pool table. The constant_pool entry at that index must be a CONSTANT_Class_info (§4.4.1) structure representing the class or interface defined by this class file.

super_class

For a class, the value of the super_class item either must be zero or must be a valid index into the constant_pool table. If the value of the super_class item is nonzero, the constant_pool entry at that index must be a CONSTANT_Class_info (§4.4.1) structure representing the direct superclass of the class defined by this class file. Neither the direct superclass nor any of its superclasses may be a final class.

If the value of the super_class item is zero, then this class file must represent the class Object, the only class or interface without a direct superclass.

For an interface, the value of the super_class item must always be a valid index into the constant_pool table. The constant_pool entry at that index must be a CONSTANT_Class_info structure representing the class Object.

interfaces_count

The value of the interfaces_count item gives the number of direct superinterfaces of this class or interface type.

interfaces[]

Each value in the interfaces array must be a valid index into the constant_pool table. The constant_pool entry at each value of interfaces[i], where $0 \leq i <$ interfaces_count, must be a CONSTANT_Class_info (§4.4.1) structure representing an interface that is a direct superinterface of this class or interface type, in the left-to-right order given in the source for the type.

fields_count

The value of the fields_count item gives the number of field_info structures in the fields table. The field_info (§4.5) structures represent all fields, both class variables and instance variables, declared by this class or interface type.

`fields[]`

> Each value in the `fields` table must be a `field_info` (§4.5)
> structure giving a complete description of a field in this class or
> interface. The `fields` table includes only those fields that are
> declared by this class or interface. It does not include items
> representing fields that are inherited from superclasses or
> superinterfaces.

`methods_count`

> The value of the `methods_count` item gives the number of
> `method_info` structures in the `methods` table.

`methods[]`

> Each value in the `methods` table must be a `method_info` (§4.6)
> structure giving a complete description of a method in this class
> or interface. If the method is not `native` or `abstract`, the Java
> virtual machine instructions implementing the method are also
> supplied.
>
> The `method_info` structures represent all methods declared
> by this class or interface type, including instance methods, class
> (`static`) methods, instance initialization methods (§3.9), and
> any class or interface initialization method (§3.9). The `methods`
> table does not include items representing methods that are
> inherited from superclasses or superinterfaces.

`attributes_count`

> The value of the `attributes_count` item gives the number of
> attributes (§4.7) in the `attributes` table of this class.

`attributes[]`

> Each value of the `attributes` table must be an attribute structure
> (§4.7).
>
> The only attributes defined by this specification as appearing
> in the `attributes` table of a `ClassFile` structure are the
> `SourceFile` attribute (§4.7.7) and the `Deprecated` (§4.7.10)
> attribute.
>
> A Java virtual machine implementation is required to silently
> ignore any or all attributes in the `attributes` table of a
> `ClassFile` structure that it does not recognize. Attributes not
> defined in this specification are not allowed to affect the

semantics of the `class` file, but only to provide additional descriptive information (§4.7.1).

4.2 The Internal Form of Fully Qualified Class and Interface Names

Class and interface names that appear in `class` file structures are always represented in a fully qualified form (§2.7.5). Such names are always represented as `CONSTANT_Utf8_info` (§4.4.7) structures and thus may be drawn, where not further constrained, from the entire Unicode character set. Class names and interfaces are referenced both from those `CONSTANT_NameAndType_info` (§4.4.6) structures that have such names as part of their descriptor (§4.3) and from all `CONSTANT_Class_info` (§4.4.1) structures.

For historical reasons the syntax of fully qualified class and interface names that appear in `class` file structures differs from the familiar syntax of fully qualified names documented in §2.7.5. In this internal form, the ASCII periods (`'.'`) that normally separate the identifiers that make up the fully qualified name are replaced by ASCII forward slashes (`'/'`). For example, the normal fully qualified name of class `Thread` is `java.lang.Thread`. In the form used in descriptors in the `class` file format, a reference to the name of class `Thread` is implemented using a `CONSTANT_Utf8_info` structure representing the string `"java/lang/Thread"`.

4.3 Descriptors

A *descriptor* is a string representing the type of a field or method. Descriptors are represented in the `class` file format using UTF-8 strings (§4.4.7) and thus may be drawn, where not further constrained, from the entire Unicode character set.

4.3.1 Grammar Notation

Descriptors are specified using a grammar. This grammar is a set of productions that describe how sequences of characters can form syntactically correct descriptors of various types. Terminal symbols of the grammar are shown in **bold fixed-width** font. Nonterminal symbols are shown in *italic* type. The definition of a nonterminal is introduced by the name of the nonterminal being defined, followed by a colon.

One or more alternative right-hand sides for the nonterminal then follow on succeeding lines. For example, the production:

FieldType:
    BaseType
    ObjectType
    ArrayType

states that a *FieldType* may represent either a *BaseType*, an *ObjectType*, or an *Array-Type*.

A nonterminal symbol on the right-hand side of a production that is followed by an asterisk (*) represents zero or more possibly different values produced from that nonterminal, appended without any intervening space. The production:

MethodDescriptor:
    (*ParameterDescriptor** **)** *ReturnDescriptor*

states that a *MethodDescriptor* represents a left parenthesis, followed by zero or more *ParameterDescriptor* values, followed by a right parenthesis, followed by a *ReturnDescriptor*.

4.3.2 Field Descriptors

A *field descriptor* represents the type of a class, instance, or local variable. It is a series of characters generated by the grammar:

FieldDescriptor:
    FieldType
ComponentType:
    FieldType
FieldType:
    BaseType
    ObjectType
    ArrayType
BaseType:
    B
    C
    D
    F
    I

> J
> S
> Z

ObjectType:
> **L<classname>;**

ArrayType:
> **[***ComponentType*

The characters of *BaseType*, the **L** and **;** of *ObjectType*, and the **[** of *Array-Type* are all ASCII characters. The **<classname>** represents a fully qualified class or interface name. For historical reasons it is encoded in internal form (§4.2).

The interpretation of the field types is as shown in Table 4.2.

Table 4.2   Interpretation of *BaseType* characters

BaseType **Character**	**Type**	**Interpretation**
B	byte	signed byte
C	char	Unicode character
D	double	double-precision floating-point value
F	float	single-precision floating-point value
I	int	integer
J	long	long integer
L<classname>;	reference	an instance of class <classname>
S	short	signed short
Z	boolean	true or false
[	reference	one array dimension

For example, the descriptor of an instance variable of type int is simply **I**. The descriptor of an instance variable of type Object is **Ljava/lang/Object;**. Note that the internal form of the fully qualified name for class Object is used. The descriptor of an instance variable that is a multidimensional double array,

```
double d[][][];
```

is

[[[D

4.3.3 Method Descriptors

A *method descriptor* represents the parameters that the method takes and the value that it returns:

MethodDescriptor:
   (*ParameterDescriptor** **)** *ReturnDescriptor*

A *parameter descriptor* represents a parameter passed to a method:

ParameterDescriptor:
   FieldType

A *return descriptor* represents the type of the value returned from a method. It is a series of characters generated by the grammar:

ReturnDescriptor:
   FieldType
   V

The character **V** indicates that the method returns no value (its return type is `void`).

A method descriptor is valid only if it represents method parameters with a total length of 255 or less, where that length includes the contribution for `this` in the case of instance or interface method invocations. The total length is calculated by summing the contributions of the individual parameters, where a parameter of type `long` or `double` contributes two units to the length and a parameter of any other type contributes one unit.

For example, the method descriptor for the method

```
Object mymethod(int i, double d, Thread t)
```

is

(IDLjava/lang/Thread;)Ljava/lang/Object;

Note that internal forms of the fully qualified names of `Thread` and `Object` are used in the method descriptor.

The method descriptor for `mymethod` is the same whether `mymethod` is a class or an instance method. Although an instance method is passed `this`, a reference to the current class instance, in addition to its intended parameters, that fact is not reflected in the method descriptor. (A reference to `this` is not passed to a class method.) The reference to `this` is passed implicitly by the method invocation instructions of the Java virtual machine used to invoke instance methods.

4.4 The Constant Pool

Java virtual machine instructions do not rely on the runtime layout of classes, interfaces, class instances, or arrays. Instead, instructions refer to symbolic information in the `constant_pool` table.

All `constant_pool` table entries have the following general format:

```
cp_info {
    u1 tag;
    u1 info[];
}
```

Each item in the `constant_pool` table must begin with a 1-byte tag indicating the kind of `cp_info` entry. The contents of the `info` array vary with the value of `tag`. The valid tags and their values are listed in Table 4.3. Each tag byte must be followed by two or more bytes giving information about the specific constant. The format of the additional information varies with the tag value.

Table 4.3   Constant pool tags

Constant Type	Value
CONSTANT_Class	7
CONSTANT_Fieldref	9
CONSTANT_Methodref	10
CONSTANT_InterfaceMethodref	11
CONSTANT_String	8
CONSTANT_Integer	3
CONSTANT_Float	4
CONSTANT_Long	5
CONSTANT_Double	6
CONSTANT_NameAndType	12
CONSTANT_Utf8	1

4.4.1 The CONSTANT_Class_info Structure

The CONSTANT_Class_info structure is used to represent a class or an interface:

```
CONSTANT_Class_info {
    u1 tag;
    u2 name_index;
}
```

The items of the CONSTANT_Class_info structure are the following:

tag

> The tag item has the value CONSTANT_Class (7).

name_index

> The value of the name_index item must be a valid index into the
> constant_pool table. The constant_pool entry at that index
> must be a CONSTANT_Utf8_info (§4.4.7) structure representing a
> valid fully qualified class or interface name (§2.8.1) encoded in
> internal form (§4.2).

Because arrays are objects, the opcodes *anewarray* and *multianewarray* can
reference array "classes" via CONSTANT_Class_info (§4.4.1) structures in the
constant_pool table. For such array classes, the name of the class is the descriptor
of the array type. For example, the class name representing a two-dimensional int
array type

```
int[][]
```

is

```
[[I
```

The class name representing the type array of class Thread

```
Thread[]
```

is

```
[Ljava/lang/Thread;
```

An array type descriptor is valid only if it represents 255 or fewer dimensions.

4.4.2 The CONSTANT_Fieldref_info, CONSTANT_Methodref_info, and CONSTANT_InterfaceMethodref_info Structures

Fields, methods, and interface methods are represented by similar structures:

```
CONSTANT_Fieldref_info {
    u1 tag;
    u2 class_index;
    u2 name_and_type_index;
}

CONSTANT_Methodref_info {
    u1 tag;
    u2 class_index;
    u2 name_and_type_index;
}

CONSTANT_InterfaceMethodref_info {
    u1 tag;
    u2 class_index;
    u2 name_and_type_index;
}
```

The items of these structures are as follows:

tag

> The tag item of a CONSTANT_Fieldref_info structure has the value CONSTANT_Fieldref (9).
>
> The tag item of a CONSTANT_Methodref_info structure has the value CONSTANT_Methodref (10).
>
> The tag item of a CONSTANT_InterfaceMethodref_info structure has the value CONSTANT_InterfaceMethodref (11).

class_index

> The value of the class_index item must be a valid index into the constant_pool table. The constant_pool entry at that index must be a CONSTANT_Class_info (§4.4.1) structure representing the class or interface type that contains the declaration of the field or method.

The class_index item of a CONSTANT_Methodref_info structure must be a class type, not an interface type. The class_index item of a CONSTANT_InterfaceMethodref_info structure must be an interface type. The class_index item of a CONSTANT_Fieldref_info structure may be either a class type or an interface type.

name_and_type_index

The value of the name_and_type_index item must be a valid index into the constant_pool table. The constant_pool entry at that index must be a CONSTANT_NameAndType_info (§4.4.6) structure. This constant_pool entry indicates the name and descriptor of the field or method. In a CONSTANT_Fieldref_info the indicated descriptor must be a field descriptor (§4.3.2). Otherwise, the indicated descriptor must be a method descriptor (§4.3.3).

If the name of the method of a CONSTANT_Methodref_info structure begins with a ' <' ('\u003c'), then the name must be the special name <init>, representing an instance initialization method (§3.9). Such a method must return no value.

4.4.3 The CONSTANT_String_info Structure

The CONSTANT_String_info structure is used to represent constant objects of the type String:

```
CONSTANT_String_info {
    u1 tag;
    u2 string_index;
}
```

The items of the CONSTANT_String_info structure are as follows:

tag

The tag item of the CONSTANT_String_info structure has the value CONSTANT_String (8).

string_index

The value of the string_index item must be a valid index into the constant_pool table. The constant_pool entry at that

index must be a CONSTANT_Utf8_info (§4.4.7) structure
representing the sequence of characters to which the String
object is to be initialized.

4.4.4 The CONSTANT_Integer_info and CONSTANT_Float_info Structures

The CONSTANT_Integer_info and CONSTANT_Float_info structures represent
4-byte numeric (int and float) constants:

```
CONSTANT_Integer_info {
    u1 tag;
    u4 bytes;
}
CONSTANT_Float_info {
    u1 tag;
    u4 bytes;
}
```

The items of these structures are as follows:

tag

> The tag item of the CONSTANT_Integer_info structure has the
> value CONSTANT_Integer (3).
>
> The tag item of the CONSTANT_Float_info structure has the
> value CONSTANT_Float (4).

bytes

> The bytes item of the CONSTANT_Integer_info structure
> represents the value of the int constant. The bytes of the value
> are stored in big-endian (high byte first) order.
>
> The bytes item of the CONSTANT_Float_info structure
> represents the value of the float constant in IEEE 754 floating-
> point single format (§3.3.2). The bytes of the single format
> representation are stored in big-endian (high byte first) order.
>
> The value represented by the CONSTANT_Float_info
> structure is determined as follows. The bytes of the value are first
> converted into an int constant *bits*. Then:

- If *bits* is 0x7f800000, the float value will be positive infinity.

- If *bits* is 0xff800000, the float value will be negative infinity.

- If *bits* is in the range `0x7f800001` through `0x7fffffff` or in the range `0xff800001` through `0xffffffff`, the `float` value will be NaN.

- In all other cases, let `s`, `e`, and `m` be three values that might be computed from *bits*:

```
int s = ((bits >> 31) == 0) ? 1 : -1;
int e = ((bits >> 23) & 0xff);
int m = (e == 0) ?
            (bits & 0x7fffff) << 1 :
            (bits & 0x7fffff) | 0x800000;
```

Then the `float` value equals the result of the mathematical expression $s \cdot m \cdot 2^{e-150}$.

4.4.5   The `CONSTANT_Long_info` and `CONSTANT_Double_info` Structures

The `CONSTANT_Long_info` and `CONSTANT_Double_info` represent 8-byte numeric (`long` and `double`) constants:

```
CONSTANT_Long_info {
    u1 tag;
    u4 high_bytes;
    u4 low_bytes;
}

CONSTANT_Double_info {
    u1 tag;
    u4 high_bytes;
    u4 low_bytes;
}
```

All 8-byte constants take up two entries in the `constant_pool` table of the `class` file. If a `CONSTANT_Long_info` or `CONSTANT_Double_info` structure is the item in the `constant_pool` table at index n, then the next usable item in the pool is located at index n+2. The `constant_pool` index n+1 must be valid but is considered unusable.[2]

The items of these structures are as follows:

---

[2] In retrospect, making 8-byte constants take two constant pool entries was a poor choice.

tag

> The tag item of the CONSTANT_Long_info structure has the
> value CONSTANT_Long (5).
>
> The tag item of the CONSTANT_Double_info structure has
> the value CONSTANT_Double (6).

high_bytes, low_bytes

> The unsigned high_bytes and low_bytes items of the
> CONSTANT_Long_info structure together represent the value of
> the long constant ((long) high_bytes << 32) + low_bytes,
> where the bytes of each of high_bytes and low_bytes are
> stored in big-endian (high byte first) order.
>
> The high_bytes and low_bytes items of the
> CONSTANT_Double_info structure together represent the double
> value in IEEE 754 floating-point double format (§3.3.2). The
> bytes of each item are stored in big-endian (high byte first) order.
>
> The value represented by the CONSTANT_Double_info
> structure is determined as follows. The high_bytes and
> low_bytes items are first converted into the long constant *bits*,
> which is equal to ((long) high_bytes << 32) + low_bytes.
> Then:

- If *bits* is 0x7ff0000000000000L, the double value will be
  positive infinity.

- If *bits* is 0xfff0000000000000L, the double value will be
  negative infinity.

- If *bits* is in the range 0x7ff0000000000001L through
  0x7fffffffffffffffL or in the range 0xfff0000000000001L
  through 0xffffffffffffffffL, the double value will be NaN.

- In all other cases, let s, e, and m be three values that might be
  computed from *bits*:

  ```
  int s = ((bits >> 63) == 0) ? 1 : -1;
  int e = (int)((bits >> 52) & 0x7ffL);
  long m = (e == 0) ?
      (bits & 0xfffffffffffffL) << 1 :
      (bits & 0xfffffffffffffL) | 0x10000000000000L;
  ```

Then the floating-point value equals the `double` value of the mathematical expression $s \cdot m \cdot 2^{e-1075}$.

4.4.6 The `CONSTANT_NameAndType_info` Structure

The `CONSTANT_NameAndType_info` structure is used to represent a field or method, without indicating which class or interface type it belongs to:

```
CONSTANT_NameAndType_info {
    u1 tag;
    u2 name_index;
    u2 descriptor_index;
}
```

The items of the `CONSTANT_NameAndType_info` structure are as follows:

`tag`

> The `tag` item of the `CONSTANT_NameAndType_info` structure has the value `CONSTANT_NameAndType` (12).

`name_index`

> The value of the `name_index` item must be a valid index into the `constant_pool` table. The `constant_pool` entry at that index must be a `CONSTANT_Utf8_info` (§4.4.7) structure representing either a valid field or method name (§2.7) stored as a simple name (§2.7.1), that is, as a Java programming language identifier (§2.2) or as the special method name `<init>` (§3.9).

`descriptor_index`

> The value of the `descriptor_index` item must be a valid index into the `constant_pool` table. The `constant_pool` entry at that index must be a `CONSTANT_Utf8_info` (§4.4.7) structure representing a valid field descriptor (§4.3.2) or method descriptor (§4.3.3).

4.4.7 The `CONSTANT_Utf8_info` Structure

The `CONSTANT_Utf8_info` structure is used to represent constant string values.

UTF-8 strings are encoded so that character sequences that contain only non-null ASCII characters can be represented using only 1 byte per character, but characters of up to 16 bits can be represented. All characters in the range '\u0001' to '\u007F' are represented by a single byte:

0	*bits 6-0*

The 7 bits of data in the byte give the value of the character represented. The null character ('\u0000') and characters in the range '\u0080' to '\u07FF' are represented by a pair of bytes x and y:

x: | 1 | 1 | 0 | *bits 10-6* | y: | 1 | 0 | *bits 5-0* |

The bytes represent the character with the value $((x \,\&\, 0x1f) << 6) + (y \,\&\, 0x3f)$.

Characters in the range '\u0800' to '\uFFFF' are represented by 3 bytes x, y, and z:

x: | 1 | 1 | 1 | 0 | *bits 15-12* | y: | 1 | 0 | *bits 11-6* | z: | 1 | 0 | *bits 5-0* |

The character with the value $((x \,\&\, 0xf) << 12) + ((y \,\&\, 0x3f) << 6) + (z \,\&\, 0x3f)$ is represented by the bytes.

The bytes of multibyte characters are stored in the class file in big-endian (high byte first) order.

There are two differences between this format and the "standard" UTF-8 format. First, the null byte (byte)0 is encoded using the 2-byte format rather than the 1-byte format, so that Java virtual machine UTF-8 strings never have embedded nulls. Second, only the 1-byte, 2-byte, and 3-byte formats are used. The Java virtual machine does not recognize the longer UTF-8 formats.

For more information regarding the UTF-8 format, see *File System Safe UCS Transformation Format (FSS_UTF)*, X/Open Preliminary Specification (X/Open Company Ltd., Document Number: P316). This information also appears in ISO/IEC 10646, Annex P.

The CONSTANT_Utf8_info structure is

```
CONSTANT_Utf8_info {
    u1 tag;
    u2 length;
    u1 bytes[length];
}
```

The items of the CONSTANT_Utf8_info structure are the following:

tag

>   The `tag` item of the `CONSTANT_Utf8_info` structure has the
>   value `CONSTANT_Utf8` (1).

length

>   The value of the `length` item gives the number of bytes in the
>   `bytes` array (not the length of the resulting string). The strings in
>   the `CONSTANT_Utf8_info` structure are not null-terminated.

bytes[]

>   The `bytes` array contains the bytes of the string. No byte may
>   have the value `(byte)0` or lie in the range `(byte)0xf0`-
>   `(byte)0xff`.

4.5 Fields

Each field is described by a `field_info` structure. No two fields in one `class` file
may have the same name and descriptor (§4.3.2). The format of this structure is

```
field_info {
    u2 access_flags;
    u2 name_index;
    u2 descriptor_index;
    u2 attributes_count;
    attribute_info attributes[attributes_count];
}
```

The items of the `field_info` structure are as follows:

access_flags

>   The value of the `access_flags` item is a mask of flags used to
>   denote access permission to and properties of this field. The
>   interpretation of each flag, when set, is as shown in Table 4.4.
>
>   Fields of classes may set any of the flags in Table 4.4.
>   However, a specific field of a class may have at most one of its
>   `ACC_PRIVATE`, `ACC_PROTECTED`, and `ACC_PUBLIC` flags set
>   (§2.7.4) and may not have both its `ACC_FINAL` and
>   `ACC_VOLATILE` flags set (§2.9.1).

Table 4.4   Field access and property flags

Flag Name	Value	Interpretation
ACC_PUBLIC	0x0001	Declared public; may be accessed from outside its package.
ACC_PRIVATE	0x0002	Declared private; usable only within the defining class.
ACC_PROTECTED	0x0004	Declared protected; may be accessed within subclasses.
ACC_STATIC	0x0008	Declared static.
ACC_FINAL	0x0010	Declared final; no further assignment after initialization.
ACC_VOLATILE	0x0040	Declared volatile; cannot be cached.
ACC_TRANSIENT	0x0080	Declared transient; not written or read by a persistent object manager.

Fields of classes may set any of the flags in Table 4.4. However, a specific field of a class may have at most one of its ACC_PRIVATE, ACC_PROTECTED, and ACC_PUBLIC flags set (§2.7.4) and may not have both its ACC_FINAL and ACC_VOLATILE flags set (§2.9.1).

All fields of interfaces must have their ACC_PUBLIC, ACC_STATIC, and ACC_FINAL flags set and may not have any of the other flags in Table 4.4 set (§2.13.3.1).

All bits of the access_flags item not assigned in Table 4.4 are reserved for future use. They should be set to zero in generated class files and should be ignored by Java virtual machine implementations.

name_index

The value of the name_index item must be a valid index into the constant_pool table. The constant_pool entry at that index must be a CONSTANT_Utf8_info (§4.4.7) structure which must represent a valid field name (§2.7) stored as a simple name (§2.7.1), that is, as a Java programming language identifier (§2.2).

descriptor_index

> The value of the `descriptor_index` item must be a valid index into the `constant_pool` table. The `constant_pool` entry at that index must be a CONSTANT_Utf8_info (§4.4.7) structure that must represent a valid field descriptor (§4.3.2).

attributes_count

> The value of the `attributes_count` item indicates the number of additional attributes (§4.7) of this field.

attributes[]

> Each value of the `attributes` table must be an attribute structure (§4.7). A field can have any number of attributes associated with it.
>
> The attributes defined by this specification as appearing in the `attributes` table of a `field_info` structure are the ConstantValue (§4.7.2), Synthetic (§4.7.6), and Deprecated (§4.7.10) attributes.
>
> A Java virtual machine implementation must recognize and correctly read ConstantValue (§4.7.2) attributes found in the `attributes` table of a `field_info` structure. A Java virtual machine implementation is required to silently ignore any or all other attributes in the `attributes` table that it does not recognize. Attributes not defined in this specification are not allowed to affect the semantics of the `class` file, but only to provide additional descriptive information (§4.7.1).

4.6 Methods

Each method, including each instance initialization method (§3.9) and the class or interface initialization method (§3.9), is described by a `method_info` structure. No two methods in one `class` file may have the same name and descriptor (§4.3.3).

The structure has the following format:

```
method_info {
    u2 access_flags;
    u2 name_index;
    u2 descriptor_index;
    u2 attributes_count;
    attribute_info attributes[attributes_count];
}
```

The items of the `method_info` structure are as follows:

`access_flags`

> The value of the `access_flags` item is a mask of flags used to denote access permission to and properties of this method. The interpretation of each flag, when set, is as shown in Table 4.5.

Table 4.5 Method access and property flags

Flag Name	Value	Interpretation
ACC_PUBLIC	0x0001	Declared `public`; may be accessed from outside its package.
ACC_PRIVATE	0x0002	Declared `private`; accessible only within the defining class.
ACC_PROTECTED	0x0004	Declared `protected`; may be accessed within subclasses.
ACC_STATIC	0x0008	Declared `static`.
ACC_FINAL	0x0010	Declared `final`; may not be overridden.
ACC_SYNCHRONIZED	0x0020	Declared `synchronized`; invocation is wrapped in a monitor lock.
ACC_NATIVE	0x0100	Declared `native`; implemented in a language other than Java.
ACC_ABSTRACT	0x0400	Declared `abstract`; no implementation is provided.
ACC_STRICT	0x0800	Declared `strictfp`; floating-point mode is FP-strict

> Methods of classes may set any of the flags in Table 4.5. However, a specific method of a class may have at most one of its ACC_PRIVATE, ACC_PROTECTED, and ACC_PUBLIC flags set (§2.7.4). If such a method has its ACC_ABSTRACT flag set it may not have any of its ACC_FINAL, ACC_NATIVE, ACC_PRIVATE, ACC_STATIC, ACC_STRICT, or ACC_SYNCHRONIZED flags set (§2.13.3.2).
>
> All interface methods must have their ACC_ABSTRACT and ACC_PUBLIC flags set and may not have any of the other flags in Table 4.5 set (§2.13.3.2).

A specific instance initialization method (§3.9) may have at most one of its `ACC_PRIVATE`, `ACC_PROTECTED`, and `ACC_PUBLIC` flags set and may also have its `ACC_STRICT` flag set, but may not have any of the other flags in Table 4.5 set.

Class and interface initialization methods (§3.9) are called implicitly by the Java virtual machine; the value of their `access_flags` item is ignored except for the settings of the `ACC_STRICT` flag.

All bits of the `access_flags` item not assigned in Table 4.5 are reserved for future use. They should be set to zero in generated `class` files and should be ignored by Java virtual machine implementations.

`name_index`

The value of the `name_index` item must be a valid index into the `constant_pool` table. The `constant_pool` entry at that index must be a `CONSTANT_Utf8_info` (§4.4.7) structure representing either one of the special method names (§3.9), `<init>` or `<clinit>`, or a valid method name in the Java programming language (§2.7), stored as a simple name (§2.7.1).

`descriptor_index`

The value of the `descriptor_index` item must be a valid index into the `constant_pool` table. The `constant_pool` entry at that index must be a `CONSTANT_Utf8_info` (§4.4.7) structure representing a valid method descriptor (§4.3.3).

`attributes_count`

The value of the `attributes_count` item indicates the number of additional attributes (§4.7) of this method.

`attributes[]`

Each value of the `attributes` table must be an attribute structure (§4.7). A method can have any number of optional attributes associated with it.

The only attributes defined by this specification as appearing in the `attributes` table of a `method_info` structure are the Code (§4.7.3), Exceptions (§4.7.4), Synthetic (§4.7.6), and Deprecated (§4.7.10) attributes.

A Java virtual machine implementation must recognize and correctly read Code (§4.7.3) and Exceptions (§4.7.4) attributes found in the attributes table of a method_info structure. A Java virtual machine implementation is required to silently ignore any or all other attributes in the attributes table of a method_info structure that it does not recognize. Attributes not defined in this specification are not allowed to affect the semantics of the class file, but only to provide additional descriptive information (§4.7.1).

4.7 Attributes

Attributes are used in the ClassFile (§4.1), field_info (§4.5), method_info (§4.6), and Code_attribute (§4.7.3) structures of the class file format. All attributes have the following general format:

```
attribute_info {
    u2 attribute_name_index;
    u4 attribute_length;
    u1 info[attribute_length];
}
```

For all attributes, the attribute_name_index must be a valid unsigned 16-bit index into the constant pool of the class. The constant_pool entry at attribute_name_index must be a CONSTANT_Utf8_info (§4.4.7) structure representing the name of the attribute. The value of the attribute_length item indicates the length of the subsequent information in bytes. The length does not include the initial six bytes that contain the attribute_name_index and attribute_length items.

Certain attributes are predefined as part of the class file specification. The predefined attributes are the SourceFile (§4.7.7), ConstantValue (§4.7.2), Code (§4.7.3), Exceptions (§4.7.4), InnerClasses (§4.7.5), Synthetic (§4.7.6), LineNumberTable (§4.7.8), LocalVariableTable (§4.7.9), and Deprecated (§4.7.10) attributes. Within the context of their use in this specification, that is, in the attributes tables of the class file structures in which they appear, the names of these predefined attributes are reserved.

Of the predefined attributes, the Code, ConstantValue, and Exceptions attributes must be recognized and correctly read by a class file reader for correct interpretation of the `class` file by a Java virtual machine implementation. The `InnerClasses` and `Synthetic` attributes must be recognized and correctly read by a `class` file reader in order to properly implement the Java and Java 2 platform class libraries (§3.12). Use of the remaining predefined attributes is optional; a `class` file reader may use the information they contain, or otherwise must silently ignore those attributes.

4.7.1 Defining and Naming New Attributes

Compilers are permitted to define and emit `class` files containing new attributes in the `attributes` tables of `class` file structures. Java virtual machine implementations are permitted to recognize and use new attributes found in the `attributes` tables of `class` file structures. However, any attribute not defined as part of this Java virtual machine specification must not affect the semantics of class or interface types. Java virtual machine implementations are required to silently ignore attributes they do not recognize.

For instance, defining a new attribute to support vendor-specific debugging is permitted. Because Java virtual machine implementations are required to ignore attributes they do not recognize, `class` files intended for that particular Java virtual machine implementation will be usable by other implementations even if those implementations cannot make use of the additional debugging information that the `class` files contain.

Java virtual machine implementations are specifically prohibited from throwing an exception or otherwise refusing to use `class` files simply because of the presence of some new attribute. Of course, tools operating on `class` files may not run correctly if given `class` files that do not contain all the attributes they require.

Two attributes that are intended to be distinct, but that happen to use the same attribute name and are of the same length, will conflict on implementations that recognize either attribute. Attributes defined other than by Sun must have names chosen according to the package naming convention defined by *The Java Language Specification*. For instance, a new attribute defined by Netscape might have the name `"com.Netscape.new-attribute"`.[3]

Sun may define additional attributes in future versions of this `class` file specification.

---

[3] The first edition of *The Java Language Specification* required that "com" be in uppercase in this example. The second edition will reverse that convention and use lowercase.

4.7.2 The `ConstantValue` Attribute

The `ConstantValue` attribute is a fixed-length attribute used in the `attributes` table of the `field_info` (§4.5) structures. A `ConstantValue` attribute represents the value of a constant field that must be (explicitly or implicitly) `static`; that is, the `ACC_STATIC` bit (Table 4.4) in the `flags` item of the `field_info` structure must be set. There can be no more than one `ConstantValue` attribute in the `attributes` table of a given `field_info` structure. The constant field represented by the `field_info` structure is assigned the value referenced by its `ConstantValue` attribute as part of the initialization of the class or interface declaring the constant field (§2.17.4). This occurs immediately prior to the invocation of the class or interface initialization method (§3.9) of that class or interface.

If a `field_info` structure representing a non-`static` field has a `Constant-Value` attribute, then that attribute must silently be ignored. Every Java virtual machine implementation must recognize `ConstantValue` attributes.

The `ConstantValue` attribute has the following format:

```
ConstantValue_attribute {
    u2 attribute_name_index;
    u4 attribute_length;
    u2 constantvalue_index;
}
```

The items of the `ConstantValue_attribute` structure are as follows:

`attribute_name_index`

> The value of the `attribute_name_index` item must be a valid index into the `constant_pool` table. The `constant_pool` entry at that index must be a `CONSTANT_Utf8_info` (§4.4.7) structure representing the string `"ConstantValue"`.

`attribute_length`

> The value of the `attribute_length` item of a `ConstantValue_attribute` structure must be 2.

`constantvalue_index`

> The value of the `constantvalue_index` item must be a valid index into the `constant_pool` table. The `constant_pool` entry at that index gives the constant value represented by this attribute. The `constant_pool` entry must be of a type appropriate to the field, as shown by Table 4.6.

Table 4.6   Constant value attribute types

Field Type	Entry Type
long	CONSTANT_Long
float	CONSTANT_Float
double	CONSTANT_Double
int, short, char, byte, boolean	CONSTANT_Integer
String	CONSTANT_String

4.7.3 The Code Attribute

The Code attribute is a variable-length attribute used in the attributes table of method_info structures. A Code attribute contains the Java virtual machine instructions and auxiliary information for a single method, instance initialization method (§3.9), or class or interface initialization method (§3.9). Every Java virtual machine implementation must recognize Code attributes. If the method is either native or abstract, its method_info structure must not have a Code attribute. Otherwise, its method_info structure must have exactly one Code attribute.

The Code attribute has the following format:

```
Code_attribute {
    u2 attribute_name_index;
    u4 attribute_length;
    u2 max_stack;
    u2 max_locals;
    u4 code_length;
    u1 code[code_length];
    u2 exception_table_length;
    {   u2 start_pc;
        u2 end_pc;
        u2 handler_pc;
        u2 catch_type;
    }   exception_table[exception_table_length];
    u2 attributes_count;
    attribute_info attributes[attributes_count];
}
```

The items of the Code_attribute structure are as follows:

`attribute_name_index`

The value of the `attribute_name_index` item must be a valid index into the `constant_pool` table. The `constant_pool` entry at that index must be a `CONSTANT_Utf8_info` (§4.4.7) structure representing the string "Code".

`attribute_length`

The value of the `attribute_length` item indicates the length of the attribute, excluding the initial six bytes.

`max_stack`

The value of the `max_stack` item gives the maximum depth (§3.6.2) of the operand stack of this method at any point during execution of the method.

`max_locals`

The value of the `max_locals` item gives the number of local variables in the local variable array allocated upon invocation of this method, including the local variables used to pass parameters to the method on its invocation.

The greatest local variable index for a value of type `long` or `double` is `max_locals−2`. The greatest local variable index for a value of any other type is `max_locals−1`.

`code_length`

The value of the `code_length` item gives the number of bytes in the `code` array for this method. The value of `code_length` must be greater than zero; the `code` array must not be empty.

`code[]`

The `code` array gives the actual bytes of Java virtual machine code that implement the method.

When the `code` array is read into memory on a byte-addressable machine, if the first byte of the array is aligned on a 4-byte boundary, the *tableswitch* and *lookupswitch* 32-bit offsets will be 4-byte aligned. (Refer to the descriptions of those instructions for more information on the consequences of `code` array alignment.)

The detailed constraints on the contents of the `code` array are extensive and are given in a separate section (§4.8).

exception_table_length

> The value of the exception_table_length item gives the number of entries in the exception_table table.

exception_table[]

> Each entry in the exception_table array describes one exception handler in the code array. The order of the handlers in the exception_table array is significant. See Section 3.10 for more details.
>
> Each exception_table entry contains the following four items:

start_pc, end_pc

> The values of the two items start_pc and end_pc indicate the ranges in the code array at which the exception handler is active. The value of start_pc must be a valid index into the code array of the opcode of an instruction. The value of end_pc either must be a valid index into the code array of the opcode of an instruction or must be equal to code_length, the length of the code array. The value of start_pc must be less than the value of end_pc.
>
> The start_pc is inclusive and end_pc is exclusive; that is, the exception handler must be active while the program counter is within the interval [start_pc, end_pc).[4]

handler_pc

> The value of the handler_pc item indicates the start of the exception handler. The value of the item must be a valid index into the code array and must be the index of the opcode of an instruction.

catch_type

> If the value of the catch_type item is nonzero, it must be a valid index into the constant_pool table. The

---

[4] The fact that end_pc is exclusive is a historical mistake in the design of the Java virtual machine: if the Java virtual machine code for a method is exactly 65535 bytes long and ends with an instruction that is 1 byte long, then that instruction cannot be protected by an exception handler. A compiler writer can work around this bug by limiting the maximum size of the generated Java virtual machine code for any method, instance initialization method, or static initializer (the size of any code array) to 65534 bytes.

constant_pool entry at that index must be a
CONSTANT_Class_info (§4.4.1) structure representing a
class of exceptions that this exception handler is designated
to catch. This class must be the class Throwable or one of its
subclasses. The exception handler will be called only if the
thrown exception is an instance of the given class or one of its
subclasses.

If the value of the catch_type item is zero, this
exception handler is called for all exceptions. This is used to
implement finally (see Section 7.13, "Compiling
finally").

attributes_count

The value of the attributes_count item indicates the number
of attributes of the Code attribute.

attributes[]

Each value of the attributes table must be an attribute structure
(§4.7). A Code attribute can have any number of optional
attributes associated with it.

Currently, the LineNumberTable (§4.7.8) and
LocalVariableTable (§4.7.9) attributes, both of which contain
debugging information, are defined and used with the Code
attribute.

A Java virtual machine implementation is permitted to
silently ignore any or all attributes in the attributes table of a
Code attribute. Attributes not defined in this specification are not
allowed to affect the semantics of the class file, but only to
provide additional descriptive information (§4.7.1).

4.7.4 The Exceptions Attribute

The Exceptions attribute is a variable-length attribute used in the attributes
table of a method_info (§4.6) structure. The Exceptions attribute indicates which
checked exceptions a method may throw. There may be at most one Exceptions
attribute in each method_info structure.

The Exceptions attribute has the following format:

```
Exceptions_attribute {
    u2 attribute_name_index;
    u4 attribute_length;
    u2 number_of_exceptions;
    u2 exception_index_table[number_of_exceptions];
}
```

The items of the Exceptions_attribute structure are as follows:

attribute_name_index

> The value of the attribute_name_index item must be a valid
> index into the constant_pool table. The constant_pool entry
> at that index must be the CONSTANT_Utf8_info (§4.4.7)
> structure representing the string "Exceptions".

attribute_length

> The value of the attribute_length item indicates the attribute
> length, excluding the initial six bytes.

number_of_exceptions

> The value of the number_of_exceptions item indicates the
> number of entries in the exception_index_table.

exception_index_table[]

> Each value in the exception_index_table array must be a
> valid index into the constant_pool table. The constant_pool
> entry referenced by each table item must be a
> CONSTANT_Class_info (§4.4.1) structure representing a class
> type that this method is declared to throw.

A method should throw an exception only if at least one of the following three
criteria is met:

- The exception is an instance of RuntimeException or one of its subclasses.

- The exception is an instance of Error or one of its subclasses.

- The exception is an instance of one of the exception classes specified in the
  exception_index_table just described, or one of their subclasses.

These requirements are not enforced in the Java virtual machine; they are
enforced only at compile time.

4.7.5 The InnerClasses Attribute

The InnerClasses attribute[5] is a variable-length attribute in the attributes table of the ClassFile (§4.1) structure. If the constant pool of a class or interface refers to any class or interface that is not a member of a package, its ClassFile structure must have exactly one InnerClasses attribute in its attributes table.

The InnerClasses attribute has the following format:

```
InnerClasses_attribute {
    u2 attribute_name_index;
    u4 attribute_length;
    u2 number_of_classes;
    { u2 inner_class_info_index;
      u2 outer_class_info_index;
      u2 inner_name_index;
      u2 inner_class_access_flags;
    } classes[number_of_classes];
}
```

The items of the InnerClasses_attribute structure are as follows:

attribute_name_index

> The value of the attribute_name_index item must be a valid index into the constant_pool table. The constant_pool entry at that index must be a CONSTANT_Utf8_info (§4.4.7) structure representing the string "InnerClasses".

attribute_length

> The value of the attribute_length item indicates the length of the attribute, excluding the initial six bytes.

number_of_classes

> The value of the number_of_classes item indicates the number of entries in the classes array.

classes[]

> Every CONSTANT_Class_info entry in the constant_pool table which represents a class or interface *C* that is not a package

---

[5] The InnerClasses attribute was introduced in JDK release 1.1 to support nested classes and interfaces.

member must have exactly one corresponding entry in the
`classes` array.

If a class has members that are classes or interfaces, its
`constant_pool` table (and hence its `InnerClasses` attribute)
must refer to each such member, even if that member is not
otherwise mentioned by the class. These rules imply that a nested
class or interface member will have `InnerClasses` information
for each enclosing class and for each immediate member.

Each `classes` array entry contains the following four items:

`inner_class_info_index`

> The value of the `inner_class_info_index` item must be
> zero or a valid index into the `constant_pool` table. The
> `constant_pool` entry at that index must be a
> `CONSTANT_Class_info` (§4.4.1) structure representing *C*.
> The remaining items in the `classes` array entry give
> information about *C*.

`outer_class_info_index`

> If *C* is not a member, the value of the
> `outer_class_info_index` item must be zero. Otherwise,
> the value of the `outer_class_info_index` item must be a
> valid index into the `constant_pool` table, and the entry at
> that index must be a `CONSTANT_Class_info` (§4.4.1)
> structure representing the class or interface of which *C* is a
> member.

`inner_name_index`

> If *C* is anonymous, the value of the `inner_name_index`
> item must be zero. Otherwise, the value of the
> `inner_name_index` item must be a valid index into the
> `constant_pool` table, and the entry at that index must be a
> `CONSTANT_Utf8_info` (§4.4.7) structure that represents the
> original simple name of *C*, as given in the source code from
> which this `class` file was compiled.

`inner_class_access_flags`

> The value of the `inner_class_access_flags` item is a
> mask of flags used to denote access permissions to and
> properties of class or interface *C* as declared in the source

code from which this `class` file was compiled. It is used by compilers to recover the original information when source code is not available. The flags are shown in Table 4.7.

Table 4.7   Nested class access and property flags

Flag Name	Value	Meaning
ACC_PUBLIC	0x0001	Marked or implicitly `public` in source.
ACC_PRIVATE	0x0002	Marked `private` in source.
ACC_PROTECTED	0x0004	Marked `protected` in source.
ACC_STATIC	0x0008	Marked or implicitly `static` in source.
ACC_FINAL	0x0010	Marked `final` in source.
ACC_INTERFACE	0x0200	Was an `interface` in source.
ACC_ABSTRACT	0x0400	Marked or implicitly `abstract` in source.

All bits of the `inner_class_access_flags` item not assigned in Table 4.7 are reserved for future use. They should be set to zero in generated `class` files and should be ignored by Java virtual machine implementations.

The Java virtual machine does not currently check the consistency of the `InnerClasses` attribute with any `class` file actually representing a class or interface referenced by the attribute.

4.7.6   The Synthetic Attribute

The `Synthetic` attribute[6] is a fixed-length attribute in the `attributes` table of `ClassFile` (§4.1), `field_info` (§4.5), and `method_info` (§4.6) structures. A class member that does not appear in the source code must be marked using a `Synthetic` attribute.

---

[6] The `Synthetic` attribute was introduced in JDK release 1.1 to support nested classes and interfaces.

The Synthetic attribute has the following format:

```
Synthetic_attribute {
    u2 attribute_name_index;
    u4 attribute_length;
}
```

The items of the Synthetic_attribute structure are as follows:

attribute_name_index

> The value of the attribute_name_index item must be a valid index into the constant_pool table. The constant_pool entry at that index must be a CONSTANT_Utf8_info (§4.4.7) structure representing the string "Synthetic".

attribute_length

> The value of the attribute_length item is zero.

4.7.7   The SourceFile Attribute

The SourceFile attribute is an optional fixed-length attribute in the attributes table of the ClassFile (§4.1) structure. There can be no more than one SourceFile attribute in the attributes table of a given ClassFile structure.

The SourceFile attribute has the following format:

```
SourceFile_attribute {
    u2 attribute_name_index;
    u4 attribute_length;
    u2 sourcefile_index;
}
```

The items of the SourceFile_attribute structure are as follows:

attribute_name_index

> The value of the attribute_name_index item must be a valid index into the constant_pool table. The constant_pool entry at that index must be a CONSTANT_Utf8_info (§4.4.7) structure representing the string "SourceFile".

attribute_length

> The value of the attribute_length item of a SourceFile_attribute structure must be 2.

sourcefile_index

> The value of the sourcefile_index item must be a valid index into the constant_pool table. The constant pool entry at that index must be a CONSTANT_Utf8_info (§4.4.7) structure representing a string.

> The string referenced by the sourcefile_index item will be interpreted as indicating the name of the source file from which this class file was compiled. It will not be interpreted as indicating the name of a directory containing the file or an absolute path name for the file; such platform-specific additional information must be supplied by the runtime interpreter or development tool at the time the file name is actually used.

4.7.8 The LineNumberTable Attribute

The LineNumberTable attribute is an optional variable-length attribute in the attributes table of a Code (§4.7.3) attribute. It may be used by debuggers to determine which part of the Java virtual machine code array corresponds to a given line number in the original source file. If LineNumberTable attributes are present in the attributes table of a given Code attribute, then they may appear in any order. Furthermore, multiple LineNumberTable attributes may together represent a given line of a source file; that is, LineNumberTable attributes need not be one-to-one with source lines.

The LineNumberTable attribute has the following format:

```
LineNumberTable_attribute {
    u2 attribute_name_index;
    u4 attribute_length;
    u2 line_number_table_length;
    { u2 start_pc;
      u2 line_number;
    } line_number_table[line_number_table_length];
}
```

The items of the LineNumberTable_attribute structure are as follows:

attribute_name_index

> The value of the attribute_name_index item must be a valid index into the constant_pool table. The constant_pool entry

at that index must be a CONSTANT_Utf8_info (§4.4.7) structure representing the string "LineNumberTable".

attribute_length

> The value of the attribute_length item indicates the length of the attribute, excluding the initial six bytes.

line_number_table_length

> The value of the line_number_table_length item indicates the number of entries in the line_number_table array.

line_number_table[]

> Each entry in the line_number_table array indicates that the line number in the original source file changes at a given point in the code array. Each line_number_table entry must contain the following two items:

> start_pc

>> The value of the start_pc item must indicate the index into the code array at which the code for a new line in the original source file begins. The value of start_pc must be less than the value of the code_length item of the Code attribute of which this LineNumberTable is an attribute.

> line_number

>> The value of the line_number item must give the corresponding line number in the original source file.

4.7.9 The LocalVariableTable Attribute

The LocalVariableTable attribute is an optional variable-length attribute of a Code (§4.7.3) attribute. It may be used by debuggers to determine the value of a given local variable during the execution of a method. If LocalVariableTable attributes are present in the attributes table of a given Code attribute, then they may appear in any order. There may be no more than one LocalVariableTable attribute per local variable in the Code attribute.

The LocalVariableTable attribute has the following format:

```
LocalVariableTable_attribute {
    u2 attribute_name_index;
    u4 attribute_length;
    u2 local_variable_table_length;
    { u2 start_pc;
      u2 length;
      u2 name_index;
      u2 descriptor_index;
      u2 index;
    } local_variable_table[
            local_variable_table_length];
}
```

The items of the LocalVariableTable_attribute structure are as follows:

attribute_name_index

> The value of the attribute_name_index item must be a valid index into the constant_pool table. The constant_pool entry at that index must be a CONSTANT_Utf8_info (§4.4.7) structure representing the string "LocalVariableTable".

attribute_length

> The value of the attribute_length item indicates the length of the attribute, excluding the initial six bytes.

local_variable_table_length

> The value of the local_variable_table_length item indicates the number of entries in the local_variable_table array.

local_variable_table[]

> Each entry in the local_variable_table array indicates a range of code array offsets within which a local variable has a value. It also indicates the index into the local variable array of the current frame at which that local variable can be found. Each entry must contain the following five items:

start_pc, length

> The given local variable must have a value at indices into the code array in the interval [start_pc, start_pc+length], that is, between start_pc and start_pc+length inclusive. The value of start_pc must be a valid index into the code array of this Code attribute and must be the index of the opcode of an instruction. Either the value of start_pc+length must be a valid index into the code array of this Code attribute and be the index of the opcode of an instruction, or it must be the first index beyond the end of that code array.

name_index, descriptor_index

> The value of the name_index item must be a valid index into the constant_pool table. The constant_pool entry at that index must contain a CONSTANT_Utf8_info (§4.4.7) structure representing a valid local variable name stored as a simple name (§2.7.1).
>
> The value of the descriptor_index item must be a valid index into the constant_pool table. The constant_pool entry at that index must contain a CONSTANT_Utf8_info (§4.4.7) structure representing a field descriptor (§4.3.2) encoding the type of a local variable in the source program.

index

> The given local variable must be at index in the local variable array of the current frame. If the local variable at index is of type double or long, it occupies both index and index+1.

4.7.10 The Deprecated Attribute

The Deprecated attribute[7] is an optional fixed-length attribute in the attributes table of ClassFile (§4.1), field_info (§4.5), and method_info (§4.6) structures. A class, interface, method, or field may be marked using a Deprecated attribute to indicate that the class, interface, method, or field has been superseded. A

---

[7] The Deprecated attribute was introduced in JDK release 1.1 to support the @deprecated tag in documentation comments.

runtime interpreter or tool that reads the `class` file format, such as a compiler, can use this marking to advise the user that a superseded class, interface, method, or field is being referred to. The presence of a `Deprecated` attribute does not alter the semantics of a class or interface.

The `Deprecated` attribute has the following format:

```
Deprecated_attribute {
    u2 attribute_name_index;
    u4 attribute_length;
}
```

The items of the `Deprecated_attribute` structure are as follows:

attribute_name_index

The value of the `attribute_name_index` item must be a valid index into the `constant_pool` table. The `constant_pool` entry at that index must be a CONSTANT_Utf8_info (§4.4.7) structure representing the string "Deprecated".

attribute_length

The value of the `attribute_length` item is zero.

4.8 Constraints on Java Virtual Machine Code

The Java virtual machine code for a method, instance initialization method (§3.9), or class or interface initialization method (§3.9) is stored in the `code` array of the Code attribute of a `method_info` structure of a `class` file. This section describes the constraints associated with the contents of the `Code_attribute` structure.

4.8.1 Static Constraints

The *static constraints* on a `class` file are those defining the well-formedness of the file. With the exception of the static constraints on the Java virtual machine code of the `class` file, these constraints have been given in the previous section. The static constraints on the Java virtual machine code in a `class` file specify how Java virtual machine instructions must be laid out in the `code` array and what the operands of individual instructions must be.

The static constraints on the instructions in the `code` array are as follows:

- The `code` array must not be empty, so the `code_length` item cannot have the value 0.

- The value of the `code_length` item must be less than 65536.

- The opcode of the first instruction in the `code` array begins at index 0.

- Only instances of the instructions documented in Section 6.4 may appear in the `code` array. Instances of instructions using the reserved opcodes (§6.2) or any opcodes not documented in this specification may not appear in the `code` array.

- For each instruction in the `code` array except the last, the index of the opcode of the next instruction equals the index of the opcode of the current instruction plus the length of that instruction, including all its operands. The *wide* instruction is treated like any other instruction for these purposes; the opcode specifying the operation that a *wide* instruction is to modify is treated as one of the operands of that *wide* instruction. That opcode must never be directly reachable by the computation.

- The last byte of the last instruction in the `code` array must be the byte at index `code_length−1`.

The static constraints on the operands of instructions in the `code` array are as follows:

- The target of each jump and branch instruction (*jsr, jsr_w, goto, goto_w, ifeq, ifne, ifle, iflt, ifge, ifgt, ifnull, ifnonnull, if_icmpeq, if_icmpne, if_icmple, if_icmplt, if_icmpge, if_icmpgt, if_acmpeq, if_acmpne*) must be the opcode of an instruction within this method. The target of a jump or branch instruction must never be the opcode used to specify the operation to be modified by a *wide* instruction; a jump or branch target may be the *wide* instruction itself.

- Each target, including the default, of each *tableswitch* instruction must be the opcode of an instruction within this method. Each *tableswitch* instruction must have a number of entries in its jump table that is consistent with the value of its *low* and *high* jump table operands, and its *low* value must be less than or equal to its *high* value. No target of a *tableswitch* instruction may be the opcode used to specify the operation to be modified by a *wide* instruction; a *tableswitch* target may be a *wide* instruction itself.

- Each target, including the default, of each *lookupswitch* instruction must be the opcode of an instruction within this method. Each *lookupswitch* instruction must have a number of *match-offset* pairs that is consistent with the value of its *npairs* operand. The *match-offset* pairs must be sorted in increasing numerical order by signed *match* value. No target of a *lookupswitch* instruction may be the opcode used to specify the operation to be modified by a *wide* instruction; a *lookupswitch* target may be a *wide* instruction itself.

- The operand of each *ldc* instruction must be a valid index into the constant_pool table. The operands of each *ldc_w* instruction must represent a valid index into the constant_pool table. In both cases the constant pool entry referenced by that index must be of type CONSTANT_Integer, CONSTANT_Float, or CONSTANT_String.

- The operands of each *ldc2_w* instruction must represent a valid index into the constant_pool table. The constant pool entry referenced by that index must be of type CONSTANT_Long or CONSTANT_Double. In addition, the subsequent constant pool index must also be a valid index into the constant pool, and the constant pool entry at that index must not be used.

- The operands of each *getfield*, *putfield*, *getstatic*, and *putstatic* instruction must represent a valid index into the constant_pool table. The constant pool entry referenced by that index must be of type CONSTANT_Fieldref.

- The indexbyte operands of each *invokevirtual*, *invokespecial*, and *invokestatic* instruction must represent a valid index into the constant_pool table. The constant pool entry referenced by that index must be of type CONSTANT_Methodref.

- Only the *invokespecial* instruction is allowed to invoke an instance initialization method (§3.9). No other method whose name begins with the character '<' ('\u003c') may be called by the method invocation instructions. In particular, the class or interface initialization method specially named <clinit> is never called explicitly from Java virtual machine instructions, but only implicitly by the Java virtual machine itself.

- The indexbyte operands of each *invokeinterface* instruction must represent a valid index into the constant_pool table. The constant pool entry referenced by that index must be of type CONSTANT_Interface-Methodref. The value of the *count* operand of each *invokeinterface* instruction must reflect the number of local variables necessary to store the arguments to be passed to the interface method, as implied by the descriptor of the CONSTANT_NameAndType_info structure referenced by the CONSTANT_InterfaceMethodref constant pool entry. The fourth operand byte of each *invokeinterface* instruction must have the value zero.

- The operands of each *instanceof*, *checkcast*, *new*, and *anewarray* instruction and the indexbyte operands of each *multianewarray* instruction must represent a valid index into the constant_pool table. The constant pool entry referenced by that index must be of type CONSTANT_Class.

- No *anewarray* instruction may be used to create an array of more than 255 dimensions.

- No *new* instruction may reference a CONSTANT_Class constant_pool table entry representing an array class. The *new* instruction cannot be used to create an array. The *new* instruction also cannot be used to create an instance of an interface or an instance of an abstract class.

- A *multianewarray* instruction must be used only to create an array of a type that has at least as many dimensions as the value of its *dimensions* operand. That is, while a *multianewarray* instruction is not required to create all of the dimensions of the array type referenced by its indexbyte operands, it must not attempt to create more dimensions than are in the array type. The *dimensions* operand of each *multianewarray* instruction must not be zero.

- The *atype* operand of each *newarray* instruction must take one of the values T_BOOLEAN (4), T_CHAR (5), T_FLOAT (6), T_DOUBLE (7), T_BYTE (8), T_SHORT (9), T_INT (10), or T_LONG (11).

- The index operand of each *iload*, *fload*, *aload*, *istore*, *fstore*, *astore*, *iinc*, and *ret* instruction must be a nonnegative integer no greater than max_locals−1.

- The implicit index of each *iload_<n>*, *fload_<n>*, *aload_<n>*, *istore_<n>*, *fstore_<n>*, and *astore_<n>* instruction must be no greater than the value of max_locals−1.

- The index operand of each *lload*, *dload*, *lstore*, and *dstore* instruction must be no greater than the value of max_locals−2.

- The implicit index of each *lload_<n>*, *dload_<n>*, *lstore_<n>*, and *dstore_<n>* instruction must be no greater than the value of max_locals−2.

- The indexbyte operands of each *wide* instruction modifying an *iload*, *fload*, *aload*, *istore*, *fstore*, *astore*, *ret*, or *iinc* instruction must represent a nonnegative integer no greater than `max_locals−1`. The indexbyte operands of each *wide* instruction modifying an *lload*, *dload*, *lstore*, or *dstore* instruction must represent a nonnegative integer no greater than `max_locals−2`.

4.8.2 Structural Constraints

The structural constraints on the `code` array specify constraints on relationships between Java virtual machine instructions. The structural constraints are as follows:

- Each instruction must only be executed with the appropriate type and number of arguments in the operand stack and local variable array, regardless of the execution path that leads to its invocation. An instruction operating on values of type `int` is also permitted to operate on values of type `boolean`, `byte`, `char`, and `short`. (As noted in §3.3.4 and §3.11.1, the Java virtual machine internally converts values of types `boolean`, `byte`, `char`, and `short` to type `int`.)

- If an instruction can be executed along several different execution paths, the operand stack must have the same depth (§3.6.2) prior to the execution of the instruction, regardless of the path taken.

- At no point during execution can the order of the local variable pair holding a value of type `long` or `double` be reversed or the pair split up. At no point can the local variables of such a pair be operated on individually.

- No local variable (or local variable pair, in the case of a value of type `long` or `double`) can be accessed before it is assigned a value.

- At no point during execution can the operand stack grow to a depth (§3.6.2) greater than that implied by the `max_stack` item.

- At no point during execution can more values be popped from the operand stack than it contains.

- Each *invokespecial* instruction must name an instance initialization method (§3.9), a method in the current class, or a method in a superclass of the current class.

- When the instance initialization method (§3.9) is invoked, an uninitialized class instance must be in an appropriate position on the operand stack. An instance initialization method must never be invoked on an initialized class instance.

- When any instance method is invoked or when any instance variable is accessed, the class instance that contains the instance method or instance variable must already be initialized.

- There must never be an uninitialized class instance on the operand stack or in a local variable when any backwards branch is taken. There must never be an uninitialized class instance in a local variable in code protected by an exception handler. However, an uninitialized class instance may be on the operand stack in code protected by an exception handler. When an exception is thrown, the contents of the operand stack are discarded.

- Each instance initialization method (§3.9), except for the instance initialization method derived from the constructor of class Object, must call either another instance initialization method of this or an instance initialization method of its direct superclass super before its instance members are accessed. However, instance fields of this that are declared in the current class may be assigned before calling any instance initialization method.

- The arguments to each method invocation must be method invocation compatible (§2.6.8) with the method descriptor (§4.3.3).

- The type of every class instance that is the target of a method invocation instruction must be assignment compatible (§2.6.7) with the class or interface type specified in the instruction.

- Each return instruction must match its method's return type. If the method returns a boolean, byte, char, short, or int, only the *ireturn* instruction may be used. If the method returns a float, long, or double, only an *freturn*, *lreturn*, or *dreturn* instruction, respectively, may be used. If the method returns a reference type, it must do so using an *areturn* instruction, and the type of the returned value must be assignment compatible (§2.6.7) with the return descriptor (§4.3.3) of the method. All instance initialization methods, class or interface initialization methods, and methods declared to return void must use only the *return* instruction.

- If *getfield* or *putfield* is used to access a protected field of a superclass, then the type of the class instance being accessed must be the same as or a subclass of the current class. If *invokevirtual* or *invokespecial* is used to access a protected method of a superclass, then the type of the class instance being accessed must be the same as or a subclass of the current class.

- The type of every class instance accessed by a *getfield* instruction or modified by a *putfield* instruction must be assignment compatible (§2.6.7) with the class type specified in the instruction.

- The type of every value stored by a *putfield* or *putstatic* instruction must be compatible with the descriptor of the field (§4.3.2) of the class instance or class being stored into. If the descriptor type is boolean, byte, char, short, or int, then the value must be an int. If the descriptor type is float, long, or double, then the value must be a float, long, or double, respectively. If the descriptor type is a reference type, then the value must be of a type that is assignment compatible (§2.6.7) with the descriptor type.

- The type of every value stored into an array of type reference by an *aastore* instruction must be assignment compatible (§2.6.7) with the component type of the array.

- Each *athrow* instruction must throw only values that are instances of class Throwable or of subclasses of Throwable.

- Execution never falls off the bottom of the code array.

- No return address (a value of type returnAddress) may be loaded from a local variable.

- The instruction following each *jsr* or *jsr_w* instruction may be returned to only by a single *ret* instruction.

- No *jsr* or *jsr_w* instruction may be used to recursively call a subroutine if that subroutine is already present in the subroutine call chain. (Subroutines can be nested when using try-finally constructs from within a finally clause. For more information on Java virtual machine subroutines, see §4.9.6.)

- Each instance of type returnAddress can be returned to at most once. If a *ret* instruction returns to a point in the subroutine call chain above the *ret* instruction corresponding to a given instance of type returnAddress, then that instance can never be used as a return address.

4.9 Verification of `class` Files

Even though Sun's compiler for the Java programming language attempts to produce only class files that satisfy all the static constraints in the previous sections, the Java virtual machine has no guarantee that any file it is asked to load was generated by that compiler or is properly formed. Applications such as Sun's HotJava World Wide Web browser do not download source code, which they then compile; these applications download already-compiled `class` files. The HotJava browser needs to determine whether the `class` file was produced by a trustworthy compiler or by an adversary attempting to exploit the virtual machine.

An additional problem with compile-time checking is version skew. A user may have successfully compiled a class, say `PurchaseStockOptions`, to be a subclass of `TradingClass`. But the definition of `TradingClass` might have changed since the time the class was compiled in a way that is not compatible with preexisting binaries. Methods might have been deleted or had their return types or modifiers changed. Fields might have changed types or changed from instance variables to class variables. The access modifiers of a method or variable may have changed from `public` to `private`. For a discussion of these issues, see Chapter 13, "Binary Compatibility," in the first edition of *The Java*™ *Language Specification* or the equivalent chapter in the second edition.

Because of these potential problems, the Java virtual machine needs to verify for itself that the desired constraints are satisfied by the `class` files it attempts to incorporate. A Java virtual machine implementation verifies that each `class` file satisfies the necessary constraints at linking time (§2.17.3). Structural constraints on the Java virtual machine code may be checked using a simple theorem prover.

Linking-time verification enhances the performance of the interpreter. Expensive checks that would otherwise have to be performed to verify constraints at run time for each interpreted instruction can be eliminated. The Java virtual machine can assume that these checks have already been performed. For example, the Java virtual machine will already know the following:

- There are no operand stack overflows or underflows.

- All local variable uses and stores are valid.

- The arguments to all the Java virtual machine instructions are of valid types.

Sun's `class` file verifier is independent of any compiler. It should certify all code generated by Sun's compiler for the Java programming language; it should also certify code that other compilers can generate, as well as code that the current compiler could not possibly generate. Any class file that satisfies the structural criteria and static constraints will be certified by the verifier.

The class file verifier is also independent of the Java programming language. Programs written in other languages can be compiled into the class file format, but will pass verification only if all the same constraints are satisfied.

4.9.1 The Verification Process

The class file verifier operates in four passes:

Pass 1: When a prospective class file is loaded (§2.17.2) by the Java virtual machine, the Java virtual machine first ensures that the file has the basic format of a class file. The first four bytes must contain the right magic number. All recognized attributes must be of the proper length. The class file must not be truncated or have extra bytes at the end. The constant pool must not contain any superficially unrecognizable information.

While class file verification properly occurs during class linking (§2.17.3), this check for basic class file integrity is necessary for any interpretation of the class file contents and can be considered to be logically part of the verification process.

Pass 2: When the class file is linked, the verifier performs all additional verification that can be done without looking at the code array of the Code attribute (§4.7.3). The checks performed by this pass include the following:

- Ensuring that final classes are not subclassed and that final methods are not overridden.

- Checking that every class (except Object) has a direct superclass.

- Ensuring that the constant pool satisfies the documented static constraints: for example, that each CONSTANT_Class_info structure in the constant pool contains in its name_index item a valid constant pool index for a CONSTANT_Utf8_info structure.

- Checking that all field references and method references in the constant pool have valid names, valid classes, and a valid type descriptor.

Note that when it looks at field and method references, this pass does not check to make sure that the given field or method actually exists in the given class, nor does it check that the type descriptors given refer to real classes. It checks only that these items are well formed. More detailed checking is delayed until passes 3 and 4.

Pass 3: During linking, the verifier checks the code array of the Code attribute for each method of the class file by performing data-flow analysis on each method. The verifier ensures that at any given point in the program, no matter what code path is taken to reach that point, the following is true:

- The operand stack is always the same size and contains the same types of values.

- No local variable is accessed unless it is known to contain a value of an appropriate type.

- Methods are invoked with the appropriate arguments.

- Fields are assigned only using values of appropriate types.

- All opcodes have appropriate type arguments on the operand stack and in the local variable array.

For further information on this pass, see Section 4.9.2, "The Bytecode Verifier."

Pass 4: For efficiency reasons, certain tests that could in principle be performed in Pass 3 are delayed until the first time the code for the method is actually invoked. In so doing, Pass 3 of the verifier avoids loading class files unless it has to.

For example, if a method invokes another method that returns an instance of class A, and that instance is assigned only to a field of the same type, the verifier does not bother to check if the class A actually exists. However, if it is assigned to a field of the type B, the definitions of both A and B must be loaded in to ensure that A is a subclass of B.

Pass 4 is a virtual pass whose checking is done by the appropriate Java virtual machine instructions. The first time an instruction that references a type is executed, the executing instruction does the following:

- Loads in the definition of the referenced type if it has not already been loaded.

- Checks that the currently executing type is allowed to reference the type.

The first time an instruction invokes a method, or accesses or modifies a field, the executing instruction does the following:

- Ensures that the referenced method or field exists in the given class.

- Checks that the referenced method or field has the indicated descriptor.

- Checks that the currently executing method has access to the referenced method or field.

The Java virtual machine does not have to check the type of the object on the operand stack. That check has already been done by Pass 3. Errors that are detected in Pass 4 cause instances of subclasses of `LinkageError` to be thrown.

A Java virtual machine implementation is allowed to perform any or all of the Pass 4 steps as part of Pass 3; see 2.17.1, "Virtual Machine Start-up" for an example and more discussion.

In one of Sun's Java virtual machine implementations, after the verification has been performed, the instruction in the Java virtual machine code is replaced with an alternative form of the instruction. This alternative instruction indicates that the verification needed by this instruction has taken place and does not need to be performed again. Subsequent invocations of the method will thus be faster. It is illegal for these alternative instruction forms to appear in `class` files, and they should never be encountered by the verifier.

4.9.2 The Bytecode Verifier

As indicated earlier, Pass 3 of the verification process is the most complex of the four passes of `class` file verification. This section looks at the verification of Java virtual machine code in Pass 3 in more detail.

The code for each method is verified independently. First, the bytes that make up the code are broken up into a sequence of instructions, and the index into the `code` array of the start of each instruction is placed in an array. The verifier then goes through the code a second time and parses the instructions. During this pass a data structure is built to hold information about each Java virtual machine instruction in the method. The operands, if any, of each instruction are checked to make sure they are valid. For instance:

- Branches must be within the bounds of the `code` array for the method.

- The targets of all control-flow instructions are each the start of an instruction. In the case of a *wide* instruction, the *wide* opcode is considered the start of the instruction, and the opcode giving the operation modified by that *wide* instruction is not considered to start an instruction. Branches into the middle of an instruction are disallowed.

- No instruction can access or modify a local variable at an index greater than or equal to the number of local variables that its method indicates it allocates.

- All references to the constant pool must be to an entry of the appropriate type. For example: the instruction *ldc* can be used only for data of type int or float or for instances of class String; the instruction *getfield* must reference a field.

- The code does not end in the middle of an instruction.

- Execution cannot fall off the end of the code.

- For each exception handler, the starting and ending point of code protected by the handler must be at the beginning of an instruction or, in the case of the ending point, immediately past the end of the code. The starting point must be before the ending point. The exception handler code must start at a valid instruction, and it may not start at an opcode being modified by the *wide* instruction.

For each instruction of the method, the verifier records the contents of the operand stack and the contents of the local variable array prior to the execution of that instruction. For the operand stack, it needs to know the stack height and the type of each value on it. For each local variable, it needs to know either the type of the contents of that local variable or that the local variable contains an unusable or unknown value (it might be uninitialized). The bytecode verifier does not need to distinguish between the integral types (e.g., byte, short, char) when determining the value types on the operand stack.

Next, a data-flow analyzer is initialized. For the first instruction of the method, the local variables that represent parameters initially contain values of the types indicated by the method's type descriptor; the operand stack is empty. All other local variables contain an illegal value. For the other instructions, which have not been examined yet, no information is available regarding the operand stack or local variables.

Finally, the data-flow analyzer is run. For each instruction, a "changed" bit indicates whether this instruction needs to be looked at. Initially, the "changed" bit is set only for the first instruction. The data-flow analyzer executes the following loop:

1. Select a virtual machine instruction whose "changed" bit is set. If no instruction remains whose "changed" bit is set, the method has successfully been verified. Otherwise, turn off the "changed" bit of the selected instruction.

2. Model the effect of the instruction on the operand stack and local variable array by doing the following:

   - If the instruction uses values from the operand stack, ensure that there are a sufficient number of values on the stack and that the top values on the stack are of an appropriate type. Otherwise, verification fails.

   - If the instruction uses a local variable, ensure that the specified local variable contains a value of the appropriate type. Otherwise, verification fails.

   - If the instruction pushes values onto the operand stack, ensure that there is sufficient room on the operand stack for the new values. Add the indicated types to the top of the modeled operand stack.

   - If the instruction modifies a local variable, record that the local variable now contains the new type.

3. Determine the instructions that can follow the current instruction. Successor instructions can be one of the following:

   - The next instruction, if the current instruction is not an unconditional control transfer instruction (for instance *goto*, *return*, or *athrow*). Verification fails if it is possible to "fall off" the last instruction of the method.

   - The target(s) of a conditional or unconditional branch or switch.

   - Any exception handlers for this instruction.

4. Merge the state of the operand stack and local variable array at the end of the execution of the current instruction into each of the successor instructions. In the special case of control transfer to an exception handler, the operand stack is set to contain a single object of the exception type indicated by the exception handler information.

   - If this is the first time the successor instruction has been visited, record that the operand stack and local variable values calculated in steps 2 and 3 are the state of the operand stack and local variable array prior to executing the successor instruction. Set the "changed" bit for the successor instruction.

- If the successor instruction has been seen before, merge the operand stack and local variable values calculated in steps 2 and 3 into the values already there. Set the "changed" bit if there is any modification to the values.

5. Continue at step 1.

To merge two operand stacks, the number of values on each stack must be identical. The types of values on the stacks must also be identical, except that differently typed reference values may appear at corresponding places on the two stacks. In this case, the merged operand stack contains a reference to an instance of the first common superclass of the two types. Such a reference type always exists because the type Object is a superclass of all class and interface types. If the operand stacks cannot be merged, verification of the method fails.

To merge two local variable array states, corresponding pairs of local variables are compared. If the two types are not identical, then unless both contain reference values, the verifier records that the local variable contains an unusable value. If both of the pair of local variables contain reference values, the merged state contains a reference to an instance of the first common superclass of the two types.

If the data-flow analyzer runs on a method without reporting a verification failure, then the method has been successfully verified by Pass 3 of the class file verifier.

Certain instructions and data types complicate the data-flow analyzer. We now examine each of these in more detail.

4.9.3 Values of Types long and double

Values of the long and double types are treated specially by the verification process.

Whenever a value of type long or double is moved into a local variable at index n, index n + 1 is specially marked to indicate that it has been reserved by the value at index n and may not be used as a local variable index. Any value previously at index n + 1 becomes unusable.

Whenever a value is moved to a local variable at index n, the index n − 1 is examined to see if it is the index of a value of type long or double. If so, the local variable at index n − 1 is changed to indicate that it now contains an unusable value. Since the local variable at index n has been overwritten, the local variable at index n − 1 cannot represent a value of type long or double.

Dealing with values of types `long` or `double` on the operand stack is simpler; the verifier treats them as single values on the stack. For example, the verification code for the *dadd* opcode (add two `double` values) checks that the top two items on the stack are both of type `double`. When calculating operand stack length, values of type `long` and `double` have length two.

Untyped instructions that manipulate the operand stack must treat values of type `double` and `long` as atomic (indivisible). For example, the verifier reports a failure if the top value on the stack is a `double` and it encounters an instruction such as *pop* or *dup*. The instructions *pop2* or *dup2* must be used instead.

4.9.4 Instance Initialization Methods and Newly Created Objects

Creating a new class instance is a multistep process. The statement

```
. . .
new myClass(i, j, k);
. . .
```

can be implemented by the following:

```
...
new     #1            // Allocate uninitialized space for myClass
dup                   // Duplicate object on the operand stack
iload_1               // Push i
iload_2               // Push j
iload_3               // Push k
invokespecial #5      // Invoke myClass.<init>
...
```

This instruction sequence leaves the newly created and initialized object on top of the operand stack. (Additional examples of compilation to the instruction set of the Java virtual machine are given in Chapter 7, "Compiling for the Java Virtual Machine.")

The instance initialization method (§3.9) for class `myClass` sees the new uninitialized object as its `this` argument in local variable 0. Before that method invokes another instance initialization method of `myClass` or its direct superclass on `this`, the only operation the method can perform on `this` is assigning fields declared within `myClass`.

When doing dataflow analysis on instance methods, the verifier initializes local variable 0 to contain an object of the current class, or, for instance initialization methods, local variable 0 contains a special type indicating an uninitialized object. After an appropriate instance initialization method is invoked (from the current class or the current superclass) on this object, all occurrences of this special type on the verifier's model of the operand stack and in the local variable array are replaced by the current class type. The verifier rejects code that uses the new object before it has been initialized or that initializes the object more than once. In addition, it ensures that every normal return of the method has invoked an instance initialization method either in the class of this method or in the direct superclass.

Similarly, a special type is created and pushed on the verifier's model of the operand stack as the result of the Java virtual machine instruction *new*. The special type indicates the instruction by which the class instance was created and the type of the uninitialized class instance created. When an instance initialization method is invoked on that class instance, all occurrences of the special type are replaced by the intended type of the class instance. This change in type may propagate to subsequent instructions as the dataflow analysis proceeds.

The instruction number needs to be stored as part of the special type, as there may be multiple not-yet-initialized instances of a class in existence on the operand stack at one time. For example, the Java virtual machine instruction sequence that implements

```
new InputStream(new Foo(), new InputStream("foo"))
```

may have two uninitialized instances of InputStream on the operand stack at once. When an instance initialization method is invoked on a class instance, only those occurrences of the special type on the operand stack or in the local variable array that are the *same object* as the class instance are replaced.

A valid instruction sequence must not have an uninitialized object on the operand stack or in a local variable during a backwards branch, or in a local variable in code protected by an exception handler or a finally clause. Otherwise, a devious piece of code might fool the verifier into thinking it had initialized a class instance when it had, in fact, initialized a class instance created in a previous pass through a loop.

4.9.5 Exception Handlers

Java virtual machine code produced by Sun's compiler for the Java programming language always generates exception handlers such that:

- Either the ranges of instructions protected by two different exception handlers always are completely disjoint, or else one is a subrange of the other. There is never a partial overlap of ranges.

- The handler for an exception will never be inside the code that is being protected.

- The only entry to an exception handler is through an exception. It is impossible to fall through or "goto" the exception handler.

These restrictions are not enforced by the `class` file verifier since they do not pose a threat to the integrity of the Java virtual machine. As long as every nonexceptional path to the exception handler causes there to be a single object on the operand stack, and as long as all other criteria of the verifier are met, the verifier will pass the code.

4.9.6 Exceptions and `finally`

Given the code fragment

```
...
try {
    startFaucet();
    waterLawn();
} finally {
    stopFaucet();
}
...
```

the Java programming language guarantees that `stopFaucet` is invoked (the faucet is turned off) whether we finish watering the lawn or whether an exception occurs while starting the faucet or watering the lawn. That is, the `finally` clause is guaranteed to be executed whether its `try` clause completes normally or completes abruptly by throwing an exception.

To implement the `try-finally` construct, Sun's compiler for the Java programming language uses the exception-handling facilities together with two special instructions: *jsr* ("jump to subroutine") and *ret* ("return from subroutine"). The `finally` clause is compiled as a subroutine within the Java virtual machine code for its method, much like the code for an exception handler. When a *jsr* instruction that invokes the subroutine is executed, it pushes its return address, the address of the instruction after the *jsr* that is being executed, onto the operand stack as a value of type `returnAddress`. The code for the subroutine stores the return address in a local variable. At the end of the subroutine, a *ret* instruction fetches the return address from the local variable and transfers control to the instruction at the return address.

Control can be transferred to the `finally` clause (the `finally` subroutine can be invoked) in several different ways. If the `try` clause completes normally, the `finally` subroutine is invoked via a *jsr* instruction before evaluating the next expression. A `break` or `continue` inside the `try` clause that transfers control outside the `try` clause executes a *jsr* to the code for the `finally` clause first. If the `try` clause executes a `return`, the compiled code does the following:

1. Saves the return value (if any) in a local variable.

2. Executes a *jsr* to the code for the `finally` clause.

3. Upon return from the `finally` clause, returns the value saved in the local variable.

The compiler sets up a special exception handler, which catches any exception thrown by the `try` clause. If an exception is thrown in the `try` clause, this exception handler does the following:

1. Saves the exception in a local variable.

2. Executes a *jsr* to the `finally` clause.

3. Upon return from the `finally` clause, rethrows the exception.

For more information about the implementation of the `try-finally` construct, see Section 7.13, "Compiling `finally`."

The code for the `finally` clause presents a special problem to the verifier. Usually, if a particular instruction can be reached via multiple paths and a particular local variable contains incompatible values through those multiple paths, then the local variable becomes unusable. However, a `finally` clause might be called from several different places, yielding several different circumstances:

- The invocation from the exception handler may have a certain local variable that contains an exception.

- The invocation to implement `return` may have some local variable that contains the return value.

- The invocation from the bottom of the `try` clause may have an indeterminate value in that same local variable.

The code for the `finally` clause itself might pass verification, but after completing the updating all the successors of the *ret* instruction, the verifier would note that the local variable that the exception handler expects to hold an exception, or that the return code expects to hold a return value, now contains an indeterminate value.

Verifying code that contains a `finally` clause is complicated. The basic idea is the following:

- Each instruction keeps track of the list of *jsr* targets needed to reach that instruction. For most code, this list is empty. For instructions inside code for the `finally` clause, it is of length one. For multiply nested `finally` code (extremely rare!), it may be longer than one.

- For each instruction and each *jsr* needed to reach that instruction, a bit vector is maintained of all local variables accessed or modified since the execution of the *jsr* instruction.

- When executing the *ret* instruction, which implements a return from a subroutine, there must be only one possible subroutine from which the instruction can be returning. Two different subroutines cannot "merge" their execution to a single *ret* instruction.

- To perform the data-flow analysis on a *ret* instruction, a special procedure is used. Since the verifier knows the subroutine from which the instruction must be returning, it can find all the *jsr* instructions that call the subroutine and merge the state of the operand stack and local variable array at the time of the *ret* instruction into the operand stack and local variable array of the instructions following the *jsr*. Merging uses a special set of values for local variables:

  - For any local variable that the bit vector (constructed above) indicates has been accessed or modified by the subroutine, use the type of the local variable at the time of the *ret*.

  - For other local variables, use the type of the local variable before the *jsr* instruction.

4.10 Limitations of the Java Virtual Machine

The following limitations of the Java virtual machine are implicit in the class file format:

- The per-class or per-interface constant pool is limited to 65535 entries by the 16-bit constant_pool_count field of the ClassFile structure (§4.1). This acts as an internal limit on the total complexity of a single class or interface.

- The amount of code per non-native, non-abstract method is limited to 65536 bytes by the sizes of the indices in the exception_table of the Code attribute (§4.7.3), in the LineNumberTable attribute (§4.7.8), and in the LocalVariableTable attribute (§4.7.9).

- The greatest number of local variables in the local variables array of a frame created upon invocation of a method is limited to 65535 by the size of the max_locals item of the Code attribute (§4.7.3) giving the code of the method. Note that values of type long and double are each considered to reserve two local variables and contribute two units toward the max_locals value, so use of local variables of those types further reduces this limit.

- The number of fields that may be declared by a class or interface is limited to 65535 by the size of the fields_count item of the ClassFile structure (§4.1). Note that the value of the fields_count item of the ClassFile structure does not include fields that are inherited from superclasses or superinterfaces.

- The number of methods that may be declared by a class or interface is limited to 65535 by the size of the methods_count item of the ClassFile structure (§4.1). Note that the value of the methods_count item of the ClassFile structure does not include methods that are inherited from superclasses or superinterfaces.

- The number of direct superinterfaces of a class or interface is limited to 65535 by the size of the interfaces_count item of the ClassFile structure (§4.1).

- The size of an operand stack in a frame (§3.6) is limited to 65535 values by the max_stack field of the Code_attribute structure (§4.7.3). Note that values of type long and double are each considered to contribute two units toward the max_stack value, so use of values of these types on the operand stack further reduces this limit.

- The number of local variables in a frame (§3.6) is limited to 65535 by the `max_locals` field of the `Code_attribute` structure (§4.7.3) and the 16-bit local variable indexing of the Java virtual machine instruction set.

- The number of dimensions in an array is limited to 255 by the size of the *dimensions* opcode of the *multianewarray* instruction and by the constraints imposed on the *multianewarray*, *anewarray*, and *newarray* instructions by §4.8.2.

- The number of method parameters is limited to 255 by the definition of a method descriptor (§4.3.3), where the limit includes one unit for `this` in the case of instance or interface method invocations. Note that a method descriptor is defined in terms of a notion of method parameter length in which a parameter of type `long` or `double` contributes two units to the length, so parameters of these types further reduce the limit.

- The length of field and method names, field and method descriptors, and other constant string values is limited to 65535 characters by the 16-bit unsigned `length` item of the `CONSTANT_Utf8_info` structure (§4.4.7). Note that the limit is on the number of bytes in the encoding and not on the number of encoded characters. UTF-8 encodes some characters using two or three bytes. Thus, strings incorporating multibyte characters are further constrained.

Loading, Linking, and Initializing

T HE Java virtual machine dynamically loads (§2.17.2), links (§2.17.3), and initializes (§2.17.4) classes and interfaces. Loading is the process of finding the binary representation of a class or interface type with a particular name and *creating* a class or interface from that binary representation. Linking is the process of taking a class or interface and combining it into the runtime state of the Java virtual machine so that it can be executed. Initialization of a class or interface consists of executing the class or interface initialization method <clinit> (§3.9).

In this chapter, Section 5.1 describes how the Java virtual machine derives symbolic references from the binary representation of a class or interface. Section 5.2 explains how the processes of loading, linking, and initialization are first initiated by the Java virtual machine. Section 5.3 specifies how binary representations of classes and interfaces are loaded by class loaders and how classes and interfaces are created. Linking is described in Section 5.4. Section 5.5 details how classes and interfaces are initialized. Finally, Section 5.6 introduces the notion of binding native methods.

5.1 The Runtime Constant Pool

The Java virtual machine maintains a per-type constant pool (§3.5.5), a runtime data structure that serves many of the purposes of the symbol table of a conventional programming language implementation.

The constant_pool table (§4.4) in the binary representation of a class or interface is used to construct the runtime constant pool upon class or interface creation (§5.3). All references in the runtime constant pool are initially symbolic. The symbolic references in the runtime constant pool are derived from structures in the binary representation of the class or interface as follows:

- A symbolic reference to a class or interface is derived from a CONSTANT_Class_info structure (§4.4.1) in the binary representation of a class or interface. Such a reference gives the name of the class or interface in the form returned by the Class.getName method, that is:

  - For a nonarray class or an interface, the name is the fully qualified name of the class or interface.

  - For an array class of *M* dimensions, the name begins with *M* occurrences of the ASCII "[" character followed by a representation of the element type:

    - If the element type is a primitive type, it is represented by the corresponding field descriptor (§4.3.2).

    - Otherwise, if the element type is a reference type, it is represented by the ASCII "L" character followed by the fully qualified name of the element type followed by the ASCII ";" character.

- Whenever this chapter refers to the name of a class or interface, it should be understood to be in the form returned by the Class.getName method.

- A symbolic reference to a field of a class (§2.9) or an interface (§2.13.3.1) is derived from a CONSTANT_Fieldref_info structure (§4.4.2) in the binary representation of a class or interface. Such a reference gives the name and descriptor of the field, as well as a symbolic reference to the class or interface in which the field is to be found.

- A symbolic reference to a method of a class (§2.10) is derived from a CONSTANT_Methodref_info structure (§4.4.2) in the binary representation of a class or interface. Such a reference gives the name and descriptor of the method, as well as a symbolic reference to the class in which the method is to be found.

- A symbolic reference to a method of an interface (§2.13) is derived from a CONSTANT_InterfaceMethodref_info structure (§4.4.2) in the binary representation of a class or interface. Such a reference gives the name and descriptor of the interface method, as well as a symbolic reference to the interface in which the method is to be found.

In addition, certain nonreference runtime values are derived from items found in the `constant_pool` table:

- A string literal (§2.3) is derived from a `CONSTANT_String_info` structure (§4.4.3) in the binary representation of a class or interface. The `CONSTANT_String_info` structure gives the sequence of Unicode characters constituting the string literal.

- The Java programming language requires that identical string literals (that is, literals that contain the same sequence of characters) must refer to the same instance of class `String`. In addition, if the method `String.intern` is called on any string, the result is a reference to the same class instance that would be returned if that string appeared as a literal. Thus,

    ```
    ("a" + "b" + "c").intern() == "abc"
    ```

  must have the value `true`.

- To derive a string literal, the Java virtual machine examines the sequence of characters given by the `CONSTANT_String_info` structure.

    - If the method `String.intern` has previously been called on an instance of class `String` containing a sequence of Unicode characters identical to that given by the `CONSTANT_String_info` structure, then the result of string literal derivation is a reference to that same instance of class `String`.

    - Otherwise, a new instance of class `String` is created containing the sequence of Unicode characters given by the `CONSTANT_String_info` structure; that class instance is the result of string literal derivation. Finally, the `intern` method of the new `String` instance is invoked.

- Runtime constant values are derived from `CONSTANT_Integer_info`, `CONSTANT_Float_info`, `CONSTANT_Long_info`, or `CONSTANT_Double_info` structures (§4.4.4, §4.4.5) in the binary representation of a class or interface. Note that `CONSTANT_Float_info` structures represent values in IEEE 754 single format and `CONSTANT_Double_info` structures represent values in IEEE 754 double format (§4.4.4, §4.4.5). The runtime constant values derived from these structures must thus be values that can be represented using IEEE 754 single and double formats, respectively.

The remaining structures in the `constant_pool` table of the binary representation of a class or interface, the `CONSTANT_NameAndType_info` (§4.4.6) and

CONSTANT_Utf8_info (§4.4.7) structures are only used indirectly when deriving symbolic references to classes, interfaces, methods, and fields, and when deriving string literals.

5.2 Virtual Machine Start-up

The Java virtual machine starts up by creating an initial class, which is specified in an implementation-dependent manner, using the bootstrap class loader (§5.3.1). The Java virtual machine then links the initial class, initializes it, and invokes its public class method void main(String[]). The invocation of this method drives all further execution. Execution of the Java virtual machine instructions constituting the main method may cause linking (and consequently creation) of additional classes and interfaces, as well as invocation of additional methods.

In some implementations of the Java virtual machine the initial class could be provided as a command line argument, as in JDK releases 1.0 and 1.1. Alternatively, the initial class could be provided by the implementation. In this case the initial class might set up a class loader that would in turn load an application, as in the Java 2 SDK, Standard Edition, v1.2. Other choices of the initial class are possible so long as they are consistent with the specification given in the previous paragraph.

5.3 Creation and Loading

Creation of a class or interface C denoted by the name N consists of the construction in the method area of the Java virtual machine (§3.5.4) of an implementation-specific internal representation of C. Class or interface creation is triggered by another class or interface D, which references C through its runtime constant pool. Class or interface creation may also be triggered by D invoking methods in certain Java class libraries (§3.12) such as reflection.

If C is not an array class, it is created by loading a binary representation of C (see Chapter 4, "The class File Format") using a class loader (§2.17.2). Array classes do not have an external binary representation; they are created by the Java virtual machine rather than by a class loader.

There are two types of class loaders: user-defined class loaders and the bootstrap class loader supplied by the Java virtual machine. Every user-defined class loader is an instance of a subclass of the abstract class ClassLoader. Applications employ class loaders in order to extend the manner in which the Java virtual machine dynamically loads and thereby creates classes. User-defined class loaders can be used to create classes that originate from user-defined sources. For example, a class could be downloaded across a network, generated on the fly, or extracted from an encrypted file.

A class loader *L* may create *C* by defining it directly or by delegating to another class loader. If *L* creates *C* directly, we say that *L* *defines C* or, equivalently, that *L* is the *defining loader* of *C*.

When one class loader delegates to another class loader, the loader that initiates the loading is not necessarily the same loader that completes the loading and defines the class. If *L* creates *C*, either by defining it directly or by delegation, we say that *L* *initiates* loading of *C* or, equivalently, that *L* is an *initiating loader* of *C*.

At run time, a class or interface is determined not by its name alone, but by a pair: its fully qualified name and its defining class loader. Each such class or interface belongs to a single *runtime package*. The runtime package of a class or interface is determined by the package name and defining class loader of the class or interface.

The Java virtual machine uses one of three procedures to create class or interface *C* denoted by *N*:

- If *N* denotes a nonarray class or an interface, one of the two following methods is used to load and thereby create *C* :

  - If *D* was defined by the bootstrap class loader, then the bootstrap class loader initiates loading of *C* (§5.3.1).

  - If *D* was defined by a user-defined class loader, then that same user-defined class loader initiates loading of *C* (§5.3.2).

- Otherwise *N* denotes an array class. An array class is created directly by the Java virtual machine (§5.3.3), not by a class loader. However, the defining class loader of *D* is used in the process of creating array class *C*.

We will sometimes represent a class or interface using the notation $<N, L_d>$, where *N* denotes the name of the class or interface and L_d denotes the defining loader of the class or interface. We will also represent a class or interface using the notation N^{L_i}, where *N* denotes the name of the class or interface and L_i denotes an initiating loader of the class or interface.

5.3.1 Loading Using the Bootstrap Class Loader

The following steps are used to load and thereby create the nonarray class or interface *C* denoted by *N* using the bootstrap class loader.

First, the Java virtual machine determines whether the bootstrap class loader has already been recorded as an initiating loader of a class or interface denoted by *N*. If so, this class or interface is *C*, and no class creation is necessary.

Otherwise, the Java virtual machine performs one of the following two operations in order to load *C*:

1. The Java virtual machine searches for a purported representation of *C* in a platform-dependent manner. Note that there is no guarantee that a purported representation found is valid or is a representation of *C*.

   Typically, a class or interface will be represented using a file in a hierarchical file system. The name of the class or interface will usually be encoded in the pathname of the file.

   This phase of loading must detect the following error:

   - If no purported representation of *C* is found, loading throws an instance of `NoClassDefFoundError` or an instance of one of its subclasses.

   Then the Java virtual machine attempts to derive a class denoted by *N* using the bootstrap class loader from the purported representation using the algorithm found in Section 5.3.5. That class is *C*.

2. The bootstrap class loader can delegate the loading of *C* to some user-defined class loader *L* by passing *N* to an invocation of a `loadClass` method on *L*. The result of the invocation is *C*. The Java virtual machine then records that the bootstrap loader is an initiating loader of *C* (§5.3.4).

5.3.2 Loading Using a User-defined Class Loader

The following steps are used to load and thereby create the nonarray class or interface *C* denoted by *N* using a user-defined class loader *L*.

First, the Java virtual machine determines whether *L* has already been recorded as an initiating loader of a class or interface denoted by *N*. If so, this class or interface is *C*, and no class creation is necessary.

Otherwise the Java virtual machine invokes `loadClass(N)` on *L*.[1] The value returned by the invocation is the created class or interface *C*. The Java virtual machine then records that *L* is an initiating loader of *C* (§5.3.4). The remainder of this section describes this process in more detail.

When the `loadClass` method of the class loader *L* is invoked with the name *N* of a class or interface *C* to be loaded, *L* must perform one of the following two operations in order to load *C* :

1. The class loader *L* can create an array of bytes representing *C* as the bytes of a `ClassFile` structure (§4.1); it then must invoke the method `defineClass` of class `ClassLoader`. Invoking `defineClass` causes the Java virtual machine to derive a class or interface denoted by *N* using *L* from the array of bytes using the algorithm found in Section 5.3.5.

2. The class loader *L* can delegate the loading of *C* to some other class loader *L'*. This is accomplished by passing the argument *N* directly or indirectly to an invocation of a method on *L'* (typically the `loadClass` method). The result of the invocation is *C*.

5.3.3 Creating Array Classes

The following steps are used to create the array class *C* denoted by *N* using class loader *L*. Class loader *L* may be either the bootstrap class loader or a user-defined class loader.

If *L* has already been recorded as an initiating loader of an array class with the same component type as *N*, that class is *C*, and no array class creation is necessary. Otherwise, the following steps are performed to create *C*:

1. If the component type is a reference type, the algorithm of this section (§5.3) is applied recursively using class loader *L* in order to load and thereby create the component type of *C*.

2. The Java virtual machine creates a new array class with the indicated component type and number of dimensions. If the component type is a reference type, *C* is marked as having been defined by the defining class loader of the component type. Otherwise, *C* is marked as having been defined by the bootstrap class loader. In any case, the Java virtual machine then records that *L* is an initiating loader for *C* (§5.3.4). If the component type is a reference type, the accessibil-

---

[1] Since JDK release 1.1 the Java virtual machine invokes the `loadClass` method of a class loader in order to cause it to load a class or interface. The argument to `loadClass` is the name of the class or interface to be loaded. There is also a two-argument version of the `loadClass` method. The second argument is a `boolean` that indicates whether the class or interface is to be linked or not. Only the two-argument version was supplied in JDK release 1.0.2, and the Java virtual machine relied on it to link the loaded class or interface. From JDK release 1.1 onward, the Java virtual machine links the class or interface directly, without relying on the class loader.

ity of the array class is determined by the accessibility of its component type. Otherwise, the accessibility of the array class is `public`.

5.3.4 Loading Constraints

Ensuring type safe linkage in the presence of class loaders requires special care. It is possible that when two different class loaders initiate loading of a class or interface denoted by *N*, the name *N* may denote a different class or interface in each loader.

When a class or interface $C = <N1, L1>$ makes a symbolic reference to a field or method of another class or interface $D = <N2, L2>$, the symbolic reference includes a descriptor specifying the type of the field, or the return and argument types of the method. It is essential that any type name *N* mentioned in the field or method descriptor denote the same class or interface when loaded by *L1* and when loaded by *L2*.

To ensure this, the Java virtual machine imposes *loading constraints* of the form $N^{L1} = N^{L2}$ during preparation (§5.4.2) and resolution (§5.4.3). To enforce these constraints, the Java virtual machine will, at certain prescribed times (see §5.3.1, §5.3.2, §5.3.3, and §5.3.5), record that a particular loader is an initiating loader of a particular class. After recording that a loader is an initiating loader of a class, the Java virtual machine must immediately check to see if any loading constraints are violated. If so, the record is retracted, the Java virtual machine throws a `LinkageError`, and the loading operation that caused the recording to take place fails.

Similarly, after imposing a loading constraint (see §5.4.2, §5.4.3.2, §5.4.3.3, and §5.4.3.4), the Java virtual machine must immediately check to see if any loading constraints are violated. If so, the newly imposed loading constraint is retracted, the Java virtual machine throws a `LinkageError`, and the operation that caused the constraint to be imposed (either resolution or preparation, as the case may be) fails.

The situations described here are the only times at which the Java virtual machine checks whether any loading constraints have been violated. A loading constraint is *violated* if, and only if, all the following four conditions hold:

- There exists a loader *L* such that *L* has been recorded by the Java virtual machine as an initiating loader of a class *C* named *N*.

- There exists a loader *L'* such that *L'* has been recorded by the Java virtual machine as an initiating loader of a class *C'* named *N*.

- The equivalence relation defined by the (transitive closure of the) set of imposed constraints implies $N^L = N^{L'}$.

- $C \neq C'$.

A full discussion of class loaders and type safety is beyond the scope of this specification. For a more comprehensive discussion, readers are referred to *Dynamic Class Loading in the Java Virtual Machine* by Sheng Liang and Gilad Bracha (Proceedings of the 1998 ACM SIGPLAN Conference on Object-Oriented Programming Systems, Languages and Applications).

5.3.5 Deriving a Class from a `class` File Representation

The following steps are used to derive the nonarray class or interface C denoted by N using loader L from a purported representation in `class` file format.

1. First, the Java virtual machine determines whether it has already recorded that L is an initiating loader of a class or interface denoted by N. If so, this creation attempt is invalid and loading throws a `LinkageError`.

2. Otherwise, the Java virtual machine attempts to parse the purported representation. However, the purported representation may not in fact be a valid representation of C.

   This phase of loading must detect the following errors:

   - If the purported representation is not in `class` file format (§4.1, pass 1 of §4.9.1), loading throws an instance of `ClassFormatError`.

   - Otherwise, if the purported representation is not of a supported major or minor version (§4.1), loading throws an instance of `UnsupportedClassVersionError`.[2]

   - Otherwise, if the purported representation does not actually represent a class named N, loading throws an instance of `NoClassDefFoundError` or an instance of one of its subclasses.

3. If C has a direct superclass, the symbolic reference from C to its direct superclass is resolved using the algorithm of Section 5.4.3.1. Note that if C is an

---

[2] `UnsupportedClassVersionError` was introduced in the Java 2 platform, Standard Edition, v1.2. In earlier versions of the platform an instance of `NoClassDefFoundError` or `ClassFormatError` was thrown in case of an unsupported version depending on whether the class was being loaded by the system class loader or a user-defined class loader.

interface it must have `Object` as its direct superclass, which must already have been loaded. Only `Object` has no direct superclass.

Any exceptions that can be thrown due to class or interface resolution can be thrown as a result of this phase of loading. In addition, this phase of loading must detect the following errors:

- If the class or interface named as the direct superclass of *C* is in fact an interface, loading throws an `IncompatibleClassChangeError`.

- Otherwise, if any of the superclasses of *C* is *C* itself, loading throws a `Class-CircularityError`.

4. If *C* has any direct superinterfaces, the symbolic references from *C* to its direct superinterfaces are resolved using the algorithm of Section 5.4.3.1.

Any exceptions that can be thrown due to class or interface resolution can be thrown as a result of this phase of loading. In addition, this phase of loading must detect the following errors:

- If any of the classes or interfaces named as direct superinterfaces of *C* is not in fact an interface, loading throws an `IncompatibleClassChangeError`.

- Otherwise, if any of the superinterfaces of *C* is *C* itself, loading throws a `ClassCircularityError`.

5. The Java virtual machine marks *C* as having *L* as its defining class loader and records that *L* is an initiating loader of *C* (§5.3.4).

5.4   Linking

Linking a class or interface (§2.17.3) involves verifying and preparing that class or interface, its direct superclass, its direct superinterfaces, and its element type (if it is an array type), if necessary. Resolution of symbolic references in the class or interface is an optional part of linking.

5.4.1   Verification

The representation of a class or interface is *verified* (§4.9) to ensure that its binary representation is structurally valid (passes 2 and 3 of §4.9.1). Verification may cause additional classes and interfaces to be loaded (§5.3) but need not cause them to be prepared or verified.

Verification must detect the following error:

- If the representation of the class or interface does not satisfy the static or structural constraints listed in Section 4.8, "Constraints on Java Virtual Machine Code," verification throws a `VerifyError`.

A class or interface must be successfully verified before it is initialized. Any attempt to initialize a class or interface that has not been successfully verified must be preceded by verification. Repeated verification of a class or interface that the Java virtual machine has previously unsuccessfully attempted to verify always fails with the same error that was thrown as a result of the initial verification attempt.

5.4.2 Preparation

Preparation involves creating the static fields for the class or interface and initializing those fields to their standard default values (§2.5.1). Preparation should not be confused with the execution of static initializers (§2.11); unlike execution of static initializers, preparation does not require the execution of any Java virtual machine code.

During preparation of a class or interface C, the Java virtual machine also imposes loading constraints (§5.3.4). Let $L1$ be the defining loader of C. For each method m declared in C that overrides a method declared in a superclass or superinterface $<D, L2>$, the Java virtual machine imposes the following loading constraints: Let $T0$ be the name of the type returned by m, and let $T1, ..., Tn$ be the names of the argument types of m. Then $Ti^{L1} = Ti^{L2}$ for $i = 0$ to n (§5.3.4).

Preparation may occur at any time following creation but must be completed prior to initialization.

5.4.3 Resolution

The process of dynamically determining concrete values from symbolic references in the runtime constant pool is known as *resolution*.

Resolution can be attempted on a symbolic reference that has already been resolved. An attempt to resolve a symbolic reference that has already successfully been resolved always succeeds trivially and always results in the same entity produced by the initial resolution of that reference.

Subsequent attempts to resolve a symbolic reference that the Java virtual machine has previously unsuccessfully attempted to resolve always fails with the same error that was thrown as a result of the initial resolution attempt.

Certain Java virtual machine instructions require specific linking checks when resolving symbolic references. For instance, in order for a *getfield* instruction to successfully resolve the symbolic reference to the field on which it operates it must complete the field resolution steps given in Section 5.4.3.2. In addition, it must also check that the field is not `static`. If it is a `static` field, a linking exception must be thrown.

Linking exceptions generated by checks that are specific to the execution of a particular Java virtual machine instruction are given in the description of that instruction and are not covered in this general discussion of resolution. Note that such exceptions, although described as part of the execution of Java virtual machine instructions rather than resolution, are still properly considered failure of resolution.

The Java virtual machine instructions *anewarray*, *checkcast*, *getfield*, *getstatic*, *instanceof*, *invokeinterface*, *invokespecial*, *invokestatic*, *invokevirtual*, *multianewarray*, *new*, *putfield*, and *putstatic* make symbolic references to the runtime constant pool. Execution of any of these instructions requires resolution of its symbolic reference.

The following sections describe the process of resolving a symbolic reference in the runtime constant pool (§5.1) of a class or interface *D*. Details of resolution differ with the kind of symbolic reference to be resolved.

5.4.3.1 Class and Interface Resolution

To resolve an unresolved symbolic reference from *D* to a class or interface *C* denoted by *N*, the following steps are performed:

1. The defining class loader of *D* is used to create a class or interface denoted by *N*. This class or interface is *C*. Any exception that can be thrown as a result of failure of class or interface creation can thus be thrown as a result of failure of class and interface resolution. The details of the process are given in Section 5.3.

2. If *C* is an array class and its element type is a reference type, then the symbolic reference to the class or interface representing the element type is resolved by invoking the algorithm in Section 5.4.3.1 recursively.

3. Finally, access permissions to *C* are checked:

- If *C* is not accessible (§5.4.4) to *D*, class or interface resolution throws an `IllegalAccessError`.

This condition can occur, for example, if *C* is a class that was originally declared to be `public` but was changed to be non-`public` after *D* was compiled.

If steps 1 and 2 succeed but step 3 fails, *C* is still valid and usable. Nevertheless, resolution fails, and *D* is prohibited from accessing *C*.

5.4.3.2 Field Resolution

To resolve an unresolved symbolic reference from *D* to a field in a class or interface *C*, the symbolic reference to *C* given by the field reference must first be resolved (§5.4.3.1). Therefore, any exception that can be thrown as a result of failure of resolution of a class or interface reference can be thrown as a result of failure of field resolution. If the reference to *C* can be successfully resolved, an exception relating to the failure of resolution of the field reference itself can be thrown.

When resolving a field reference, field resolution first attempts to look up the referenced field in *C* and its superclasses:

1. If *C* declares a field with the name and descriptor specified by the field reference, field lookup succeeds. The declared field is the result of the field lookup.

2. Otherwise, field lookup is applied recursively to the direct superinterfaces of the specified class or interface *C*.

3. Otherwise, if *C* has a superclass *S*, field lookup is applied recursively to *S*.

4. Otherwise, field lookup fails.

If field lookup fails, field resolution throws a `NoSuchFieldError`. Otherwise, if field lookup succeeds but the referenced field is not accessible (§5.4.4) to *D*, field resolution throws an `IllegalAccessError`.

Otherwise, let <*E*, *L1*> be the class or interface in which the referenced field is actually declared and let *L2* be the defining loader of *D*. Let *T* be the name of the type of the referenced field. The Java virtual machine must impose the loading constraint that $T^{L1} = T^{L2}$ (§5.3.4).

5.4.3.3 Method Resolution

To resolve an unresolved symbolic reference from *D* to a method in a class *C*, the symbolic reference to *C* given by the method reference is first resolved (§5.4.3.1). Therefore, any exceptions that can be thrown due to resolution of a class reference can be thrown as a result of method resolution. If the reference to C can be successfully resolved, exceptions relating to the resolution of the method reference itself can be thrown.

When resolving a method reference:

1. Method resolution checks whether C is a class or an interface.

   - If C is an interface, method resolution throws an `IncompatibleClass-ChangeError`.

2. Method resolution attempts to look up the referenced method in C and its superclasses:

   - If C declares a method with the name and descriptor specified by the method reference, method lookup succeeds.

   - Otherwise, if C has a superclass, step 2 of method lookup is recursively invoked on the direct superclass of C.

3. Otherwise, method lookup attempts to locate the referenced method in any of the superinterfaces of the specified class C.

   - If any superinterface of C declares a method with the name and descriptor specified by the method reference, method lookup succeeds.

   - Otherwise, method lookup fails.

If method lookup fails, method resolution throws a `NoSuchMethodError`. If method lookup succeeds and the method is `abstract`, but C is not `abstract`, method resolution throws an `AbstractMethodError`. Otherwise, if the referenced method is not accessible (§5.4.4) to D, method resolution throws an `IllegalAccessError`.

Otherwise, let $<E, L1>$ be the class or interface in which the referenced method is actually declared and let $L2$ be the defining loader of D. Let $T0$ be the name of the type returned by the referenced method, and let $T1, ..., Tn$ be the names of the argument types of the referenced method. The Java virtual machine must impose the loading constraints $Ti^{L1} = Ti^{L2}$ for $i = 0$ to n (§5.3.4).

5.4.3.4 Interface Method Resolution

To resolve an unresolved symbolic reference from D to an interface method in an interface C, the symbolic reference to C given by the interface method reference is first resolved (§5.4.3.1). Therefore, any exceptions that can be thrown as a result of failure of resolution of an interface reference can be thrown as a result of failure of interface method resolution. If the reference to *C* can be successfully resolved, exceptions relating to the resolution of the interface method reference itself can be thrown.

When resolving an interface method reference:

- If *C* is not an interface, interface method resolution throws an `Incompatible-ClassChangeError`.

- Otherwise, if the referenced method does not have the same name and descriptor as a method in *C* or in one of the superinterfaces of *C*, or in class `Object`, interface method resolution throws a `NoSuchMethodError`.

Otherwise, let <*E*, *L1*> be the interface in which the referenced interface method is actually declared and let *L2* be the defining loader of *D*. Let *T0* be the name of the type returned by the referenced method, and let *T1*, ..., *Tn* be the names of the argument types of the referenced method. The Java virtual machine must impose the loading constraints $Ti^{L1} = Ti^{L2}$ for $i = 0$ to n (§5.3.4).

5.4.4 Access Control

A class or interface *C* is *accessible* to a class or interface *D* if and only if either of the following conditions are true:

- *C* is `public`.
- *C* and *D* are members of the same runtime package (§5.3).

A field or method *R* is *accessible* to a class or interface *D* if and only if any of the following conditions is true:

- *R* is `public`.
- *R* is `protected` and is declared in a class *C*, and *D* is either a subclass of *C* or *C* itself.
- *R* is either `protected` or package private (that is, neither `public` nor `protected` nor `private`), and is declared by a class in the same runtime package as *D*.
- *R* is `private` and is declared in *D*.

This discussion of access control omits a related restriction on the target of a `protected` field access or method invocation (the target must be of class *D* or a subtype of *D*). That requirement is checked as part of the verification process (§5.4.1); it is not part of link-time access control.

5.5 Initialization

Initialization of a class or interface consists of invoking its static initializers (§2.11) and the initializers for static fields (§2.9.2) declared in the class. This process is described in more detail in §2.17.4 and §2.17.5.

A class or interface may be initialized only as a result of:

- The execution of any one of the Java virtual machine instructions *new*, *getstatic*, *putstatic*, or *invokestatic* that references the class or interface. Each of these instructions corresponds to one of the conditions in §2.17.4. All of the previously listed instructions reference a class directly or indirectly through either a field reference or a method reference. Upon execution of a *new* instruction, the referenced class or interface is initialized if it has not been initialized already. Upon execution of a *getstatic, putstatic,* or *invokestatic* instruction, the class or interface that declared the resolved field or method is initialized if it has not been initialized already.

- Invocation of certain reflective methods in the class library (§3.12), for example, in class `Class` or in package `java.lang.reflect`.

- The initialization of one of its subclasses.

- Its designation as the initial class at Java virtual machine start-up (§5.2).

Prior to initialization a class or interface must be linked, that is, verified, prepared, and optionally resolved.

5.6 Binding Native Method Implementations

Binding is the process by which a function written in a language other than the Java programming language and implementing a `native` method is integrated into the Java virtual machine so that it can be executed. Although this process is traditionally referred to as linking, the term binding is used in the specification to avoid confusion with linking of classes or interfaces by the Java virtual machine.

CHAPTER 6

The Java Virtual Machine
Instruction Set

A Java virtual machine instruction consists of an opcode specifying the operation
to be performed, followed by zero or more operands embodying values to be operated upon. This chapter gives details about the format of each Java virtual machine
instruction and the operation it performs.

6.1 Assumptions: The Meaning of "Must"

The description of each instruction is always given in the context of Java virtual
machine code that satisfies the static and structural constraints of Chapter 4, "The
`class` File Format." In the description of individual Java virtual machine instructions, we frequently state that some situation "must" or "must not" be the case: "The
value2 must be of type `int`." The constraints of Chapter 4 guarantee that all such
expectations will in fact be met. If some constraint (a "must" or "must not") in an
instruction description is not satisfied at run time, the behavior of the Java virtual
machine is undefined.

The Java virtual machine checks that Java virtual machine code satisfies the
static and structural constraints at link time using a `class` file verifier (see Section
4.9, "Verification of `class` Files"). Thus, a Java virtual machine will only attempt
to execute code from valid `class` files. Performing verification at link time is
attractive in that the checks are performed just once, substantially reducing the
amount of work that must be done at run time. Other implementation strategies
are possible, provided that they comply with *The Java Language Specification* and
The Java Virtual Machine Specification.

6.2 Reserved Opcodes

In addition to the opcodes of the instructions specified later in this chapter, which are used in class files (see Chapter 4, "The class File Format"), three opcodes are reserved for internal use by a Java virtual machine implementation. If Sun extends the instruction set of the Java virtual machine in the future, these reserved opcodes are guaranteed not to be used.

Two of the reserved opcodes, numbers 254 (0xfe) and 255 (0xff), have the mnemonics *impdep1* and *impdep2*, respectively. These instructions are intended to provide "back doors" or traps to implementation-specific functionality implemented in software and hardware, respectively. The third reserved opcode, number 202 (0xca), has the mnemonic *breakpoint* and is intended to be used by debuggers to implement breakpoints.

Although these opcodes have been reserved, they may be used only inside a Java virtual machine implementation. They cannot appear in valid class files. Tools such as debuggers or JIT code generators (§3.13) that might directly interact with Java virtual machine code that has been already loaded and executed may encounter these opcodes. Such tools should attempt to behave gracefully if they encounter any of these reserved instructions.

6.3 Virtual Machine Errors

A Java virtual machine implementation throws an object that is an instance of a subclass of the class VirtualMachineError when an internal error or resource limitation prevents it from correctly implementing the Java programming language. The Java virtual machine specification cannot predict where resource limitations or internal errors may be encountered and does not mandate precisely when they can be reported. Thus, any of the virtual machine errors listed as subclasses of VirtualMachineError in Section 2.16.4 may be thrown at any time during the operation of the Java virtual machine.

6.4 Format of Instruction Descriptions

Java virtual machine instructions are represented in this chapter by entries of the form shown in Figure 6.1, in alphabetical order and each beginning on a new page.

Each cell in the instruction format diagram represents a single 8-bit byte. The instruction's *mnemonic* is its name. Its opcode is its numeric representation and is

mnemonic   *mnemonic*

Operation   Short description of the instruction

Format
mnemonic
operand1
operand2
...

Operation

Forms   *mnemonic* = opcode

Operand   ..., *value1, value2* $\Rightarrow$
Stack   ..., *value3*

Description A longer description detailing constraints on operand stack contents or constant pool entries, the operation performed, the type of the results, etc.

Linking   If any linking exceptions may be thrown by the execution of this
Exceptions instruction, they are set off one to a line, in the order in which they must be thrown.

Runtime   If any runtime exceptions can be thrown by the execution of an
Exceptions instruction, they are set off one to a line, in the order in which they must be thrown.

Other than the linking and runtime exceptions, if any, listed for an instruction, that instruction must not throw any runtime exceptions except for instances of `VirtualMachineError` or its subclasses.

Notes   Comments not strictly part of the specification of an instruction are set aside as notes at the end of the description.

Figure 6.1 An example instruction page

given in both decimal and hexadecimal forms. Only the numeric representation is actually present in the Java virtual machine code in a `class` file.

Keep in mind that there are "operands" generated at compile time and embedded within Java virtual machine instructions, as well as "operands" calculated at run time and supplied on the operand stack. Although they are supplied from several different areas, all these operands represent the same thing: values to be operated upon by the Java virtual machine instruction being executed. By implicitly taking many of its operands from its operand stack, rather than representing them explicitly in its compiled code as additional operand bytes, register numbers, etc., the Java virtual machine's code stays compact.

Some instructions are presented as members of a family of related instructions sharing a single description, format, and operand stack diagram. As such, a family of instructions includes several opcodes and opcode mnemonics; only the family mnemonic appears in the instruction format diagram, and a separate forms line lists all member mnemonics and opcodes. For example, the forms line for the *lconst_<l>* family of instructions, giving mnemonic and opcode information for the two instructions in that family (*lconst_0* and *lconst_1*), is

Forms   *lconst_0* = 9 (0x9)
                 lconst_1 = 10 (0xa)

In the description of the Java virtual machine instructions, the effect of an instruction's execution on the operand stack (§3.6.2) of the current frame (§3.6) is represented textually, with the stack growing from left to right and each value represented separately. Thus,

Operand   ..., *value1*, *value2* $\Rightarrow$
Stack   ..., *result*

shows an operation that begins by having *value2* on top of the operand stack with *value1* just beneath it. As a result of the execution of the instruction, *value1* and *value2* are popped from the operand stack and replaced by *result* value, which has been calculated by the instruction. The remainder of the operand stack, represented by an ellipsis (...), is unaffected by the instruction's execution.

Values of types `long` and `double` are represented by a single entry on the operand stack.[1]

---

[1] Note that, in the first edition of this specification, values on the operand stack of types `long` and `double` were each represented in the stack diagram by two entries.

aaload   *aaload*

Operation   Load reference from array

Format

aaload

Forms   *aaload* = 50 (0x32)

Operand   ..., *arrayref*, *index* ⇒
Stack   ..., *value*

Description   The *arrayref* must be of type reference and must refer to an array
whose components are of type reference. The *index* must be of
type int. Both *arrayref* and *index* are popped from the operand
stack. The reference *value* in the component of the array at *index*
is retrieved and pushed onto the operand stack.

Runtime   If *arrayref* is null, *aaload* throws a NullPointerException.
Exceptions
Otherwise, if *index* is not within the bounds of the array referenced
by *arrayref*, the *aaload* instruction throws an ArrayIndex-
OutOfBoundsException.

aastore   *aastore*

Operation   Store into `reference` array

Format

aastore

Forms   *aastore* = 83 (0x53)

Operand   ..., *arrayref*, *index*, *value* ⇒
Stack   ...

Description The *arrayref* must be of type `reference` and must refer to an array whose components are of type `reference`. The *index* must be of type `int` and *value* must be of type `reference`. The *arrayref*, *index*, and *value* are popped from the operand stack. The `reference` *value* is stored as the component of the array at *index*.

The type of *value* must be assignment compatible (§2.6.7) with the type of the components of the array referenced by *arrayref*. Assignment of a value of reference type S (source) to a variable of reference type T (target) is allowed only when the type S supports all the operations defined on type T. The detailed rules follow:

- If S is a class type, then:
  - If T is a class type, then S must be the same class (§2.8.1) as T, or S must be a subclass of T;
  - If T is an interface type, S must implement (§2.13) interface T.
- If S is an interface type, then:
  - If T is a class type, then T must be `Object` (§2.4.7).
  - If T is an interface type, then T must be the same interface as S or a superinterface of S (§2.13.2).

aastore (*cont.*)   *aastore* (*cont.*)

- If *S* is an array type, namely, the type *SC*[], that is, an array of components of type *SC*, then:

  - If *T* is a class type, then *T* must be Object (§2.4.7).

  - If *T* is an array type *TC*[], that is, an array of components of type *TC*, then one of the following must be true:

    - *TC* and *SC* are the same primitive type (§2.4.1).

    - *TC* and *SC* are reference types (§2.4.6), and type *SC* is assignable to *TC* by these runtime rules.

  - If *T* is an interface type, *T* must be one of the interfaces implemented by arrays (§2.15).

Runtime Exceptions

If *arrayref* is null, *aastore* throws a NullPointerException.

Otherwise, if *index* is not within the bounds of the array referenced by *arrayref*, the *aastore* instruction throws an ArrayIndexOutOf-BoundsException.

Otherwise, if *arrayref* is not null and the actual type of *value* is not assignment compatible (§2.6.7) with the actual type of the components of the array, *aastore* throws an ArrayStoreException.

aconst_null   *aconst_null*

Operation   Push null

Format
aconst_null

Forms   *aconst_null* = 1 (0x1)

Operand $\ldots \Rightarrow$
Stack $\ldots, null$

Description   Push the null object reference onto the operand stack.

Notes   The Java virtual machine does not mandate a concrete value for null.

aload *aload*

Operation   Load reference from local variable

Format

aload
index

Forms   *aload* = 25 (0x19)

Operand   ... ⇒
Stack   ..., *objectref*

Description   The *index* is an unsigned byte that must be an index into the local variable array of the current frame (§3.6). The local variable at *index* must contain a reference. The *objectref* in the local variable at *index* is pushed onto the operand stack.

Notes   The *aload* instruction cannot be used to load a value of type returnAddress from a local variable onto the operand stack. This asymmetry with the *astore* instruction is intentional.

The *aload* opcode can be used in conjunction with the *wide* instruction to access a local variable using a two-byte unsigned index.

aload_<n>   *aload_<n>*

Operation   Load `reference` from local variable

Format
aload_<n>

Forms   *aload_0* = 42 (0x2a)
                   aload_1 = 43 (0x2b)
                   aload_2 = 44 (0x2c)
                   aload_3 = 45 (0x2d)

Operand   ... $\Rightarrow$
Stack   ..., *objectref*

Description   The *<n>* must be an index into the local variable array of the current
                   frame (§3.6). The local variable at *<n>* must contain a `reference`.
                   The *objectref* in the local variable at *index* is pushed onto the oper-
                   and stack.

Notes   An *aload_<n>* instruction cannot be used to load a value of type
                   `returnAddress` from a local variable onto the operand stack. This
                   asymmetry with the corresponding *astore_<n>* instruction is inten-
                   tional. Each of the *aload_<n>* instructions is the same as *aload* with
                   an *index* of *<n>*, except that the operand *<n>* is implicit.

anewarray *anewarray*

Operation   Create new array of `reference`

Format

anewarray
indexbyte1
indexbyte2

Forms   *anewarray* = 189 (0xbd)

Operand   ..., *count* ⇒
Stack   ..., *arrayref*

Description   The *count* must be of type `int`. It is popped off the operand stack. The *count* represents the number of components of the array to be created. The unsigned *indexbyte1* and *indexbyte2* are used to construct an index into the runtime constant pool of the current class (§3.6), where the value of the index is (*indexbyte1* << 8) | *indexbyte2*. The runtime constant pool item at that index must be a symbolic reference to a class, array, or interface type. The named class, array, or interface type is resolved (§5.4.3.1). A new array with components of that type, of length *count*, is allocated from the garbage-collected heap, and a `reference` *arrayref* to this new array object is pushed onto the operand stack. All components of the new array are initialized to `null`, the default value for `reference` types (§2.5.1).

Linking   During resolution of the symbolic reference to the class, array, or
Exceptions   interface type, any of the exceptions documented in §5.4.3.1 can be thrown.

Runtime   Otherwise, if *count* is less than zero, the *anewarray* instruction
Exception   throws a `NegativeArraySizeException`.

Notes   The *anewarray* instruction is used to create a single dimension of an array of object references or part of a multidimensional array.

areturn   *areturn*

Operation   Return reference from method

Format | *areturn* |

Forms   *areturn* = 176 (0xb0)

Operand   ..., *objectref* ⇒
Stack   [empty]

Description   The *objectref* must be of type reference and must refer to an
                    object of a type that is assignment compatible (§2.6.7) with the
                    type represented by the return descriptor (§4.3.3) of the current
                    method. If the current method is a synchronized method, the
                    monitor acquired or reentered on invocation of the method is
                    released or exited (respectively) as if by execution of a *monitorexit*
                    instruction. If no exception is thrown, *objectref* is popped from the
                    operand stack of the current frame (§3.6) and pushed onto the oper-
                    and stack of the frame of the invoker. Any other values on the oper-
                    and stack of the current method are discarded.

                    The interpreter then reinstates the frame of the invoker and returns
                    control to the invoker.

Runtime   If the current method is a synchronized method and the current
Exceptions   thread is not the owner of the monitor acquired or reentered on
                    invocation of the method, *areturn* throws an IllegalMonitor-
                    StateException. This can happen, for example, if a synchro-
                    nized method contains a *monitorexit* instruction, but no
                    monitorenter instruction, on the object on which the method is syn-
                    chronized.

                    Otherwise, if the virtual machine implementation enforces the rules
                    on structured use of locks described in §8.13 and if the first of those
                    rules is violated during invocation of the current method, then
                    areturn throws an IllegalMonitorStateException.

arraylength *arraylength*

Operation   Get length of array

Format

arraylength

Forms   *arraylength* = 190 (0xbe)

Operand   ..., *arrayref* ⇒
Stack   ..., *length*

Description   The *arrayref* must be of type `reference` and must refer to an array. It is popped from the operand stack. The *length* of the array it references is determined. That *length* is pushed onto the operand stack as an `int`.

Runtime   If the *arrayref* is `null`, the *arraylength* instruction throws a
Exception   `NullPointerException`.

astore   *astore*

Operation   Store reference into local variable

Format
astore
index

Forms   *astore* = 58 (0x3a)

Operand   ..., *objectref* $\Rightarrow$
Stack
                  ...

Description   The *index* is an unsigned byte that must be an index into the local
                  variable array of the current frame (§3.6). The *objectref* on the top
                  of the operand stack must be of type `returnAddress` or of type
                  `reference`. It is popped from the operand stack, and the value of
                  the local variable at *index* is set to *objectref*.

Notes   The *astore* instruction is used with an *objectref* of type `return-`
                  `Address` when implementing the `finally` clauses of the Java pro-
                  gramming language (see Section 7.13, "Compiling `finally`"). The
                  aload instruction cannot be used to load a value of type `return-`
                  `Address` from a local variable onto the operand stack. This asym-
                  metry with the *astore* instruction is intentional.

                  The *astore* opcode can be used in conjunction with the *wide* instruc-
                  tion to access a local variable using a two-byte unsigned index.

astore_<n>   *astore_<n>*

Operation   Store `reference` into local variable

Format
astore_<n>

Forms   *astore_0* = 75 (0x4b)
astore_1 = 76 (0x4c)
astore_2 = 77 (0x4d)
astore_3 = 78 (0x4e)

**Operand
Stack**   ..., *objectref* $\Rightarrow$
...

Description   The *<n>* must be an index into the local variable array of the current frame (§3.6). The *objectref* on the top of the operand stack must be of type `returnAddress` or of type `reference`. It is popped from the operand stack, and the value of the local variable at *<n>* is set to *objectref*.

Notes   An *astore_<n>* instruction is used with an *objectref* of type `returnAddress` when implementing the `finally` clauses of the Java programming language (see Section 7.13, "Compiling `finally`"). An *aload_<n>* instruction cannot be used to load a value of type `returnAddress` from a local variable onto the operand stack. This asymmetry with the corresponding *astore_<n>* instruction is intentional.

Each of the *astore_<n>* instructions is the same as *astore* with an *index* of *<n>*, except that the operand *<n>* is implicit.

athrow   *athrow*

Operation   Throw exception or error

Format

athrow

Forms   *athrow* = 191 (0xbf)

Operand   ..., *objectref* ⇒
Stack   *objectref*

Description   The *objectref* must be of type `reference` and must refer to an object that is an instance of class `Throwable` or of a subclass of `Throwable`. It is popped from the operand stack. The *objectref* is then thrown by searching the current method (§3.6) for the first exception handler that matches the class of *objectref*, as given by the algorithm in §3.10.

If an exception handler that matches *objectref* is found, it contains the location of the code intended to handle this exception. The `pc` register is reset to that location, the operand stack of the current frame is cleared, *objectref* is pushed back onto the operand stack, and execution continues.

If no matching exception handler is found in the current frame, that frame is popped. If the current frame represents an invocation of a `synchronized` method, the monitor acquired or reentered on invocation of the method is released or exited (respectively) as if by execution of a *monitorexit* instruction. Finally, the frame of its invoker is reinstated, if such a frame exists, and the *objectref* is rethrown. If no such frame exists, the current thread exits.

Runtime   If *objectref* is `null`, *athrow* throws a `NullPointerException`
Exceptions   instead of *objectref*.

athrow (*cont.*)   *athrow* (*cont.*)
                                                       athrow (*cont.*)

Otherwise, if the method of the current frame is a `synchronized` method and the current thread is not the owner of the monitor acquired or reentered on invocation of the method, *athrow* throws an `IllegalMonitorStateException` instead of the object previously being thrown. This can happen, for example, if an abruptly completing `synchronized` method contains a *monitorexit* instruction, but no *monitorenter* instruction, on the object on which the method is synchronized.

Otherwise, if the virtual machine implementation enforces the rules on structured use of locks described in §8.13 and if the first of those rules is violated during invocation of the current method, then *athrow* throws an `IllegalMonitorStateException` instead of the object previously being thrown.

Notes   The operand stack diagram for the *athrow* instruction may be misleading: If a handler for this exception is matched in the current method, the *athrow* instruction discards all the values on the operand stack, then pushes the thrown object onto the operand stack. However, if no handler is matched in the current method and the exception is thrown farther up the method invocation chain, then the operand stack of the method (if any) that handles the exception is cleared and *objectref* is pushed onto that empty operand stack. All intervening frames from the method that threw the exception up to, but not including, the method that handles the exception are discarded.

baload   *baload*

Operation   Load `byte` or `boolean` from array

Format

baload

Forms   *baload* = 51 (0x33)

Operand   ..., *arrayref*, *index* $\Rightarrow$
Stack   ..., *value'*

Description   The *arrayref* must be of type `reference` and must refer to an array
                   whose components are of type `byte` or of type `boolean`. The *index*
                   must be of type `int`. Both *arrayref* and *index* are popped from the
                   operand stack. If the components of the array are of type `byte`, the
                   component of the array at *index* is retrieved and sign-extended to
                   an `int` *value*. If the components of the array are of type `boolean`,
                   the component of the array at *index* is retrieved and zero-extended
                   to an `int` *value*. In either case the resulting *value* is pushed onto the
                   operand stack.

Runtime   If *arrayref* is `null`, *baload* throws a `NullPointerException`.
Exceptions
                   Otherwise, if *index* is not within the bounds of the array referenced
                   by *arrayref*, the *baload* instruction throws an `ArrayIndex-`
                   `OutOfBoundsException`.

Notes   The *baload* instruction is used to load values from both `byte` and
                   `boolean` arrays. In Sun's implementation of the Java virtual
                   machine, `boolean` arrays (arrays of type `T_BOOLEAN`; see §3.2 and
                   the description of the *newarray* instruction in this chapter) are
                   implemented as arrays of 8-bit values. Other implementations may
                   implement packed `boolean` arrays; the *baload* instruction of such
                   implementations must be used to access those arrays.

bastore   *bastore*

Operation   Store into `byte` or `boolean` array

Format

bastore

Forms   *bastore* = 84 (0x54)

Operand   ..., *arrayref*, *index*, *value* ⇒
Stack   ...

Description   The *arrayref* must be of type `reference` and must refer to an array
                   whose components are of type `byte` or of type `boolean`. The *index*
                   and the *value* must both be of type `int`. The *arrayref*, *index*, and
                   value are popped from the operand stack. If the components of the
                   array are of type `byte`, the `int` *value* is truncated to a `byte` and
                   stored as the component of the array indexed by *index*. If the com-
                   ponents of the array are of type `boolean`, the `int` *value* is truncated
                   to its low order bit then zero-extended to the storage size for com-
                   ponents of `boolean` arrays used by the implementation. The result
                   is stored as the component of the array indexed by *index*.

Runtime   If *arrayref* is `null`, *bastore* throws a `NullPointerException`.
Exceptions
                   Otherwise, if *index* is not within the bounds of the array referenced
                   by *arrayref*, the *bastore* instruction throws an `ArrayIndexOutOf-`
                   `BoundsException`.

Notes   The *bastore* instruction is used to store values into both `byte` and
                   `boolean` arrays. In Sun's implementation of the Java virtual
                   machine, `boolean` arrays (arrays of type T_BOOLEAN; see §3.2 and
                   the description of the *newarray* instruction in this chapter) are
                   implemented as arrays of 8-bit values. Other implementations may
                   implement packed `boolean` arrays; in such implementations the
                   bastore instruction must be able to store `boolean` values into
                   packed `boolean` arrays as well as `byte` values into `byte` arrays.

bipush   *bipush*

Operation   Push byte

Format

| *bipush* |
| *byte* |

Forms   *bipush* = 16 (0x10)

Operand   ... $\Rightarrow$
Stack   ..., *value*

Description   The immediate *byte* is sign-extended to an int *value*. That *value* is pushed onto the operand stack.

caload *caload*

Operation Load char from array

Format

caload

Forms *caload* = 52 (0x34)

Operand ..., *arrayref*, *index* ⇒
Stack ..., *value*

Description The *arrayref* must be of type reference and must refer to an array whose components are of type char. The *index* must be of type int. Both *arrayref* and *index* are popped from the operand stack. The component of the array at *index* is retrieved and zero-extended to an int *value*. That *value* is pushed onto the operand stack.

Runtime If *arrayref* is null, *caload* throws a NullPointerException.
Exceptions
Otherwise, if *index* is not within the bounds of the array referenced by *arrayref*, the *caload* instruction throws an ArrayIndexOutOf-BoundsException.

castore   *castore*

Operation   Store into char array

Format

castore

Forms   *castore* = 85 (0x55)

Operand   ..., *arrayref*, *index*, *value* ⇒
Stack   ...

Description   The *arrayref* must be of type reference and must refer to an array
                  whose components are of type char. The *index* and the *value* must
                  both be of type int. The *arrayref*, *index*, and *value* are popped
                  from the operand stack. The int *value* is truncated to a char and
                  stored as the component of the array indexed by *index*.

Runtime   If *arrayref* is null, *castore* throws a NullPointerException.
Exceptions
                  Otherwise, if *index* is not within the bounds of the array referenced
                  by *arrayref*, the *castore* instruction throws an ArrayIndexOutOf-
                  BoundsException.

checkcast   *checkcast*

Operation   Check whether object is of given type

Format

checkcast
indexbyte1
indexbyte2

Forms   *checkcast* = 192 (0xc0)

Operand   ..., *objectref* ⇒
Stack   ..., *objectref*

Description The *objectref* must be of type `reference`. The unsigned *indexbyte1*
and *indexbyte2* are used to construct an index into the runtime constant pool of the current class (§3.6), where the value of the index is
(*indexbyte1* << 8) | *indexbyte2*. The runtime constant pool item at
the index must be a symbolic reference to a class, array, or interface
type. The named class, array, or interface type is resolved
(§5.4.3.1).

If *objectref* is `null` or can be cast to the resolved class, array, or
interface type, the operand stack is unchanged; otherwise, the
checkcast instruction throws a `ClassCastException`.

The following rules are used to determine whether an *objectref* that
is not `null` can be cast to the resolved type: if S is the class of the
object referred to by *objectref* and T is the resolved class, array, or
interface type, *checkcast* determines whether *objectref* can be cast to
type T as follows:

- If S is an ordinary (nonarray) class, then:

  - If T is a class type, then S must be the same class (§2.8.1)
    as T, or a subclass of T.

  - If T is an interface type, then S must implement (§2.13)
    interface T.

checkcast (*cont.*)   *checkcast* (*cont.*)

- If *S* is an interface type, then:

  - If *T* is a class type, then *T* must be Object (§2.4.7).

  - If *T* is an interface type, then *T* must be the same interface as *S* or a superinterface of *S* (§2.13.2).

- If *S* is a class representing the array type *SC*[], that is, an array of components of type *SC*, then:

  - If *T* is a class type, then *T* must be Object (§2.4.7).

  - If *T* is an array type *TC*[], that is, an array of components of type *TC*, then one of the following must be true:

    - *TC* and *SC* are the same primitive type (§2.4.1).

    - *TC* and *SC* are reference types (§2.4.6), and type *SC* can be cast to *TC* by recursive application of these rules.

  - If *T* is an interface type, *T* must be one of the interfaces implemented by arrays (§2.15).

Linking Exceptions

During resolution of the symbolic reference to the class, array, or interface type, any of the exceptions documented in Section 5.4.3.1 can be thrown.

Runtime Exception

Otherwise, if *objectref* cannot be cast to the resolved class, array, or interface type, the *checkcast* instruction throws a ClassCast-Exception.

Notes

The *checkcast* instruction is very similar to the *instanceof* instruction. It differs in its treatment of null, its behavior when its test fails (*checkcast* throws an exception, *instanceof* pushes a result code), and its effect on the operand stack.

d2f   *d2f*

Operation   Convert `double` to `float`

Format

d2f

Forms   *d2f* = 144 (0x90)

Operand   ..., *value* $\Rightarrow$
Stack   ..., *result*

Description   The *value* on the top of the operand stack must be of type `double`. It is popped from the operand stack and undergoes value set conversion (§3.8.3) resulting in *value'*. Then *value'* is converted to a `float` *result* using IEEE 754 round to nearest mode. The *result* is pushed onto the operand stack.

Where an *d2f* instruction is FP-strict (§3.8.2), the result of the conversion is always rounded to the nearest representable value in the float value set (§3.3.2).

Where an *d2f* instruction is not FP-strict, the result of the conversion may be taken from the float-extended-exponent value set (§3.3.2); it is not necessarily rounded to the nearest representable value in the float value set.

A finite *value'* too small to be represented as a `float` is converted to a zero of the same sign; a finite *value'* too large to be represented as a `float` is converted to an infinity of the same sign. A `double` NaN is converted to a `float` NaN.

Notes   The *d2f* instruction performs a narrowing primitive conversion (§2.6.3). It may lose information about the overall magnitude of *value'* and may also lose precision.

d2i   *d2i*

Operation   Convert double to int

Format | *d2i* |
                     |-------|

Forms   *d2i* = 142 (0x8e)

Operand   ..., *value* ⇒
Stack   ..., *result*

Description   The *value* on the top of the operand stack must be of type double.
                     It is popped from the operand stack and undergoes value set con-
                     version (§3.8.3) resulting in *value'*. Then *value'* is converted to an
                     int. The *result* is pushed onto the operand stack:

- If the *value'* is NaN, the *result* of the conversion is an int 0.

- Otherwise, if the *value'* is not an infinity, it is rounded to an
  integer value *V*, rounding towards zero using IEEE 754 round
  towards zero mode. If this integer value *V* can be represented as
  an int, then the *result* is the int value *V*.

- Otherwise, either the *value'* must be too small (a negative value
  of large magnitude or negative infinity), and the *result* is the
  smallest representable value of type int, or the *value'* must be
  too large (a positive value of large magnitude or positive infinity),
  and the *result* is the largest representable value of type int.

Notes   The *d2i* instruction performs a narrowing primitive conversion
                     (§2.6.3). It may lose information about the overall magnitude of
                     value' and may also lose precision.

d2l   *d2l*

Operation   Convert double to long

Format

d2l

Forms   *d2l* = 143 (0x8f)

Operand   ..., *value* ⇒
Stack   ..., *result*

Description   The *value* on the top of the operand stack must be of type double. It is popped from the operand stack and undergoes value set conversion (§3.8.3) resulting in *value'*. Then *value'* is converted to a long. The *result* is pushed onto the operand stack:

- If the *value'* is NaN, the *result* of the conversion is a long 0.

- Otherwise, if the *value'* is not an infinity, it is rounded to an integer value V, rounding towards zero using IEEE 754 round towards zero mode. If this integer value V can be represented as a long, then the *result* is the long value V.

- Otherwise, either the *value'* must be too small (a negative value of large magnitude or negative infinity), and the *result* is the smallest representable value of type long, or the *value'* must be too large (a positive value of large magnitude or positive infinity), and the *result* is the largest representable value of type long.

Notes   The *d2l* instruction performs a narrowing primitive conversion (§2.6.3). It may lose information about the overall magnitude of *value'* and may also lose precision.

dadd   *dadd*

Operation   Add `double`

Format

dadd

Forms   *dadd* = 99 (0x63)

Operand   ..., *value1*, *value2* ⇒
Stack   ..., *result*

Description Both *value1* and *value2* must be of type `double`. The values are popped from the operand stack and undergo value set conversion (§3.8.3), resulting in *value1′* and *value2′*. The `double` *result* is *value1′* + *value2′*. The *result* is pushed onto the operand stack.

The result of a *dadd* instruction is governed by the rules of IEEE arithmetic:

- If either *value1′* or *value2′* is NaN, the result is NaN.

- The sum of two infinities of opposite sign is NaN.

- The sum of two infinities of the same sign is the infinity of that sign.

- The sum of an infinity and any finite value is equal to the infinity.

- The sum of two zeroes of opposite sign is positive zero.

- The sum of two zeroes of the same sign is the zero of that sign.

- The sum of a zero and a nonzero finite value is equal to the non-zero value.

- The sum of two nonzero finite values of the same magnitude and opposite sign is positive zero.

dadd (*cont.*)   *dadd* (*cont.*)

- In the remaining cases, where neither operand is an infinity, a zero, or NaN and the values have the same sign or have different magnitudes, the sum is computed and rounded to the nearest representable value using IEEE 754 round to nearest mode. If the magnitude is too large to represent as a `double`, we say the operation overflows; the result is then an infinity of appropriate sign. If the magnitude is too small to represent as a `double`, we say the operation underflows; the result is then a zero of appropriate sign.

The Java virtual machine requires support of gradual underflow as defined by IEEE 754. Despite the fact that overflow, underflow, or loss of precision may occur, execution of a *dadd* instruction never throws a runtime exception.

daload   *daload*

Operation	Load double from array

Format

daload

Forms   *daload* = 49 (0x31)

**Operand
Stack**

..., *arrayref*, *index* ⇒
..., *value*

Description   The *arrayref* must be of type reference and must refer to an array whose components are of type double. The *index* must be of type int. Both *arrayref* and *index* are popped from the operand stack. The double *value* in the component of the array at *index* is retrieved and pushed onto the operand stack.

**Runtime
Exceptions**

If *arrayref* is null, *daload* throws a NullPointerException.

Otherwise, if *index* is not within the bounds of the array referenced by *arrayref*, the *daload* instruction throws an ArrayIndexOutOf-BoundsException.

dastore *dastore*

Operation   Store into `double` array

Format

dastore

Forms   *dastore* = 82 (0x52)

**Operand
Stack**   ..., *arrayref*, *index*, *value* ⇒

...

Description   The *arrayref* must be of type `reference` and must refer to an array whose components are of type `double`. The *index* must be of type `int`, and *value* must be of type `double`. The *arrayref*, *index*, and *value* are popped from the operand stack. The `double` *value* undergoes value set conversion (§3.8.3), resulting in *value'*, which is stored as the component of the array indexed by *index*.

**Runtime
Exceptions**   If *arrayref* is `null`, *dastore* throws a `NullPointerException`.

Otherwise, if *index* is not within the bounds of the array referenced by *arrayref*, the *dastore* instruction throws an `ArrayIndex-OutOfBoundsException`.

dcmp<op>   *dcmp<op>*

Operation   Compare double

Format
dcmp<op>

Forms   *dcmpg* = 152 (0x98)
                   dcmpl = 151 (0x97)

Operand   ..., *value1*, *value2* ⇒
Stack   ..., *result*

Description   Both *value1* and *value2* must be of type double. The values are
                   popped from the operand stack and undergo value set conversion
                   (§3.8.3), resulting in *value1'* and *value2'*. A floating-point compari-
                   son is performed:

                   • If *value1'* is greater than *value2'*, the int value *1* is pushed onto
                     the operand stack.

                   • Otherwise, if *value1'* is equal to *value2'*, the int value *0* is
                     pushed onto the operand stack.

                   • Otherwise, if *value1'* is less than *value2'*, the int value – *1* is
                     pushed onto the operand stack.

                   • Otherwise, at least one of *value1'* or *value2'* is NaN. The *dcmpg*
                     instruction pushes the int value *1* onto the operand stack and
                     the *dcmpl* instruction pushes the int value –*1* onto the operand
                     stack.

                   Floating-point comparison is performed in accordance with IEEE
                   754. All values other than NaN are ordered, with negative infinity
                   less than all finite values and positive infinity greater than all finite
                   values. Positive zero and negative zero are considered equal.

dcmp<op> (cont.)   *dcmp<op> (cont.)*

Notes   The *dcmpg* and *dcmpl* instructions differ only in their treatment of a comparison involving NaN. NaN is unordered, so any `double` comparison fails if either or both of its operands are NaN. With both *dcmpg* and *dcmpl* available, any `double` comparison may be compiled to push the same *result* onto the operand stack whether the comparison fails on non-NaN values or fails because it encountered a NaN. For more information, see Section 7.5, "More Control Examples."

dconst_<d>   *dconst_<d>*

Operation   Push double

Format
dconst_<d>

Forms   *dconst_0* = 14 (0xe)
                 dconst_1 = 15 (0xf)

Operand   ... $\Rightarrow$
Stack   ..., *<d>*

Description Push the double constant *<d>* (*0.0* or *1.0*) onto the operand stack.

ddiv   *ddiv*

Operation   Divide `double`

Format

ddiv

Forms   *ddiv* = 111 (0x6f)

Operand   ..., *value1*, *value2* $\Rightarrow$
Stack   ..., *result*

Description   Both *value1* and *value2* must be of type `double`. The values are popped from the operand stack and undergo value set conversion (§3.8.3), resulting in *value1'* and *value2'*. The `double` *result* is *value1'* / *value2'*. The *result* is pushed onto the operand stack.

The result of a *ddiv* instruction is governed by the rules of IEEE arithmetic:

- If either *value1'* or *value2'* is NaN, the result is NaN.

- If neither *value1'* nor *value2'* is NaN, the sign of the result is positive if both values have the same sign, negative if the values have different signs.

- Division of an infinity by an infinity results in NaN.

- Division of an infinity by a finite value results in a signed infinity, with the sign-producing rule just given.

- Division of a finite value by an infinity results in a signed zero, with the sign-producing rule just given.

- Division of a zero by a zero results in NaN; division of zero by any other finite value results in a signed zero, with the sign-producing rule just given.

- Division of a nonzero finite value by a zero results in a signed infinity, with the sign-producing rule just given.

- In the remaining cases, where neither operand is an infinity, a zero, or NaN, the quotient is computed and rounded to the nearest double using IEEE 754 round to nearest mode. If the magnitude is too large to represent as a double, we say the operation overflows; the result is then an infinity of appropriate sign. If the magnitude is too small to represent as a double, we say the operation underflows; the result is then a zero of appropriate sign.

The Java virtual machine requires support of gradual underflow as defined by IEEE 754. Despite the fact that overflow, underflow, division by zero, or loss of precision may occur, execution of a *ddiv* instruction never throws a runtime exception.

dload *dload*

Operation Load `double` from local variable

Format

dload
index

Forms *dload* = 24 (0x18)

Operand ... ⇒
Stack ..., *value*

Description The *index* is an unsigned byte. Both *index* and *index + 1* must be indices into the local variable array of the current frame (§3.6). The local variable at *index* must contain a `double`. The *value* of the local variable at *index* is pushed onto the operand stack.

Notes The *dload* opcode can be used in conjunction with the *wide* instruction to access a local variable using a two-byte unsigned index.

dload_<n>   *dload_<n>*

Operation   Load double from local variable

Format

dload_<n>

Forms   *dload_0* = 38 (0x26)
                  dload_1 = 39 (0x27)
                  dload_2 = 40 (0x28)
                  dload_3 = 41 (0x29)

Operand   ... $\Rightarrow$
Stack   ..., *value*

Description   Both *<n>* and *<n>* + *1* must be indices into the local variable array
                  of the current frame (§3.6). The local variable at *<n>* must contain
                  a double. The *value* of the local variable at *<n>* is pushed onto the
                  operand stack.

Notes   Each of the *dload_<n>* instructions is the same as *dload* with an
                  index of *<n>*, except that the operand *<n>* is implicit.

dmul *dmul*

Operation   Multiply `double`

Format

dmul

Forms   *dmul* = 107 (0x6b)

Operand   ..., *value1*, *value2* $\Rightarrow$
Stack   ..., *result*

Description   Both *value1* and *value2* must be of type `double`. The values are popped from the operand stack and undergo value set conversion (§3.8.3), resulting in *value1'* and *value2'*. The `double` *result* is *value1'* * *value2'*. The *result* is pushed onto the operand stack.

The result of a *dmul* instruction is governed by the rules of IEEE arithmetic:

- If either *value1'* or *value2'* is NaN, the result is NaN.

- If neither *value1'* nor *value2'* is NaN, the sign of the result is positive if both values have the same sign and negative if the values have different signs.

- Multiplication of an infinity by a zero results in NaN.

- Multiplication of an infinity by a finite value results in a signed infinity, with the sign-producing rule just given.

- In the remaining cases, where neither an infinity nor NaN is involved, the product is computed and rounded to the nearest representable value using IEEE 754 round to nearest mode. If the magnitude is too large to represent as a `double`, we say the operation overflows; the result is then an infinity of appropriate sign. If the magnitude is too small to represent as a `double`, we say the operation underflows; the result is then a zero of appropriate sign.

dmul (*cont.*)   **dmul** (*cont.*)

The Java virtual machine requires support of gradual underflow as defined by IEEE 754. Despite the fact that overflow, underflow, or loss of precision may occur, execution of a *dmul* instruction never throws a runtime exception.

dneg *dneg*

Operation   Negate `double`

Format

dneg

Forms   *dneg* = 119 (0x77)

Operand   ..., *value* ⇒
Stack   ..., *result*

Description   The *value* must be of type `double`. It is popped from the operand stack and undergoes value set conversion (§3.8.3), resulting in *value'*. The `double` *result* is the arithmetic negation of *value'*. The *result* is pushed onto the operand stack.

For `double` values, negation is not the same as subtraction from zero. If x is +0.0, then 0.0−x equals +0.0, but −x equals −0.0. Unary minus merely inverts the sign of a `double`.

Special cases of interest:

- If the operand is NaN, the result is NaN (recall that NaN has no sign).

- If the operand is an infinity, the result is the infinity of opposite sign.

- If the operand is a zero, the result is the zero of opposite sign.

drem   *drem*

Operation   Remainder double

Format | *drem* |

Forms   *drem* = 115 (0x73)

Operand   ..., *value1*, *value2* ⇒
Stack   ..., *result*

Description   Both *value1* and *value2* must be of type double. The values are
                  popped from the operand stack and undergo value set conversion
                  (§3.8.3), resulting in *value1′* and *value2′*. The *result* is calculated
                  and pushed onto the operand stack as a double.

                  The result of a *drem* instruction is not the same as that of the so-
                  called remainder operation defined by IEEE 754. The IEEE 754
                  "remainder" operation computes the remainder from a rounding
                  division, not a truncating division, and so its behavior is *not* analo-
                  gous to that of the usual integer remainder operator. Instead, the
                  Java virtual machine defines *drem* to behave in a manner analogous
                  to that of the Java virtual machine integer remainder instructions
                  (*irem* and *lrem*); this may be compared with the C library function
                  fmod.

                  The result of a *drem* instruction is governed by these rules:

                  • If either *value1′* or *value2′* is NaN, the result is NaN.

                  • If neither *value1′* nor *value2′* is NaN, the sign of the result equals
                    the sign of the dividend.

                  • If the dividend is an infinity or the divisor is a zero or both, the
                    result is NaN.

                  • If the dividend is finite and the divisor is an infinity, the result
                    equals the dividend.

drem (*cont.*)   *drem* (*cont.*)

- If the dividend is a zero and the divisor is finite, the result equals the dividend.

- In the remaining cases, where neither operand is an infinity, a zero, or NaN, the floating-point remainder *result* from a dividend *value1*′ and a divisor *value2*′ is defined by the mathematical relation *result* = *value1*′ − (*value2*′ ∗ *q*), where *q* is an integer that is negative only if *value1*′ / *value2*′ is negative, and positive only if *value1*′ / *value2*′ is positive, and whose magnitude is as large as possible without exceeding the magnitude of the true mathematical quotient of *value1*′ and *value2*′.

Despite the fact that division by zero may occur, evaluation of a *drem* instruction never throws a runtime exception. Overflow, underflow, or loss of precision cannot occur.

Notes   The IEEE 754 remainder operation may be computed by the library routine `Math.IEEEremainder`.

dreturn   *dreturn*

Operation   Return double from method

Format
dreturn

Forms   *dreturn* = 175 (0xaf)

Operand   ..., *value* ⇒
Stack   [empty]

Description The current method must have return type double. The *value* must
                 be of type double. If the current method is a synchronized
                 method, the monitor acquired or reentered on invocation of the
                 method is released or exited (respectively) as if by execution of a
                 monitorexit instruction. If no exception is thrown, *value* is popped
                 from the operand stack of the current frame (§3.6) and undergoes
                 value set conversion (§3.8.3), resulting in *value'*. The *value'* is
                 pushed onto the operand stack of the frame of the invoker. Any
                 other values on the operand stack of the current method are dis-
                 carded.

                 The interpreter then returns control to the invoker of the method,
                 reinstating the frame of the invoker.

Runtime   If the current method is a synchronized method and the current
Exceptions   thread is not the owner of the monitor acquired or reentered on
                 invocation of the method, *dreturn* throws an IllegalMonitor-
                 StateException. This can happen, for example, if a synchro-
                 nized method contains a *monitorexit* instruction, but no
                 monitorenter instruction, on the object on which the method is syn-
                 chronized.

                 Otherwise, if the virtual machine implementation enforces the rules
                 on structured use of locks described in §8.13 and if the first of those
                 rules is violated during invocation of the current method, then
                 dreturn throws an IllegalMonitorStateException.

dstore *dstore*

Operation Store double into local variable

Format

dstore
index

Forms *dstore* = 57 (0x39)

Operand ..., *value* $\Rightarrow$
Stack ...

Description The *index* is an unsigned byte. Both *index* and *index* + *1* must be indices into the local variable array of the current frame (§3.6). The *value* on the top of the operand stack must be of type double. It is popped from the operand stack and undergoes value set conversion (§3.8.3), resulting in *value'*. The local variables at *index* and *index* + *1* are set to *value'*.

Notes The *dstore* opcode can be used in conjunction with the *wide* instruction to access a local variable using a two-byte unsigned index.

dstore_<n>   *dstore_<n>*

Operation   Store double into local variable

Format | *dstore_<n>* |

Forms   *dstore_0* = 71 (0x47)
                  dstore_1 = 72 (0x48)
                  dstore_2 = 73 (0x49)
                  dstore_3 = 74 (0x4a)

Operand   ..., *value* $\Rightarrow$
Stack   ...

Description   Both *<n>* and *<n>* + *1* must be indices into the local variable array of the current frame (§3.6). The *value* on the top of the operand stack must be of type double. It is popped from the operand stack and undergoes value set conversion (§3.8.3), resulting in *value'*. The local variables at *<n>* and *<n>* + *1* are set to *value'*.

Notes   Each of the *dstore_<n>* instructions is the same as *dstore* with an *index* of *<n>*, except that the operand *<n>* is implicit.

dsub   *dsub*

Operation   Subtract double

Format

dsub

Forms   *dsub* = 103 (0x67)

Operand   ..., *value1*, *value2* ⇒
Stack   ..., *result*

Description   Both *value1* and *value2* must be of type double. The values are popped from the operand stack and undergo value set conversion (§3.8.3), resulting in *value1'* and *value2'*. The double *result* is *value1'* − *value2'*. The *result* is pushed onto the operand stack.

For double subtraction, it is always the case that a−b produces the same result as a+(−b). However, for the *dsub* instruction, subtraction from zero is not the same as negation, because if x is +0.0, then 0.0−x equals +0.0, but −x equals −0.0.

The Java virtual machine requires support of gradual underflow as defined by IEEE 754. Despite the fact that overflow, underflow, or loss of precision may occur, execution of a *dsub* instruction never throws a runtime exception.

dup *dup*

Operation   Duplicate the top operand stack value

Format

dup

Forms   *dup* = 89 (0x59)

Operand   ..., *value* $\Rightarrow$
Stack   ..., *value*, *value*

Description   Duplicate the top value on the operand stack and push the duplicated value onto the operand stack.

The *dup* instruction must not be used unless *value* is a value of a category 1 computational type (§3.11.1).

dup_x1 *dup_x1*

Operation   Duplicate the top operand stack value and insert two values down

Format

dup_x1

Forms   *dup_x1* = 90 (0x5a)

Operand   ..., *value2*, *value1* $\Rightarrow$
Stack   ..., *value1*, *value2*, *value1*

Description   Duplicate the top value on the operand stack and insert the duplicated value two values down in the operand stack.

The *dup_x1* instruction must not be used unless both *value1* and *value2* are values of a category 1 computational type (§3.11.1).

dup_x2 *dup_x2*

Operation   Duplicate the top operand stack value and insert two or three values down

Format

dup_x2

Forms   *dup_x2* = 91 (0x5b)

Operand Stack   Form 1:

..., *value3*, *value2*, *value1* ⇒
..., *value1*, *value3*, *value2*, *value1*

where *value1*, *value2*, and *value3* are all values of a category 1 computational type (§3.11.1).

Form 2:

..., *value2*, *value1* ⇒
..., *value1*, *value2*, *value1*

where *value1* is a value of a category 1 computational type and *value2* is a value of a category 2 computational type (§3.11.1).

Description   Duplicate the top value on the operand stack and insert the duplicated value two or three values down in the operand stack.

dup2 *dup2*

Operation   Duplicate the top one or two operand stack values

Format

dup2

Forms   *dup2* = 92 (0x5c)

Operand   Form 1:
Stack
..., *value2*, *value1* $\Rightarrow$
..., *value2*, *value1*, *value2*, *value1*

where both *value1* and *value2* are values of a category 1 computational type (§3.11.1).

Form 2:

..., *value* $\Rightarrow$
..., *value*, *value*

where *value* is a value of a category 2 computational type (§3.11.1).

Description   Duplicate the top one or two values on the operand stack and push the duplicated value or values back onto the operand stack in the original order.

dup2_x1   *dup2_x1*

Operation   Duplicate the top one or two operand stack values and insert two or
three values down

Format

dup2_x1

Forms   *dup2_x1* = 93 (0x5d)

**Operand
Stack**

Form 1:

..., *value3*, *value2*, *value1* ⇒
..., *value2*, *value1*, *value3*, *value2*, *value1*

where *value1*, *value2*, and *value3* are all values of a category 1
computational type (§3.11.1).

Form 2:

..., *value2*, *value1* ⇒
..., *value1*, *value2*, *value1*

where *value1* is a value of a category 2 computational type and
value2 is a value of a category 1 computational type (§3.11.1).

Description   Duplicate the top one or two values on the operand stack and insert
the duplicated values, in the original order, one value beneath the
original value or values in the operand stack.

dup2_x2   *dup2_x2*

Operation   Duplicate the top one or two operand stack values and insert two, three, or four values down

Format

dup2_x2

Forms   *dup2_x2* = 94 (0x5e)

Operand   Form 1:
Stack
..., *value4, value3, value2, value1* ⇒
..., *value2, value1, value4, value3, value2, value1*

where *value1*, *value2*, *value3*, and *value4* are all values of a category 1 computational type (§3.11.1).

Form 2:

..., *value3, value2, value1* ⇒
..., *value1, value3, value2, value1*

where *value1* is a value of a category 2 computational type and *value2* and *value3* are both values of a category 1 computational type (§3.11.1).

Form 3:

..., *value3, value2, value1* ⇒
..., *value2, value1, value3, value2, value1*

where *value1* and *value2* are both values of a category 1 computational type and *value3* is a value of a category 2 computational type (§3.11.1).

Form 4:

..., *value2, value1* ⇒
..., *value1, value2, value1*

where *value1* and *value2* are both values of a category 2 computational type (§3.11.1).

dup2_x2 (cont.)   *dup2_x2* (cont.)

Description   Duplicate the top one or two values on the operand stack and insert the duplicated values, in the original order, into the operand stack.

f2d   *f2d*

Operation   Convert `float` to `double`

Format
f2d

Forms   *f2d* = 141 (0x8d)

Operand   ..., *value* ⇒
Stack   ..., *result*

Description The *value* on the top of the operand stack must be of type `float`. It
is popped from the operand stack and undergoes value set conver-
sion (§3.8.3), resulting in *value'*. Then *value'* is converted to a double *result*. This *result* is pushed onto the operand stack.

Notes   Where an *f2d* instruction is FP-strict (§3.8.2) it performs a widening primitive conversion (§2.6.2). Because all values of the float
value set (§3.3.2) are exactly representable by values of the double
value set (§3.3.2), such a conversion is exact.

Where an *f2d* instruction is not FP-strict, the result of the conversion may be taken from the double-extended-exponent value set; it
is not necessarily rounded to the nearest representable value in the
double value set. However, if the operand *value* is taken from the
float-extended-exponent value set and the target result is constrained to the double value set, rounding of *value* may be required.

f2i   *f2i*

Operation   Convert float to int

Format

f2i

Forms   *f2i* = 139 (0x8b)

Operand   ..., *value* ⇒
Stack   ..., *result*

Description The *value* on the top of the operand stack must be of type float. It is popped from the operand stack and undergoes value set conversion (§3.8.3), resulting in *value'*. Then *value'* is converted to an int *result*. This *result* is pushed onto the operand stack:

- If the *value'* is NaN, the *result* of the conversion is an int 0.

- Otherwise, if the *value'* is not an infinity, it is rounded to an integer value *V*, rounding towards zero using IEEE 754 round towards zero mode. If this integer value *V* can be represented as an int, then the *result* is the int value *V*.

- Otherwise, either the *value'* must be too small (a negative value of large magnitude or negative infinity), and the *result* is the smallest representable value of type int, or the *value'* must be too large (a positive value of large magnitude or positive infinity), and the *result* is the largest representable value of type int.

Notes   The *f2i* instruction performs a narrowing primitive conversion (§2.6.3). It may lose information about the overall magnitude of *value'* and may also lose precision.

f2l   *f2l*

Operation   Convert float to long

Format

f2l

Forms   *f2l* = 140 (0x8c)

Operand   ..., *value* ⇒
Stack   ..., *result*

Description   The *value* on the top of the operand stack must be of type float. It
                   is popped from the operand stack and undergoes value set conver-
                   sion (§3.8.3), resulting in *value'*. Then *value'* is converted to a long
                   result. This *result* is pushed onto the operand stack:

   • If the *value'* is NaN, the *result* of the conversion is a long 0.

   • Otherwise, if the *value'* is not an infinity, it is rounded to an
     integer value *V*, rounding towards zero using IEEE 754 round
     towards zero mode. If this integer value *V* can be represented
     as a long, then the *result* is the long value *V*.

   • Otherwise, either the *value'* must be too small (a negative value
     of large magnitude or negative infinity), and the *result* is the
     smallest representable value of type long, or the *value'* must be
     too large (a positive value of large magnitude or positive infinity),
     and the *result* is the largest representable value of type long.

Notes   The *f2l* instruction performs a narrowing primitive conversion
                   (§2.6.3). It may lose information about the overall magnitude of
                   value' and may also lose precision.

fadd   *fadd*

Operation	Add `float`

Format

fadd

Forms   *fadd* = 98 (0x62)

Operand   ..., *value1, value2* ⇒
Stack   ..., *result*

Description Both *value1* and *value2* must be of type `float`. The values are popped from the operand stack and undergo value set conversion (§3.8.3), resulting in *value1'* and *value2'*. The `float` *result* is *value1'* + *value2'*. The *result* is pushed onto the operand stack.

The result of an *fadd* instruction is governed by the rules of IEEE arithmetic:

- If either *value1'* or *value2'* is NaN, the result is NaN.

- The sum of two infinities of opposite sign is NaN.

- The sum of two infinities of the same sign is the infinity of that sign.

- The sum of an infinity and any finite value is equal to the infinity.

- The sum of two zeroes of opposite sign is positive zero.

- The sum of two zeroes of the same sign is the zero of that sign.

- The sum of a zero and a nonzero finite value is equal to the non-zero value.

- The sum of two nonzero finite values of the same magnitude and opposite sign is positive zero.

fadd (*cont.*)   *fadd* (*cont.*)

- In the remaining cases, where neither operand is an infinity, a zero, or NaN and the values have the same sign or have different magnitudes, the sum is computed and rounded to the nearest representable value using IEEE 754 round to nearest mode. If the magnitude is too large to represent as a float, we say the operation overflows; the result is then an infinity of appropriate sign. If the magnitude is too small to represent as a float, we say the operation underflows; the result is then a zero of appropriate sign.

The Java virtual machine requires support of gradual underflow as defined by IEEE 754. Despite the fact that overflow, underflow, or loss of precision may occur, execution of an *fadd* instruction never throws a runtime exception.

faload   *faload*

Operation   Load float from array

Format | *faload* |
                  |----------|

Forms   *faload* = 48 (0x30)

Operand   ..., *arrayref*, *index* ⇒
Stack   ..., *value*

Description   The *arrayref* must be of type reference and must refer to an array
                  whose components are of type float. The *index* must be of type
                  int. Both *arrayref* and *index* are popped from the operand stack.
                  The float *value* in the component of the array at *index* is retrieved
                  and pushed onto the operand stack.

Runtime   If *arrayref* is null, *faload* throws a NullPointerException.
Exceptions
                  Otherwise, if *index* is not within the bounds of the array referenced
                  by *arrayref*, the *faload* instruction throws an ArrayIndexOutOf-
                  BoundsException.

fastore   *fastore*

Operation   Store into `float` array

Format | *fastore* |

Forms   *fastore* = 81 (0x51)

Operand   ..., *arrayref*, *index*, *value* ⇒
Stack   ...

Description   The *arrayref* must be of type `reference` and must refer to an array whose components are of type `float`. The *index* must be of type `int`, and the *value* must be of type `float`. The *arrayref*, *index*, and *value* are popped from the operand stack. The `float` *value* undergoes value set conversion (§3.8.3), resulting in *value'*, and *value'* is stored as the component of the array indexed by *index*.

Runtime   If *arrayref* is `null`, *fastore* throws a `NullPointerException`.
Exceptions   Otherwise, if *index* is not within the bounds of the array referenced by *arrayref*, the *fastore* instruction throws an `ArrayIndexOutOf-BoundsException`.

fcmp<op>   *fcmp<op>*
fcmp<op>

Operation   Compare `float`

Format
fcmp<op>

Forms   *fcmpg* = 150 (0x96)
                  fcmpl = 149 (0x95)

Operand   ..., *value1*, *value2* ⇒
Stack   ..., *result*

Description   Both *value1* and *value2* must be of type `float`. The values are
                  popped from the operand stack and undergo value set conversion
                  (§3.8.3), resulting in *value1'* and *value2'*. A floating-point compari-
                  son is performed:

- If *value1'* is greater than *value2'*, the `int` value *1* is pushed onto
  the operand stack.

- Otherwise, if *value1'* is equal to *value2'*, the `int` value *0* is
  pushed onto the operand stack.

- Otherwise, if *value1'* is less than *value2'*, the `int` value *−1* is
  pushed onto the operand stack.

- Otherwise, at least one of *value1'* or *value2'* is NaN. The *fcmpg*
  instruction pushes the `int` value *1* onto the operand stack and
  the *fcmpl* instruction pushes the `int` value *−1* onto the operand
  stack.

Floating-point comparison is performed in accordance with IEEE
754. All values other than NaN are ordered, with negative infinity
less than all finite values and positive infinity greater than all finite
values. Positive zero and negative zero are considered equal.

fcmp<op> (*cont.*)   *fcmp<op>* (*cont.*)

Notes   The *fcmpg* and *fcmpl* instructions differ only in their treatment of a
                 comparison involving NaN. NaN is unordered, so any `float` com-
                 parison fails if either or both of its operands are NaN. With both
                 fcmpg and *fcmpl* available, any `float` comparison may be com-
                 piled to push the same *result* onto the operand stack whether the
                 comparison fails on non-NaN values or fails because it encountered
                 a NaN. For more information, see Section 7.5, "More Control
                 Examples."

fconst_<f>   *fconst_<f>*

Operation   Push `float`

Format
fconst_<f>

Forms   *fconst_0* = 11 (0xb)
                  fconst_1 = 12 (0xc)
                  fconst_2 = 13 (0xd)

Operand   ... ⇒
Stack   ..., *<f>*

Description   Push the `float` constant *<f>* (*0.0*, *1.0*, or *2.0*) onto the operand stack.

fdiv   *fdiv*

Operation   Divide `float`

Format

fdiv

Forms   *fdiv* = 110 (0x6e)

Operand   ..., *value1, value2* ⇒
Stack   ..., *result*

Description   Both *value1* and *value2* must be of type `float`. The values are
popped from the operand stack and undergo value set conversion
(§3.8.3), resulting in *value1′* and *value2′*. The `float` *result* is
value1′ / *value2′*. The *result* is pushed onto the operand stack.

The result of an *fdiv* instruction is governed by the rules of IEEE
arithmetic:

- If either *value1′* or *value2′* is NaN, the result is NaN.

- If neither *value1′* nor *value2′* is NaN, the sign of the result is
positive if both values have the same sign, negative if the values
have different signs.

- Division of an infinity by an infinity results in NaN.

- Division of an infinity by a finite value results in a signed infinity,
with the sign-producing rule just given.

- Division of a finite value by an infinity results in a signed zero,
with the sign-producing rule just given.

- Division of a zero by a zero results in NaN; division of zero by any
other finite value results in a signed zero, with the sign-producing
rule just given.

- Division of a nonzero finite value by a zero results in a signed
infinity, with the sign-producing rule just given.

fdiv (*cont.*)   *fdiv* (*cont.*)

- In the remaining cases, where neither operand is an infinity, a zero, or NaN, the quotient is computed and rounded to the nearest float using IEEE 754 round to nearest mode. If the magnitude is too large to represent as a float, we say the operation overflows; the result is then an infinity of appropriate sign. If the magnitude is too small to represent as a float, we say the operation underflows; the result is then a zero of appropriate sign.

The Java virtual machine requires support of gradual underflow as defined by IEEE 754. Despite the fact that overflow, underflow, division by zero, or loss of precision may occur, execution of an *fdiv* instruction never throws a runtime exception.

fload *fload*

Operation   Load `float` from local variable

Format

fload
index

Forms   *fload* = 23 (0x17)

Operand   ... $\Rightarrow$
Stack   ..., *value*

Description   The *index* is an unsigned byte that must be an index into the local variable array of the current frame (§3.6). The local variable at *index* must contain a `float`. The *value* of the local variable at *index* is pushed onto the operand stack.

Notes   The *fload* opcode can be used in conjunction with the *wide* instruction to access a local variable using a two-byte unsigned index.

fload_<n>   fload_<n>

Operation   Load float from local variable

Format

fload_<n>

Forms   fload_0 = 34 (0x22)
                 fload_1 = 35 (0x23)
                 fload_2 = 36 (0x24)
                 fload_3 = 37 (0x25)

Operand   ... ⇒
Stack   ..., value

Description The <n> must be an index into the local variable array of the current frame (§3.6). The local variable at <n> must contain a float. The value of the local variable at <n> is pushed onto the operand stack.

Notes   Each of the fload_<n> instructions is the same as fload with an index of <n>, except that the operand <n> is implicit.

fmul *fmul*

Operation   Multiply `float`

Format

fmul

Forms   *fmul* = 106 (0x6a)

Operand   ..., *value1*, *value2* $\Rightarrow$
Stack   ..., *result*

Description Both *value1* and *value2* must be of type `float`. The values are
popped from the operand stack and undergo value set conversion
(§3.8.3), resulting in *value1'* and *value2'*. The `float` *result* is
value1' * *value2'*. The *result* is pushed onto the operand stack.

The result of an *fmul* instruction is governed by the rules of IEEE
arithmetic:

- If either *value1'* or *value2'* is NaN, the result is NaN.

- If neither *value1'* nor *value2'* is NaN, the sign of the result is
  positive if both values have the same sign, and negative if the
  values have different signs.

- Multiplication of an infinity by a zero results in NaN.

- Multiplication of an infinity by a finite value results in a signed
  infinity, with the sign-producing rule just given.

- In the remaining cases, where neither an infinity nor NaN is
  involved, the product is computed and rounded to the nearest
  representable value using IEEE 754 round to nearest mode. If the
  magnitude is too large to represent as a `float`, we say the operation overflows; the result is then an infinity of appropriate sign.
  If the magnitude is too small to represent as a `float`, we say the
  operation underflows; the result is then a zero of appropriate sign.

fmul (*cont.*)   *fmul* (*cont.*)

The Java virtual machine requires support of gradual underflow as defined by IEEE 754. Despite the fact that overflow, underflow, or loss of precision may occur, execution of an *fmul* instruction never throws a runtime exception.

fneg *fneg*

Operation Negate `float`

Format

fneg

Forms *fneg* = 118 (0x76)

Operand ..., *value* ⇒
Stack ..., *result*

Description The *value* must be of type `float`. It is popped from the operand stack and undergoes value set conversion (§3.8.3), resulting in *value′*. The `float` *result* is the arithmetic negation of *value′*. This *result* is pushed onto the operand stack.

For `float` values, negation is not the same as subtraction from zero. If x is +0.0, then 0.0−x equals +0.0, but −x equals −0.0. Unary minus merely inverts the sign of a `float`.

Special cases of interest:

- If the operand is NaN, the result is NaN (recall that NaN has no sign).

- If the operand is an infinity, the result is the infinity of opposite sign.

- If the operand is a zero, the result is the zero of opposite sign.

frem   *frem*

Operation   Remainder `float`

Format | *frem* |

Forms   *frem* = 114 (0x72)

Operand   ..., *value1*, *value2* $\Rightarrow$
Stack   ..., *result*

Description   Both *value1* and *value2* must be of type `float`. The values are
                  popped from the operand stack and undergo value set conversion
                  (§3.8.3), resulting in *value1'* and *value2'*. The *result* is calculated
                  and pushed onto the operand stack as a `float`.

                  The *result* of an *frem* instruction is not the same as that of the so-
                  called remainder operation defined by IEEE 754. The IEEE 754
                  "remainder" operation computes the remainder from a rounding
                  division, not a truncating division, and so its behavior is *not* analo-
                  gous to that of the usual integer remainder operator. Instead, the
                  Java virtual machine defines *frem* to behave in a manner analogous
                  to that of the Java virtual machine integer remainder instructions
                  (*irem* and *lrem*); this may be compared with the C library function
                  `fmod`.

                  The result of an *frem* instruction is governed by these rules:

                  • If either *value1'* or *value2'* is NaN, the result is NaN.

                  • If neither *value1'* nor *value2'* is NaN, the sign of the result equals
                    the sign of the dividend.

                  • If the dividend is an infinity or the divisor is a zero or both, the
                    result is NaN.

                  • If the dividend is finite and the divisor is an infinity, the result
                    equals the dividend.

frem (*cont.*)   *frem* (*cont.*)

- If the dividend is a zero and the divisor is finite, the result equals the dividend.

- In the remaining cases, where neither operand is an infinity, a zero, or NaN, the floating-point remainder *result* from a dividend *value1'* and a divisor *value2'* is defined by the mathematical relation $result = value1' - (value2' * q)$, where q is an integer that is negative only if *value1'* / *value2'* is negative and positive only if *value1'* / *value2'* is positive, and whose magnitude is as large as possible without exceeding the magnitude of the true mathematical quotient of *value1'* and *value2'*.

Despite the fact that division by zero may occur, evaluation of an *frem* instruction never throws a runtime exception. Overflow, underflow, or loss of precision cannot occur.

Notes   The IEEE 754 remainder operation may be computed by the library routine `Math.IEEEremainder`.

freturn   *freturn*

Operation   Return float from method

Format

freturn

Forms   *freturn* = 174 (0xae)

Operand   ..., *value* ⇒
Stack   [empty]

Description   The current method must have return type float. The *value* must
be of type float. If the current method is a synchronized
method, the monitor acquired or reentered on invocation of the
method is released or exited (respectively) as if by execution of a
monitorexit instruction. If no exception is thrown, *value* is popped
from the operand stack of the current frame (§3.6) and undergoes
value set conversion (§3.8.3), resulting in *value'*. The *value'* is
pushed onto the operand stack of the frame of the invoker. Any
other values on the operand stack of the current method are discarded.

The interpreter then returns control to the invoker of the method,
reinstating the frame of the invoker.

Runtime   If the current method is a synchronized method and the current
Exceptions   thread is not the owner of the monitor acquired or reentered on
invocation of the method, *freturn* throws an IllegalMonitor-
StateException. This can happen, for example, if a synchronized method contains a *monitorexit* instruction, but no
monitorenter instruction, on the object on which the method is synchronized.

Otherwise, if the virtual machine implementation enforces the rules
on structured use of locks described in §8.13 and if the first of those
rules is violated during invocation of the current method, then
freturn throws an IllegalMonitorStateException.

fstore *fstore*

Operation Store `float` into local variable

Format

fstore
index

Forms *fstore* = 56 (0x38)

Operand ..., *value* $\Rightarrow$
Stack ...

Description The *index* is an unsigned byte that must be an index into the local variable array of the current frame (§3.6). The *value* on the top of the operand stack must be of type `float`. It is popped from the operand stack and undergoes value set conversion (§3.8.3), resulting in *value'*. The value of the local variable at *index* is set to *value'*.

Notes The *fstore* opcode can be used in conjunction with the *wide* instruction to access a local variable using a two-byte unsigned index.

fstore_<n>

fstore_<n>

Operation   Store float into local variable

Format

fstore_<n>

Forms   *fstore_0* = 67 (0x43)
fstore_1 = 68 (0x44)
fstore_2 = 69 (0x45)
fstore_3 = 70 (0x46)

Operand   ..., *value* ⇒
Stack   ...

Description   The *<n>* must be an index into the local variable array of the current frame (§3.6). The *value* on the top of the operand stack must be of type float. It is popped from the operand stack and undergoes value set conversion (§3.8.3), resulting in *value'*. The value of the local variable at *<n>* is set to *value'*.

Notes   Each of the *fstore_<n>* is the same as *fstore* with an *index* of *<n>*, except that the operand *<n>* is implicit.

fsub *fsub*

Operation   Subtract float

Format

fsub

Forms   *fsub* = 102 (0x66)

Operand   ..., *value1, value2* ⇒
Stack   ..., *result*

Description   Both *value1* and *value2* must be of type float. The values are popped from the operand stack and undergo value set conversion (§3.8.3), resulting in *value1′* and *value2′*. The float *result* is *value1′* − *value2′*. The *result* is pushed onto the operand stack.

For float subtraction, it is always the case that a−b produces the same result as a+(−b). However, for the *fsub* instruction, subtraction from zero is not the same as negation, because if x is +0.0, then 0.0−x equals +0.0, but −x equals −0.0.

The Java virtual machine requires support of gradual underflow as defined by IEEE 754. Despite the fact that overflow, underflow, or loss of precision may occur, execution of an *fsub* instruction never throws a runtime exception.

getfield   *getfield*

Operation   Fetch field from object

Format

getfield
indexbyte1
indexbyte2

Forms   *getfield* = 180 (0xb4)

Operand   ..., *objectref* ⇒
Stack   ..., *value*

Description   The *objectref*, which must be of type `reference`, is popped from
                    the operand stack. The unsigned *indexbyte1* and *indexbyte2* are
                    used to construct an index into the runtime constant pool of the
                    current class (§3.6), where the value of the index is (*indexbyte1* <<
                    8) | *indexbyte2*. The runtime constant pool item at that index must
                    be a symbolic reference to a field (§5.1), which gives the name and
                    descriptor of the field as well as a symbolic reference to the class in
                    which the field is to be found. The referenced field is resolved
                    (§5.4.3.2). The *value* of the referenced field in *objectref* is fetched
                    and pushed onto the operand stack.

                    The class of *objectref* must not be an array. If the field is `protected`
                    (§4.6), and it is either a member of the current class or a member of
                    a superclass of the current class, then the class of *objectref* must be
                    either the current class or a subclass of the current class.

Linking   During resolution of the symbolic reference to the field, any of the
Exceptions   errors pertaining to field resolution documented in Section 5.4.3.2
                    can be thrown.

                    Otherwise, if the resolved field is a `static` field, *getfield* throws an
                    `IncompatibleClassChangeError`.

getfield (*cont.*)   *getfield* (*cont.*)

Runtime   Otherwise, if *objectref* is `null`, the *getfield* instruction throws a
Exception   `NullPointerException`.

Notes   The *getfield* instruction cannot be used to access the `length` field of
                   an array. The *arraylength* instruction is used instead.

getstatic   *getstatic*

Operation   Get static field from class

Format

getstatic
indexbyte1
indexbyte2

Forms   *getstatic* = 178 (0xb2)

Operand   ..., ⇒
Stack   ..., *value*

Description The unsigned *indexbyte1* and *indexbyte2* are used to construct an
                 index into the runtime constant pool of the current class (§3.6),
                 where the value of the index is (*indexbyte1* << 8) | *indexbyte2*. The
                 runtime constant pool item at that index must be a symbolic refer-
                 ence to a field (§5.1), which gives the name and descriptor of the
                 field as well as a symbolic reference to the class or interface in
                 which the field is to be found. The referenced field is resolved
                 (§5.4.3.2).

                 On successful resolution of the field, the class or interface that
                 declared the resolved field is initialized (§5.5) if that class or inter-
                 face has not already been initialized.

                 The *value* of the class or interface field is fetched and pushed onto
                 the operand stack.

Linking   During resolution of the symbolic reference to the class or interface
Exceptions   field, any of the exceptions pertaining to field resolution docu-
                 mented in Section 5.4.3.2 can be thrown.

                 Otherwise, if the resolved field is not a static (class) field or an
                 interface field, *getstatic* throws an IncompatibleClassChange-
                 Error.

getstatic (*cont.*)   *getstatic* (*cont.*)

Runtime   Otherwise, if execution of this *getstatic* instruction causes initial-
Exception   ization of the referenced class or interface, *getstatic* may throw an
                 Error as detailed in Section 2.17.5.

goto   *goto*

Operation   Branch always

Format

goto
branchbyte1
branchbyte2

Forms   *goto* = 167 (0xa7)

**Operand
Stack**   No change

Description   The unsigned bytes *branchbyte1* and *branchbyte2* are used to
                  construct a signed 16-bit *branchoffset*, where *branchoffset* is
                  (*branchbyte1* << 8) | *branchbyte2*. Execution proceeds at that offset
                  from the address of the opcode of this *goto* instruction. The target
                  address must be that of an opcode of an instruction within the
                  method that contains this *goto* instruction.

goto_w *goto_w*

Operation   Branch always (wide index)

Format

goto_w
branchbyte1
branchbyte2
branchbyte3
branchbyte4

Forms   *goto_w* = 200 (0xc8)

Operand   No change
Stack

Description   The unsigned bytes *branchbyte1*, *branchbyte2*, *branchbyte3*, and *branchbyte4* are used to construct a signed 32-bit *branchoffset*, where *branchoffset* is (*branchbyte1* << 24) | (*branchbyte2* << 16) | (*branchbyte3* << 8) | *branchbyte4*. Execution proceeds at that offset from the address of the opcode of this *goto_w* instruction. The target address must be that of an opcode of an instruction within the method that contains this *goto_w* instruction.

Notes   Although the *goto_w* instruction takes a 4-byte branch offset, other factors limit the size of a method to 65535 bytes (§4.10). This limit may be raised in a future release of the Java virtual machine.

i2b   *i2b*

Operation   Convert int to byte

Format

i2b

Forms   *i2b* = 145 (0x91)

Operand   ..., *value* ⇒
Stack   ..., *result*

Description The *value* on the top of the operand stack must be of type int. It is
                 popped from the operand stack, truncated to a byte, then sign-
                 extended to an int *result*. That *result* is pushed onto the operand
                 stack.

Notes   The *i2b* instruction performs a narrowing primitive conversion
                 (§2.6.3). It may lose information about the overall magnitude of
                 value. The *result* may also not have the same sign as *value*.

i2c *i2c*

Operation   Convert int to char

Format

i2c

Forms   *i2c* = 146 (0x92)

Operand   ..., *value* ⇒
Stack   ..., *result*

Description   The *value* on the top of the operand stack must be of type int. It is popped from the operand stack, truncated to char, then zero-extended to an int *result*. That *result* is pushed onto the operand stack.

Notes   The *i2c* instruction performs a narrowing primitive conversion (§2.6.3). It may lose information about the overall magnitude of *value*. The *result* (which is always positive) may also not have the same sign as *value*.

i2d   *i2d*

Operation	Convert int to double

Format

i2d

Forms   *i2d* = 135 (0x87)

Operand   ..., *value* ⇒
Stack   ..., *result*

Description   The *value* on the top of the operand stack must be of type int. It is
popped from the operand stack and converted to a double *result*.
The *result* is pushed onto the operand stack.

Notes   The *i2d* instruction performs a widening primitive conversion
(§2.6.2). Because all values of type int are exactly representable
by type double, the conversion is exact.

i2f   *i2f*

Operation   Convert int to float

Format

i2f

Forms   *i2f* = 134 (0x86)

Operand   ..., *value* $\Rightarrow$
Stack   ..., *result*

Description   The *value* on the top of the operand stack must be of type int. It is
                  popped from the operand stack and converted to the float *result*
                  using IEEE 754 round to nearest mode. The *result* is pushed onto
                  the operand stack.

Notes   The *i2f* instruction performs a widening primitive conversion
                  (§2.6.2), but may result in a loss of precision because values of type
                  float have only 24 significand bits.

i2l   *i2l*

Operation   Convert int to long

Format | *i2l* |

Forms   *i2l* = 133 (0x85)

Operand   ..., *value* ⇒
Stack   ..., *result*

Description   The *value* on the top of the operand stack must be of type int. It is popped from the operand stack and sign-extended to a long *result*. That *result* is pushed onto the operand stack.

Notes   The *i2l* instruction performs a widening primitive conversion (§2.6.2). Because all values of type int are exactly representable by type long, the conversion is exact.

i2s *i2s*

Operation   Convert `int` to `short`

Format

i2s

Forms   *i2s* = 147 (0x93)

Operand   ..., *value* ⇒
Stack   ..., *result*

Description   The *value* on the top of the operand stack must be of type `int`. It is popped from the operand stack, truncated to a `short`, then sign-extended to an `int` *result*. That *result* is pushed onto the operand stack.

Notes   The *i2s* instruction performs a narrowing primitive conversion (§2.6.3). It may lose information about the overall magnitude of *value*. The *result* may also not have the same sign as *value*.

iadd   *iadd*

Operation   Add int

Format

iadd

Forms   *iadd* = 96 (0x60)

Operand   ..., *value1*, *value2* $\Rightarrow$
Stack   ..., *result*

Description   Both *value1* and *value2* must be of type int. The values are popped from the operand stack. The int *result* is *value1* + *value2*. The *result* is pushed onto the operand stack.

The result is the 32 low-order bits of the true mathematical result in a sufficiently wide two's-complement format, represented as a value of type int. If overflow occurs, then the sign of the result may not be the same as the sign of the mathematical sum of the two values.

Despite the fact that overflow may occur, execution of an *iadd* instruction never throws a runtime exception.

iaload   *iaload*

Operation   Load int from array

Format

iaload

Forms   *iaload* = 46 (0x2e)

Operand   ..., *arrayref*, *index* $\Rightarrow$
Stack   ..., *value*

Description The *arrayref* must be of type `reference` and must refer to an array whose components are of type `int`. The *index* must be of type `int`. Both *arrayref* and *index* are popped from the operand stack. The `int` *value* in the component of the array at *index* is retrieved and pushed onto the operand stack.

Runtime   If *arrayref* is `null`, *iaload* throws a `NullPointerException`.
Exceptions
Otherwise, if *index* is not within the bounds of the array referenced by *arrayref*, the *iaload* instruction throws an `ArrayIndexOutOf-BoundsException`.

iand   *iand*

Operation   Boolean AND int

Format | iand |

Forms   *iand* = 126 (0x7e)

Operand   ..., *value1, value2* $\Rightarrow$
Stack   ..., *result*

Description Both *value1* and *value2* must be of type int. They are popped from
                 the operand stack. An int *result* is calculated by taking the bitwise
                 AND (conjunction) of *value1* and *value2*. The *result* is pushed onto
                 the operand stack.

iastore   *iastore*

Operation   Store into `int` array

Format

iastore

Forms   *iastore* = 79 (0x4f)

Operand   ..., *arrayref*, *index*, *value* ⇒

Stack   ...

Description The *arrayref* must be of type `reference` and must refer to an array whose components are of type `int`. Both *index* and *value* must be of type `int`. The *arrayref*, *index*, and *value* are popped from the operand stack. The `int` *value* is stored as the component of the array indexed by *index*.

Runtime   If *arrayref* is `null`, *iastore* throws a `NullPointerException`.

Exceptions   Otherwise, if *index* is not within the bounds of the array referenced by *arrayref*, the *iastore* instruction throws an `ArrayIndexOutOf-BoundsException`.

iconst_<i>   *iconst_<i>*
iconst_<i>

Operation   Push int constant

Format

iconst_<i>

Forms   *iconst_m1* = 2 (0x2)
                   iconst_0 = 3 (0x3)
                   iconst_1 = 4 (0x4)
                   iconst_2 = 5 (0x5)
                   iconst_3 = 6 (0x6)
                   iconst_4 = 7 (0x7)
                   iconst_5 = 8 (0x8)

Operand   ... $\Rightarrow$
Stack   ..., *<i>*

Description   Push the int constant *<i>* (*−1, 0, 1, 2, 3, 4* or *5*) onto the operand
                   stack.

Notes   Each of this family of instructions is equivalent to *bipush <i>* for
                   the respective value of *<i>*, except that the operand *<i>* is implicit.

idiv *idiv*

Operation	Divide `int`

Format

idiv

Forms *idiv* = 108 (0x6c)

Operand Stack ..., *value1*, *value2* $\Rightarrow$
..., *result*

Description Both *value1* and *value2* must be of type `int`. The values are popped from the operand stack. The `int` *result* is the value of the Java programming language expression *value1* / *value2*. The *result* is pushed onto the operand stack.

An `int` division rounds towards 0; that is, the quotient produced for `int` values in *n/d* is an `int` value *q* whose magnitude is as large as possible while satisfying $|d \cdot q| \le |n|$. Moreover, *q* is positive when $|n| \ge |d|$ and *n* and *d* have the same sign, but *q* is negative when $|n| \ge |d|$ and *n* and *d* have opposite signs.

There is one special case that does not satisfy this rule: if the dividend is the negative integer of largest possible magnitude for the `int` type, and the divisor is *−1*, then overflow occurs, and the result is equal to the dividend. Despite the overflow, no exception is thrown in this case.

Runtime Exception If the value of the divisor in an `int` division is 0, *idiv* throws an `ArithmeticException`.

if_acmp<cond>   *if_acmp<cond>*

Operation   Branch if `reference` comparison succeeds

Format

| *if_acmp<cond>* |
| *branchbyte1* |
| *branchbyte2* |

Forms   *if_acmpeq* = 165 (0xa5)
                  if_acmpne = 166 (0xa6)

Operand   ..., *value1*, *value2* ⇒
Stack   ...

Description   Both *value1* and *value2* must be of type `reference`. They are both
                  popped from the operand stack and compared. The results of the
                  comparison are as follows:

                  • *eq*   succeeds if and only if *value1* = *value2*

                  • *ne*   succeeds if and only if *value1* ≠ *value2*

                  If the comparison succeeds, the unsigned *branchbyte1* and
                  branchbyte2 are used to construct a signed 16-bit offset, where the
                  offset is calculated to be (*branchbyte1* << 8) | *branchbyte2*. Execu-
                  tion then proceeds at that offset from the address of the opcode of
                  this *if_acmp<cond>* instruction. The target address must be that of
                  an opcode of an instruction within the method that contains this
                  if_acmp<cond> instruction.

                  Otherwise, if the comparison fails, execution proceeds at the
                  address of the instruction following this *if_acmp<cond>* instruc-
                  tion.

if_icmp<cond>   *if_icmp<cond>*

Operation   Branch if `int` comparison succeeds

Format

if_icmp<cond>
branchbyte1
branchbyte2

Forms   *if_icmpeq* = 159 (0x9f)
if_icmpne = 160 (0xa0)
if_icmplt = 161 (0xa1)
if_icmpge = 162 (0xa2)
if_icmpgt = 163 (0xa3)
if_icmple = 164 (0xa4)

Operand   ..., *value1*, *value2* $\Rightarrow$
Stack   ...

Description Both *value1* and *value2* must be of type `int`. They are both popped
from the operand stack and compared. All comparisons are signed.
The results of the comparison are as follows:

- *eq*   succeeds if and only if *value1* = *value2*

- *ne*   succeeds if and only if *value1* ≠ *value2*

- *lt*   succeeds if and only if *value1* < *value2*

- *le*   succeeds if and only if *value1* ≤ *value2*

- *gt*   succeeds if and only if *value1* > *value2*

- *ge*   succeeds if and only if *value1* ≥ *value2*

if_icmp<cond> (*cont.*)   *if_icmp<cond>* (*cont.*)

If the comparison succeeds, the unsigned *branchbyte1* and *branchbyte2* are used to construct a signed 16-bit offset, where the offset is calculated to be (*branchbyte1* << 8) | *branchbyte2*. Execution then proceeds at that offset from the address of the opcode of this *if_icmp<cond>* instruction. The target address must be that of an opcode of an instruction within the method that contains this *if_icmp<cond>* instruction.

Otherwise, execution proceeds at the address of the instruction following this *if_icmp<cond>* instruction.

if<cond>   *if<cond>*

Operation   Branch if int comparison with zero succeeds

Format

if<cond>
branchbyte1
branchbyte2

Forms   *ifeq* = 153 (0x99)
             ifne = 154 (0x9a)
             iflt = 155 (0x9b)
             ifge = 156 (0x9c)
             ifgt = 157 (0x9d)
             ifle = 158 (0x9e)

Operand   ..., *value* $\Rightarrow$
Stack   ...

Description   The *value* must be of type int. It is popped from the operand stack and compared against zero. All comparisons are signed. The results of the comparisons are as follows:

- *eq*   succeeds if and only if *value* = 0

- *ne*   succeeds if and only if *value* ≠ 0

- *lt*   succeeds if and only if *value* < 0

- *le*   succeeds if and only if *value* ≤ 0

- *gt*   succeeds if and only if *value* > 0

- *ge*   succeeds if and only if *value* ≥ 0

if<cond> (*cont.*)   *if<cond>* (*cont.*)

If the comparison succeeds, the unsigned *branchbyte1* and *branchbyte2* are used to construct a signed 16-bit offset, where the offset is calculated to be (*branchbyte1* << 8) | *branchbyte2*. Execution then proceeds at that offset from the address of the opcode of this *if<cond>* instruction. The target address must be that of an opcode of an instruction within the method that contains this *if<cond>* instruction.

Otherwise, execution proceeds at the address of the instruction following this *if<cond>* instruction.

ifnonnull   *ifnonnull*

Operation   Branch if `reference` not `null`

Format

ifnonnull
branchbyte1
branchbyte2

Forms   *ifnonnull* = 199 (0xc7)

Operand   ..., *value* ⇒
Stack   ...

Description The *value* must be of type `reference`. It is popped from the oper-
and stack. If *value* is not `null`, the unsigned *branchbyte1* and
branchbyte2 are used to construct a signed 16-bit offset, where the
offset is calculated to be (*branchbyte1* << 8) | *branchbyte2*. Execu-
tion then proceeds at that offset from the address of the opcode of
this *ifnonnull* instruction. The target address must be that of an
opcode of an instruction within the method that contains this *ifnonnull* instruction.

Otherwise, execution proceeds at the address of the instruction following this *ifnonnull* instruction.

ifnull   *ifnull*

Operation   Branch if `reference` is `null`

Format

ifnull
branchbyte1
branchbyte2

Forms   *ifnull* = 198 (0xc6)

Operand   ..., *value* ⇒
Stack   ...

Description   The *value* must of type `reference`. It is popped from the operand
                   stack. If *value* is `null`, the unsigned *branchbyte1* and *branchbyte2*
                   are used to construct a signed 16-bit offset, where the offset is cal-
                   culated to be (*branchbyte1* << 8) | *branchbyte2*. Execution then pro-
                   ceeds at that offset from the address of the opcode of this *ifnull*
                   instruction. The target address must be that of an opcode of an
                   instruction within the method that contains this *ifnull* instruction.

                   Otherwise, execution proceeds at the address of the instruction fol-
                   lowing this *ifnull* instruction.

iinc   *iinc*

Operation	Increment local variable by constant

Format

iinc
index
const

Forms   *iinc* = 132 (0x84)

Operand Stack   No change

Description   The *index* is an unsigned byte that must be an index into the local variable array of the current frame (§3.6). The *const* is an immediate signed byte. The local variable at *index* must contain an int. The value *const* is first sign-extended to an int, and then the local variable at *index* is incremented by that amount.

Notes   The *iinc* opcode can be used in conjunction with the *wide* instruction to access a local variable using a two-byte unsigned index and to increment it by a two-byte immediate value.

iload   *iload*

Operation   Load int from local variable

Format

iload
index

Forms   *iload* = 21 (0x15)

Operand   ... ⇒
Stack   ..., *value*

Description   The *index* is an unsigned byte that must be an index into the local
                   variable array of the current frame (§3.6). The local variable at
                   index must contain an int. The *value* of the local variable at *index*
                   is pushed onto the operand stack.

Notes   The *iload* opcode can be used in conjunction with the *wide* instruc-
                   tion to access a local variable using a two-byte unsigned index.

iload_<n> *iload_<n>*

Operation   Load int from local variable

Format

iload_<n>

Forms   *iload_0* = 26 (0x1a)
iload_1 = 27 (0x1b)
iload_2 = 28 (0x1c)
iload_3 = 29 (0x1d)

Operand   ... $\Rightarrow$
Stack   ..., *value*

Description The *<n>* must be an index into the local variable array of the current frame (§3.6). The local variable at *<n>* must contain an int. The *value* of the local variable at *<n>* is pushed onto the operand stack.

Notes   Each of the *iload_<n>* instructions is the same as *iload* with an *index* of *<n>*, except that the operand *<n>* is implicit.

imul   *imul*

Operation   *Multiply* int

Format
imul

Forms   *imul* = 104 (0x68)

Operand   ..., *value1*, *value2* ⇒
Stack   ..., *result*

Description   Both *value1* and *value2* must be of type int. The values are popped from the operand stack. The int *result* is *value1* * *value2*. The *result* is pushed onto the operand stack.

The result is the 32 low-order bits of the true mathematical result in a sufficiently wide two's-complement format, represented as a value of type int. If overflow occurs, then the sign of the result may not be the same as the sign of the mathematical sum of the two values.

Despite the fact that overflow may occur, execution of an *imul* instruction never throws a runtime exception.

ineg   *ineg*

Operation   Negate `int`

Format

ineg

Forms   *ineg* = 116 (0x74)

Operand   ..., *value* $\Rightarrow$
Stack   ..., *result*

Description   The *value* must be of type `int`. It is popped from the operand stack. The `int` *result* is the arithmetic negation of *value*, *−value*. The *result* is pushed onto the operand stack.

For `int` values, negation is the same as subtraction from zero. Because the Java virtual machine uses two's-complement representation for integers and the range of two's-complement values is not symmetric, the negation of the maximum negative `int` results in that same maximum negative number. Despite the fact that overflow has occurred, no exception is thrown.

For all `int` values x, −x equals (~x) + 1.

instanceof   *instanceof*

Operation   Determine if object is of given type

Format

instanceof
indexbyte1
indexbyte2

Forms   *instanceof* = 193 (0xc1)

Operand   ..., *objectref* ⇒
Stack   ..., *result*

Description   The *objectref*, which must be of type reference, is popped from
                  the operand stack. The unsigned *indexbyte1* and *indexbyte2* are
                  used to construct an index into the runtime constant pool of the cur-
                  rent class (§3.6), where the value of the index is (*indexbyte1* << 8) |
                  indexbyte2. The runtime constant pool item at the index must be a
                  symbolic reference to a class, array, or interface type. The named
                  class, array, or interface type is resolved (§5.4.3.1).

                  If *objectref* is not null and is an instance of the resolved class or
                  array or implements the resolved interface, the *instanceof* instruc-
                  tion pushes an int *result* of 1 as an int on the operand stack. Other-
                  wise, it pushes an int *result* of 0.

                  The following rules are used to determine whether an *objectref* that
                  is not null is an instance of the resolved type: If *S* is the class of
                  the object referred to by *objectref* and *T* is the resolved class, array,
                  or interface type, *instanceof* determines whether *objectref* is an
                  instance of *T* as follows:

                  • If *S* is an ordinary (nonarray) class, then:

                     • If *T* is a class type, then *S* must be the same class (§2.8.1) as
                       T or a subclass of *T*.

                     • If *T* is an interface type, then *S* must implement (§2.13) inter-
                       face *T*.

instanceof (*cont.*)   *instanceof* (*cont.*)

- If S is an interface type, then:

  - If *T* is a class type, then *T* must be Object (§2.4.7).

  - If *T* is an interface type, then *T* must be the same interface as *S*, or a superinterface of *S* (§2.13.2).

- If *S* is a class representing the array type *SC*[], that is, an array of components of type *SC*, then:

  - If *T* is a class type, then *T* must be Object (§2.4.7).

  - If *T* is an array type *TC*[], that is, an array of components of type *TC*, then one of the following must be true:

    - *TC* and *SC* are the same primitive type (§2.4.1).

    - *TC* and *SC* are reference types (§2.4.6), and type *SC* can be cast to *TC* by these runtime rules.

  - If *T* is an interface type, *T* must be one of the interfaces implemented by arrays (§2.15).

Linking Exceptions   During resolution of symbolic reference to the class, array, or interface type, any of the exceptions documented in Section 5.4.3.1 can be thrown.

Notes   The *instanceof* instruction is very similar to the *checkcast* instruction. It differs in its treatment of null, its behavior when its test fails (*checkcast* throws an exception, *instanceof* pushes a result code), and its effect on the operand stack.

invokeinterface   *invokeinterface*

Operation   Invoke interface method

Format

invokeinterface
indexbyte1
indexbyte2
count
0

Forms   *invokeinterface* = 185 (0xb9)

Operand   ..., *objectref*, [*arg1*, [*arg2* ...]] $\Rightarrow$
Stack
                 ...

Description The unsigned *indexbyte1* and *indexbyte2* are used to construct an
                 index into the runtime constant pool of the current class (§3.6),
                 where the value of the index is (*indexbyte1* << 8) | *indexbyte2*.
                 The runtime constant pool item at that index must be a symbolic
                 reference to an interface method (§5.1), which gives the name and
                 descriptor (§4.3.3) of the interface method as well as a symbolic
                 reference to the interface in which the interface method is to be
                 found. The named interface method is resolved (§5.4.3.4). The
                 interface method must not be an instance initialization method
                 (§3.9) or the class or interface initialization method (§3.9).

                 The *count* operand is an unsigned byte that must not be zero. The
                 objectref must be of type `reference` and must be followed on the
                 operand stack by *nargs* argument values, where the number, type,
                 and order of the values must be consistent with the descriptor of the
                 resolved interface method. The value of the fourth operand byte
                 must always be zero.

                 Let *C* be the class of *objectref*. The actual method to be invoked is
                 selected by the following lookup procedure:

invokeinterface (*cont.*) *invokeinterface* (*cont.*)

- If *C* contains a declaration for an instance method with the same name and descriptor as the resolved method, then this is the method to be invoked, and the lookup procedure terminates.

- Otherwise, if *C* has a superclass, this same lookup procedure is performed recursively using the direct superclass of *C*; the method to be invoked is the result of the recursive invocation of this lookup procedure.

- Otherwise, an `AbstractMethodError` is raised.

If the method is `synchronized`, the monitor associated with *object-ref* is acquired or reentered.

If the method is not `native`, the *nargs* argument values and *object-ref* are popped from the operand stack. A new frame is created on the Java virtual machine stack for the method being invoked. The *objectref* and the argument values are consecutively made the values of local variables of the new frame, with *objectref* in local variable *0*, *arg1* in local variable *1* (or, if *arg1* is of type `long` or `double`, in local variables *1* and *2*), and so on. Any argument value that is of a floating-point type undergoes value set conversion (§3.8.3) prior to being stored in a local variable. The new frame is then made current, and the Java virtual machine `pc` is set to the opcode of the first instruction of the method to be invoked. Execution continues with the first instruction of the method.

If the method is `native` and the platform-dependent code that implements it has not yet been bound (§5.6) into the Java virtual machine, that is done. The *nargs* argument values and *objectref* are popped from the operand stack and are passed as parameters to the code that implements the method. Any argument value that is of a floating-point type undergoes value set conversion (§3.8.3) prior to being passed as a parameter. The parameters are passed and the code is invoked in an implementation-dependent manner. When the platform-dependent code returns:

invokeinterface (cont.)   *invokeinterface* (cont.)

invokeinterface (cont.)

- If the native method is synchronized, the monitor associated with *objectref* is released or exited as if by execution of a *monitor-exit* instruction.

- If the native method returns a value, the return value of the platform-dependent code is converted in an implementation-dependent way to the return type of the native method and pushed onto the operand stack.

Linking Exceptions   During resolution of the symbolic reference to the interface method, any of the exceptions documented in §5.4.3.4 can be thrown.

Runtime Exceptions   Otherwise, if *objectref* is null, the *invokeinterface* instruction throws a NullPointerException.

Otherwise, if the class of *objectref* does not implement the resolved interface, *invokeinterface* throws an IncompatibleClassChange-Error.

Otherwise, if no method matching the resolved name and descriptor is selected, *invokeinterface* throws an AbstractMethodError.

Otherwise, if the selected method is not public, *invokeinterface* throws an IllegalAccessError.

Otherwise, if the selected method is abstract, *invokeinterface* throws an AbstractMethodError.

Otherwise, if the selected method is native and the code that implements the method cannot be bound, *invokeinterface* throws an UnsatisfiedLinkError.

invokeinterface (*cont.*) *invokeinterface* (*cont.*)

invokeinterface (*cont.*)

Notes   The *count* operand of the *invokeinterface* instruction records a measure of the number of argument values, where an argument value of type `long` or type `double` contributes two units to the *count* value and an argument of any other type contributes one unit. This information can also be derived from the descriptor of the selected method. The redundancy is historical.

The fourth operand byte exists to reserve space for an additional operand used in certain of Sun's implementations, which replace the *invokeinterface* instruction by a specialized pseudo-instruction at run time. It must be retained for backwards compatibility.

The *nargs* argument values and *objectref* are not one-to-one with the first *nargs* + *1* local variables. Argument values of types `long` and `double` must be stored in two consecutive local variables, thus more than *nargs* local variables may be required to pass *nargs* argument values to the invoked method.

invokespecial   *invokespecial*

Operation   Invoke instance method; special handling for superclass, private, and instance initialization method invocations

Format

invokespecial
indexbyte1
indexbyte2

Forms   *invokespecial* = 183 (0xb7)

Operand   ..., *objectref*, [*arg1*, [*arg2* ...]] $\Rightarrow$
Stack   ...

Description   The unsigned *indexbyte1* and *indexbyte2* are used to construct an index into the runtime constant pool of the current class (§3.6), where the value of the index is (*indexbyte1* << 8) | *indexbyte2*. The runtime constant pool item at that index must be a symbolic reference to a method (§5.1), which gives the name and descriptor (§4.3.3) of the method as well as a symbolic reference to the class in which the method is to be found. The named method is resolved (§5.4.3.3). Finally, if the resolved method is `protected` (§4.6), and it is either a member of the current class or a member of a super-class of the current class, then the class of *objectref* must be either the current class or a subclass of the current class.

Next, the resolved method is selected for invocation unless all of the following conditions are true:

- The `ACC_SUPER` flag (see Table 4.1, "Class access and property modifiers") is set for the current class.

- The class of the resolved method is a superclass of the current class.

- The resolved method is not an instance initialization method (§3.9).

invokespecial (*cont.*) *invokespecial* (*cont.*)

If the above conditions are true, the actual method to be invoked is selected by the following lookup procedure. Let *C* be the direct superclass of the current class:

- If *C* contains a declaration for an instance method with the same name and descriptor as the resolved method, then this method will be invoked. The lookup procedure terminates.

- Otherwise, if *C* has a superclass, this same lookup procedure is performed recursively using the direct superclass of *C*. The method to be invoked is the result of the recursive invocation of this lookup procedure.

- Otherwise, an `AbstractMethodError` is raised.

The *objectref* must be of type `reference` and must be followed on the operand stack by *nargs* argument values, where the number, type, and order of the values must be consistent with the descriptor of the selected instance method.

If the method is `synchronized`, the monitor associated with *objectref* is acquired or reentered.

If the method is not `native`, the *nargs* argument values and *objectref* are popped from the operand stack. A new frame is created on the Java virtual machine stack for the method being invoked. The *objectref* and the argument values are consecutively made the values of local variables of the new frame, with *objectref* in local variable *0*, *arg1* in local variable *1* (or, if *arg1* is of type `long` or `double`, in local variables *1* and *2*), and so on. Any argument value that is of a floating-point type undergoes value set conversion (§3.8.3) prior to being stored in a local variable. The new frame is then made current, and the Java virtual machine `pc` is set to the opcode of the first instruction of the method to be invoked. Execution continues with the first instruction of the method.

invokespecial (*cont.*)   *invokespecial* (*cont.*)

If the method is `native` and the platform-dependent code that implements it has not yet been bound (§5.6) into the Java virtual machine, that is done. The *nargs* argument values and *objectref* are popped from the operand stack and are passed as parameters to the code that implements the method. Any argument value that is of a floating-point type undergoes value set conversion (§3.8.3) prior to being passed as a parameter. The parameters are passed and the code is invoked in an implementation-dependent manner. When the platform-dependent code returns, the following take place:

- If the `native` method is `synchronized`, the monitor associated with *objectref* is released or exited as if by execution of a *monitor-exit* instruction.

- If the `native` method returns a value, the return value of the platform-dependent code is converted in an implementation-dependent way to the return type of the `native` method and pushed onto the operand stack.

Linking Exceptions   During resolution of the symbolic reference to the method, any of the exceptions pertaining to method resolution documented in Section 5.4.3.3 can be thrown.

Otherwise, if the resolved method is an instance initialization method, and the class in which it is declared is not the class symbolically referenced by the instruction, a `NoSuchMethodError` is thrown.

Otherwise, if the resolved method is a class (`static`) method, the *invokespecial* instruction throws an `IncompatibleClassChange-Error`.

Otherwise, if no method matching the resolved name and descriptor is selected, *invokespecial* throws an `AbstractMethodError`.

Otherwise, if the selected method is `abstract`, *invokespecial* throws an `AbstractMethodError`.

invokespecial (*cont.*)   *invokespecial* (*cont.*)

Runtime   Otherwise, if *objectref* is `null`, the *invokespecial* instruction throws
Exceptions   a `NullPointerException`.

Otherwise, if the selected method is `native` and the code that implements the method cannot be bound, *invokespecial* throws an `UnsatisfiedLinkError`.

Notes   The difference between the *invokespecial* and the *invokevirtual* instructions is that *invokevirtual* invokes a method based on the class of the object. The *invokespecial* instruction is used to invoke instance initialization methods (§3.9) as well as `private` methods and methods of a superclass of the current class.

The *invokespecial* instruction was named *invokenonvirtual* prior to Sun's JDK release 1.0.2.

The *nargs* argument values and *objectref* are not one-to-one with the first *nargs* + *1* local variables. Argument values of types `long` and `double` must be stored in two consecutive local variables, thus more than *nargs* local variables may be required to pass *nargs* argument values to the invoked method.

invokestatic   *invokestatic*
invokestatic

Operation   Invoke a class (`static`) method

Format

invokestatic
indexbyte1
indexbyte2

Forms   *invokestatic* = 184 (0xb8)

Operand   ..., [arg1, [arg2 ...]] ⇒
Stack   ...

Description   The unsigned *indexbyte1* and *indexbyte2* are used to construct an
index into the runtime constant pool of the current class (§3.6),
where the value of the index is (*indexbyte1* << 8) | *indexbyte2*.
The runtime constant pool item at that index must be a symbolic
reference to a method (§5.1), which gives the name and descriptor
(§4.3.3) of the method as well as a symbolic reference to the class
in which the method is to be found. The named method is resolved
(§5.4.3.3). The method must not be the class or interface initialization method (§3.9). It must be `static`, and therefore cannot be
`abstract`.

On successful resolution of the method, the class that declared the
resolved field is initialized (§5.5) if that class has not already been
initialized.

The operand stack must contain *nargs* argument values, where the
number, type, and order of the values must be consistent with the
descriptor of the resolved method.

If the method is `synchronized`, the monitor associated with the
resolved class is acquired or reentered.

invokestatic (*cont.*)   *invokestatic* (*cont.*)

If the method is not `native`, the *nargs* argument values are popped from the operand stack. A new frame is created on the Java virtual machine stack for the method being invoked. The *nargs* argument values are consecutively made the values of local variables of the new frame, with *arg1* in local variable *0* (or, if *arg1* is of type `long` or `double`, in local variables *0* and *1*) and so on. Any argument value that is of a floating-point type undergoes value set conversion (§3.8.3) prior to being stored in a local variable. The new frame is then made current, and the Java virtual machine `pc` is set to the opcode of the first instruction of the method to be invoked. Execution continues with the first instruction of the method.

If the method is `native` and the platform-dependent code that implements it has not yet been bound (§5.6) into the Java virtual machine, that is done. The *nargs* argument values are popped from the operand stack and are passed as parameters to the code that implements the method. Any argument value that is of a floating-point type undergoes value set conversion (§3.8.3) prior to being passed as a parameter. The parameters are passed and the code is invoked in an implementation-dependent manner. When the platform-dependent code returns, the following take place:

- If the `native` method is `synchronized`, the monitor associated with the resolved class is released or exited as if by execution of a *monitorexit* instruction.

- If the `native` method returns a value, the return value of the platform-dependent code is converted in an implementation-dependent way to the return type of the `native` method and pushed onto the operand stack.

Linking Exceptions   During resolution of the symbolic reference to the method, any of the exceptions pertaining to method resolution documented in Section 5.4.3.3 can be thrown.

invokestatic (*cont.*)   *invokestatic* (*cont.*)

Otherwise, if the resolved method is an instance method, the *invokestatic* instruction throws an `IncompatibleClassChange-Error`.

Runtime   Otherwise, if execution of this *invokestatic* instruction causes ini-
Exceptions   tialization of the referenced class, *invokestatic* may throw an `Error` as detailed in Section 2.17.5.

Otherwise, if the resolved method is `native` and the code that implements the method cannot be bound, *invokestatic* throws an `UnsatisfiedLinkError`.

Notes   The *nargs* argument values are not one-to-one with the first *nargs* local variables. Argument values of types `long` and `double` must be stored in two consecutive local variables, thus more than *nargs* local variables may be required to pass *nargs* argument values to the invoked method.

invokevirtual *invokevirtual*

Operation   Invoke instance method; dispatch based on class

Format

| invokevirtual |
| indexbyte1 |
| indexbyte2 |

Forms   *invokevirtual* = 182 (0xb6)

Operand   ..., *objectref*, [*arg1*, [*arg2* ...]] ⇒
Stack   ...

Description   The unsigned *indexbyte1* and *indexbyte2* are used to construct an index into the runtime constant pool of the current class (§3.6), where the value of the index is (*indexbyte1* << 8) | *indexbyte2*. The runtime constant pool item at that index must be a symbolic reference to a method (§5.1), which gives the name and descriptor (§4.3.3) of the method as well as a symbolic reference to the class in which the method is to be found. The named method is resolved (§5.4.3.3). The method must not be an instance initialization method (§3.9) or the class or interface initialization method (§3.9). Finally, if the resolved method is protected (§4.6), and it is either a member of the current class or a member of a superclass of the current class, then the class of *objectref* must be either the current class or a subclass of the current class.

Let *C* be the class of *objectref*. The actual method to be invoked is selected by the following lookup procedure:

- If *C* contains a declaration for an instance method with the same name and descriptor as the resolved method, and the resolved method is accessible from *C*, then this is the method to be invoked, and the lookup procedure terminates.

invokevirtual (*cont.*)   *invokevirtual* (*cont.*)

- Otherwise, if *C* has a superclass, this same lookup procedure is performed recursively using the direct superclass of *C*; the method to be invoked is the result of the recursive invocation of this lookup procedure.

- Otherwise, an `AbstractMethodError` is raised.

The *objectref* must be followed on the operand stack by *nargs* argument values, where the number, type, and order of the values must be consistent with the descriptor of the selected instance method.

If the method is `synchronized`, the monitor associated with *objectref* is acquired or reentered.

If the method is not `native`, the *nargs* argument values and *objectref* are popped from the operand stack. A new frame is created on the Java virtual machine stack for the method being invoked. The *objectref* and the argument values are consecutively made the values of local variables of the new frame, with *objectref* in local variable *0*, *arg1* in local variable *1* (or, if *arg1* is of type `long` or `double`, in local variables *1* and 2), and so on. Any argument value that is of a floating-point type undergoes value set conversion (§3.8.3) prior to being stored in a local variable. The new frame is then made current, and the Java virtual machine `pc` is set to the opcode of the first instruction of the method to be invoked. Execution continues with the first instruction of the method.

If the method is `native` and the platform-dependent code that implements it has not yet been bound (§5.6) into the Java virtual machine, that is done. The *nargs* argument values and *objectref* are popped from the operand stack and are passed as parameters to the code that implements the method. Any argument value that is of a floating-point type undergoes value set conversion (§3.8.3) prior to being passed as a parameter. The parameters are passed and the code is invoked in an implementation-dependent manner. When the platform-dependent code returns, the following take place:

invokevirtual (*cont.*)   *invokevirtual* (*cont.*)

- If the `native` method is `synchronized`, the monitor associated with *objectref* is released or exited as if by execution of a *monitorexit* instruction.

- If the `native` method returns a value, the return value of the platform-dependent code is converted in an implementation-dependent way to the return type of the `native` method and pushed onto the operand stack.

Linking Exceptions   During resolution of the symbolic reference to the method, any of the exceptions pertaining to method resolution documented in Section 5.4.3.3 can be thrown.

Otherwise, if the resolved method is a class (`static`) method, the *invokevirtual* instruction throws an `IncompatibleClassChange-Error`.

Runtime Exceptions   Otherwise, if *objectref* is `null`, the *invokevirtual* instruction throws a `NullPointerException`.

Otherwise, if no method matching the resolved name and descriptor is selected, *invokevirtual* throws an `AbstractMethodError`.

Otherwise, if the selected method is `abstract`, *invokevirtual* throws an `AbstractMethodError`.

Otherwise, if the selected method is `native` and the code that implements the method cannot be bound, *invokevirtual* throws an `UnsatisfiedLinkError`.

Notes   The *nargs* argument values and *objectref* are not one-to-one with the first *nargs* + *1* local variables. Argument values of types `long` and `double` must be stored in two consecutive local variables, thus more than *nargs* local variables may be required to pass *nargs* argument values to the invoked method.

ior   *ior*

Operation   Boolean OR int

Format | *ior* |

Forms   *ior* = 128 (0x80)

Operand   ..., *value1, value2* $\Rightarrow$
Stack   ..., *result*

Description   Both *value1* and *value2* must be of type int. They are popped from
                  the operand stack. An int *result* is calculated by taking the bitwise
                  inclusive OR of *value1* and *value2*. The *result* is pushed onto the
                  operand stack.

irem *irem*

Operation   Remainder `int`

Format

irem

Forms   *irem* = 112 (0x70)

Operand   ..., *value1, value2* ⇒
Stack   ..., *result*

Description   Both *value1* and *value2* must be of type `int`. The values are popped from the operand stack. The `int` *result* is *value1* − (*value1* / *value2*) * *value2*. The *result* is pushed onto the operand stack.

The result of the *irem* instruction is such that `(a/b)*b + (a%b)` is equal to `a`. This identity holds even in the special case in which the dividend is the negative `int` of largest possible magnitude for its type and the divisor is −1 (the remainder is 0). It follows from this rule that the result of the remainder operation can be negative only if the dividend is negative and can be positive only if the dividend is positive. Moreover, the magnitude of the result is always less than the magnitude of the divisor.

Runtime   If the value of the divisor for an `int` remainder operator is 0, *irem*
Exception throws an `ArithmeticException`.

ireturn   *ireturn*

Operation   Return int from method

Format

ireturn

Forms   *ireturn* = 172 (0xac)

Operand   ..., *value* ⇒
Stack   [empty]

Description   The current method must have return type boolean, byte, short, char, or int. The *value* must be of type int. If the current method is a synchronized method, the monitor acquired or reentered on invocation of the method is released or exited (respectively) as if by execution of a *monitorexit* instruction. If no exception is thrown, *value* is popped from the operand stack of the current frame (§3.6) and pushed onto the operand stack of the frame of the invoker. Any other values on the operand stack of the current method are discarded.

The interpreter then returns control to the invoker of the method, reinstating the frame of the invoker.

Runtime   If the current method is a synchronized method and the current
Exceptions   thread is not the owner of the monitor acquired or reentered on invocation of the method, *ireturn* throws an IllegalMonitor-StateException. This can happen, for example, if a synchronized method contains a *monitorexit* instruction, but no *monitorenter* instruction, on the object on which the method is synchronized.

Otherwise, if the virtual machine implementation enforces the rules on structured use of locks described in Section 8.13 and if the first of those rules is violated during invocation of the current method, then *ireturn* throws an IllegalMonitorStateException.

ishl

Operation   Shift left `int`

Format

ishl

Forms   *ishl* = 120 (0x78)

**Operand
Stack**   ..., *value1*, *value2* $\Rightarrow$
..., *result*

Description   Both *value1* and *value2* must be of type `int`. The values are popped from the operand stack. An `int` *result* is calculated by shifting *value1* left by *s* bit positions, where *s* is the value of the low 5 bits of *value2*. The *result* is pushed onto the operand stack.

Notes   This is equivalent (even if overflow occurs) to multiplication by 2 to the power *s*. The shift distance actually used is always in the range 0 to 31, inclusive, as if *value2* were subjected to a bitwise logical AND with the mask value 0x1f.

ishr   *ishr*

Operation	Arithmetic shift right `int`

Format

ishr

Forms   *ishr* = 122 (0x7a)

Operand   ..., *value1*, *value2* $\Rightarrow$
Stack   ..., *result*

Description Both *value1* and *value2* must be of type `int`. The values are popped from the operand stack. An `int` *result* is calculated by shifting *value1* right by *s* bit positions, with sign extension, where *s* is the value of the low 5 bits of *value2*. The *result* is pushed onto the operand stack.

Notes   The resulting value is $\lfloor value1 / 2^s \rfloor$, where *s* is *value2* & 0x1f. For nonnegative *value1*, this is equivalent to truncating `int` division by 2 to the power *s*. The shift distance actually used is always in the range 0 to 31, inclusive, as if *value2* were subjected to a bitwise logical AND with the mask value 0x1f.

istore *istore*

Operation   Store `int` into local variable

Format

istore
index

Forms   *istore* = 54 (0x36)

Operand   ..., *value* ⇒
Stack   ...

Description   The *index* is an unsigned byte that must be an index into the local variable array of the current frame (§3.6). The *value* on the top of the operand stack must be of type `int`. It is popped from the operand stack, and the value of the local variable at *index* is set to *value*.

Notes   The *istore* opcode can be used in conjunction with the *wide* instruction to access a local variable using a two-byte unsigned index.

istore_<n> *istore_<n>*

Operation Store `int` into local variable

Format

istore_<n>

Forms *istore_0* = 59 (0x3b)
istore_1 = 60 (0x3c)
istore_2 = 61 (0x3d)
istore_3 = 62 (0x3e)

Operand ..., *value* ⇒
Stack ...

Description The *<n>* must be an index into the local variable array of the current frame (§3.6). The *value* on the top of the operand stack must be of type `int`. It is popped from the operand stack, and the value of the local variable at *<n>* is set to *value*.

Notes Each of the *istore_<n>* instructions is the same as *istore* with an *index* of *<n>*, except that the operand *<n>* is implicit.

isub $\qquad$ *isub*

Operation $\quad$ Subtract `int`

Format

isub

Forms $\quad$ *isub* = 100 (0x64)

Operand
Stack $\quad$ ..., *value1*, *value2* $\Rightarrow$
$\quad\quad\quad\quad$ ..., *result*

Description $\quad$ Both *value1* and *value2* must be of type `int`. The values are popped from the operand stack. The `int` *result* is *value1* − *value2*. The *result* is pushed onto the operand stack.

For `int` subtraction, a − b produces the same result as a + (−b). For `int` values, subtraction from zero is the same as negation.

The result is the 32 low-order bits of the true mathematical result in a sufficiently wide two's-complement format, represented as a value of type `int`. If overflow occurs, then the sign of the result may not be the same as the sign of the mathematical sum of the two values.

Despite the fact that overflow may occur, execution of an *isub* instruction never throws a runtime exception.

iushr   *iushr*

Operation   Logical shift right `int`

Format

iushr

Forms   *iushr* = 124 (0x7c)

Operand   ..., *value1*, *value2* ⇒
Stack   ..., *result*

Description Both *value1* and *value2* must be of type `int`. The values are popped
                 from the operand stack. An `int` *result* is calculated by shifting
                 value1 right by s bit positions, with zero extension, where s is the
                 value of the low 5 bits of *value2*. The *result* is pushed onto the
                 operand stack.

Notes   If *value1* is positive and s is *value2* & 0x1f, the result is the same as
                 that of *value1* >> s; if *value1* is negative, the result is equal to the
                 value of the expression (*value1* >> s) + (2 << ~s). The addition of
                 the (2 << ~s) term cancels out the propagated sign bit. The shift
                 distance actually used is always in the range 0 to 31, inclusive.

ixor   *ixor*

Operation   Boolean XOR `int`

Format

ixor

Forms   *ixor* = 130 (0x82)

Operand   ..., *value1, value2* $\Rightarrow$
Stack   ..., *result*

Description   Both *value1* and *value2* must be of type `int`. They are popped from the operand stack. An `int` *result* is calculated by taking the bitwise exclusive OR of *value1* and *value2*. The *result* is pushed onto the operand stack.

jsr   *jsr*

Operation   Jump subroutine

Format
jsr
branchbyte1
branchbyte2

Forms   *jsr* = 168 (0xa8)

Operand   ... $\Rightarrow$
Stack   ..., *address*

Description The *address* of the opcode of the instruction immediately following
                 this *jsr* instruction is pushed onto the operand stack as a value of
                 type returnAddress. The unsigned *branchbyte1* and *branchbyte2*
                 are used to construct a signed 16-bit offset, where the offset is
                 (*branchbyte1* << 8) | *branchbyte2*. Execution proceeds at that offset
                 from the address of this *jsr* instruction. The target address must be
                 that of an opcode of an instruction within the method that contains
                 this *jsr* instruction.

Notes   The *jsr* instruction is used with the *ret* instruction in the implemen-
                 tation of the finally clauses of the Java programming language
                 (see Section 7.13, "Compiling finally"). Note that *jsr* pushes the
                 address onto the operand stack and *ret* gets it out of a local variable.
                 This asymmetry is intentional.

jsr_w   *jsr_w*
jsr_w

Operation   Jump subroutine (wide index)

Format

jsr_w
branchbyte1
branchbyte2
branchbyte3
branchbyte4

Forms   *jsr_w* = 201 (0xc9)

Operand   ... ⇒
Stack   ..., *address*

Description   The *address* of the opcode of the instruction immediately following
this *jsr_w* instruction is pushed onto the operand stack as a value of
type `returnAddress`. The unsigned *branchbyte1*, *branchbyte2*,
branchbyte3, and *branchbyte4* are used to construct a signed 32-bit
offset, where the offset is (*branchbyte1* << 24) | (*branchbyte2* <<
16) | (*branchbyte3* << 8) | *branchbyte4*. Execution proceeds at that
offset from the address of this *jsr_w* instruction. The target address
must be that of an opcode of an instruction within the method that
contains this *jsr_w* instruction.

Notes   The *jsr_w* instruction is used with the *ret* instruction in the implementation of the `finally` clauses of the Java programming lan-
guage (see Section 7.13, "Compiling `finally`"). Note that *jsr_w*
pushes the address onto the operand stack and *ret* gets it out of a
local variable. This asymmetry is intentional.

Although the *jsr_w* instruction takes a 4-byte branch offset, other
factors limit the size of a method to 65535 bytes (§4.10). This limit
may be raised in a future release of the Java virtual machine.

l2d   *l2d*

Operation	Convert `long` to `double`

Format

l2d

Forms   *l2d* = 138 (0x8a)

Operand   ..., *value* ⇒
Stack   ..., *result*

Description The *value* on the top of the operand stack must be of type `long`. It is popped from the operand stack and converted to a `double` *result* using IEEE 754 round to nearest mode. The *result* is pushed onto the operand stack.

Notes   The *l2d* instruction performs a widening primitive conversion (§2.6.2) that may lose precision because values of type `double` have only 53 significand bits.

l2f   *l2f*

Operation   Convert `long` to `float`

Format

l2f

Forms   *l2f* = 137 (0x89)

Operand   ..., *value* $\Rightarrow$
Stack   ..., *result*

Description The *value* on the top of the operand stack must be of type `long`. It
is popped from the operand stack and converted to a `float` *result*
using IEEE 754 round to nearest mode. The *result* is pushed onto
the operand stack.

Notes   The *l2f* instruction performs a widening primitive conversion
(§2.6.2) that may lose precision because values of type `float` have
only 24 significand bits.

l2i   *l2i*

Operation   Convert long to int

Format

l2i

Forms   *l2i* = 136 (0x88)

Operand   ..., *value* ⟹
Stack   ..., *result*

Description The *value* on the top of the operand stack must be of type long. It is popped from the operand stack and converted to an int *result* by taking the low-order 32 bits of the long value and discarding the high-order 32 bits. The *result* is pushed onto the operand stack.

Notes   The *l2i* instruction performs a narrowing primitive conversion (§2.6.3). It may lose information about the overall magnitude of *value*. The *result* may also not have the same sign as *value*.

ladd   *ladd*

Operation   Add long

Format | *ladd* |

Forms   *ladd* = 97 (0x61)

Operand   ..., *value1*, *value2* ⇒
Stack   ..., *result*

Description   Both *value1* and *value2* must be of type long. The values are popped from the operand stack. The long *result* is *value1* + *value2*. The *result* is pushed onto the operand stack.

The result is the 64 low-order bits of the true mathematical result in a sufficiently wide two's-complement format, represented as a value of type long. If overflow occurs, the sign of the result may not be the same as the sign of the mathematical sum of the two values.

Despite the fact that overflow may occur, execution of an *ladd* instruction never throws a runtime exception.

laload   *laload*

Operation   Load long from array

Format | *laload* |

Forms   *laload* = 47 (0x2f)

Operand   ..., *arrayref*, *index* $\Rightarrow$
Stack   ..., *value*

Description   The *arrayref* must be of type reference and must refer to an array
                  whose components are of type long. The *index* must be of type
                  int. Both *arrayref* and *index* are popped from the operand stack.
                  The long *value* in the component of the array at *index* is retrieved
                  and pushed onto the operand stack.

Runtime   If *arrayref* is null, *laload* throws a NullPointerException.
Exceptions
                  Otherwise, if *index* is not within the bounds of the array referenced
                  by *arrayref*, the *laload* instruction throws an ArrayIndexOutOf-
                  BoundsException.

land   *land*

Operation   Boolean AND `long`

Format

land

Forms   *land* = 127 (0x7f)

Operand   ..., *value1*, *value2* $\Rightarrow$
Stack   ..., *result*

Description   Both *value1* and *value2* must be of type `long`. They are popped from the operand stack. A `long` *result* is calculated by taking the bitwise AND of *value1* and *value2*. The *result* is pushed onto the operand stack.

lastore   *lastore*

Operation   Store into long array

Format

lastore

Forms   *lastore* = 80 (0x50)

Operand   ..., *arrayref*, *index*, *value* $\Rightarrow$
Stack   ...

Description   The *arrayref* must be of type reference and must refer to an array
whose components are of type long. The *index* must be of type
int, and *value* must be of type long. The *arrayref*, *index*, and
value are popped from the operand stack. The long *value* is stored
as the component of the array indexed by *index*.

Runtime   If *arrayref* is null, *lastore* throws a NullPointerException.
Exceptions
Otherwise, if *index* is not within the bounds of the array referenced
by *arrayref*, the *lastore* instruction throws an ArrayIndexOutOf-
BoundsException.

lcmp *lcmp*

Operation   Compare `long`

Format

lcmp

Forms   *lcmp* = 148 (0x94)

Operand   ..., *value1*, *value2* $\Rightarrow$
Stack   ..., *result*

Description Both *value1* and *value2* must be of type `long`. They are both popped from the operand stack, and a signed integer comparison is performed. If *value1* is greater than *value2*, the `int` value 1 is pushed onto the operand stack. If *value1* is equal to *value2*, the `int` value 0 is pushed onto the operand stack. If *value1* is less than *value2*, the `int` value −1 is pushed onto the operand stack.

lconst_<l>   *lconst_<l>*

Operation   Push long constant

Format | *lconst_<l>* |

Forms   *lconst_0* = 9 (0x9)
lconst_1 = 10 (0xa)

Operand   ... $\Rightarrow$
Stack   ..., *<l>*

Description   Push the long constant *<l>* (*0* or *1*) onto the operand stack.

ldc   *ldc*

Operation   Push item from runtime constant pool

Format

ldc
index

Forms   *ldc* = 18 (0x12)

Operand   ... $\Rightarrow$
Stack   ..., *value*

Description   The *index* is an unsigned byte that must be a valid index into the runtime constant pool of the current class (§3.6). The runtime constant pool entry at *index* either must be a runtime constant of type int or float, or must be a symbolic reference to a string literal (§5.1).

If the runtime constant pool entry is a runtime constant of type int or float, the numeric *value* of that runtime constant is pushed onto the operand stack as an int or float, respectively.

Otherwise, the runtime constant pool entry must be a reference to an instance of class String representing a string literal (§5.1). A reference to that instance, *value*, is pushed onto the operand stack.

Notes   The *ldc* instruction can only be used to push a value of type float taken from the float value set (§3.3.2) because a constant of type float in the constant pool (§4.4.4) must be taken from the float value set.

ldc_w   *ldc_w*

Operation   Push item from runtime constant pool (wide index)

Format

ldc_w
indexbyte1
indexbyte2

Forms   *ldc_w* = 19 (0x13)

Operand   ... ⇒
Stack   ..., *value*

Description The unsigned *indexbyte1* and *indexbyte2* are assembled into an
                 unsigned 16-bit index into the runtime constant pool of the current
                 class (§3.6), where the value of the index is calculated as
                 (*indexbyte1* << 8) | *indexbyte2*. The index must be a valid index
                 into the runtime constant pool of the current class. The runtime
                 constant pool entry at the index either must be a runtime constant
                 of type `int` or `float`, or must be a symbolic reference to a string
                 literal (§5.1).

                 If the runtime constant pool entry is a runtime constant of type `int`
                 or `float`, the numeric *value* of that runtime constant is pushed onto
                 the operand stack as an `int` or `float`, respectively.

                 Otherwise, the runtime constant pool entry must be a reference to
                 an instance of class `String` representing a string literal (§5.1). A
                 `reference` to that instance, *value*, is pushed onto the operand
                 stack.

Notes   The *ldc_w* instruction is identical to the *ldc* instruction except for
                 its wider runtime constant pool index.

                 The *ldc_w* instruction can only be used to push a value of type
                 `float` taken from the float value set (§3.3.2) because a constant of
                 type `float` in the constant pool (§4.4.4) must be taken from the
                 float value set.

ldc2_w *ldc2_w*

Operation   Push long or double from runtime constant pool (wide index)

Format

ldc2_w
indexbyte1
indexbyte2

Forms   *ldc2_w* = 20 (0x14)

Operand   ... ⇒
Stack   ..., *value*

Description   The unsigned *indexbyte1* and *indexbyte2* are assembled into an unsigned 16-bit index into the runtime constant pool of the current class (§3.6), where the value of the index is calculated as (*indexbyte1* << 8) | *indexbyte2*. The index must be a valid index into the runtime constant pool of the current class. The runtime constant pool entry at the index must be a runtime constant of type long or double (§5.1). The numeric *value* of that runtime constant is pushed onto the operand stack as a long or double, respectively.

Notes   Only a wide-index version of the *ldc2_w* instruction exists; there is no *ldc2* instruction that pushes a long or double with a single-byte index.

The *ldc2_w* instruction can only be used to push a value of type double taken from the double value set (§3.3.2) because a constant of type double in the constant pool (§4.4.5) must be taken from the double value set.

ldiv   *ldiv*

Operation   Divide long

Format

ldiv

Forms   *ldiv* = 109 (0x6d)

Operand   ..., *value1*, *value2* $\Rightarrow$
Stack   ..., *result*

Description   Both *value1* and *value2* must be of type long. The values are popped from the operand stack. The long *result* is the value of the Java programming language expression *value1* / *value2*. The *result* is pushed onto the operand stack.

A long division rounds towards 0; that is, the quotient produced for long values in *n* / *d* is a long value *q* whose magnitude is as large as possible while satisfying $|d \cdot q| \le |n|$. Moreover, *q* is positive when $|n| \ge |d|$ and *n* and *d* have the same sign, but *q* is negative when $|n| \ge |d|$ and *n* and *d* have opposite signs.

There is one special case that does not satisfy this rule: if the dividend is the negative integer of largest possible magnitude for the long type and the divisor is −1, then overflow occurs and the result is equal to the dividend; despite the overflow, no exception is thrown in this case.

Runtime   If the value of the divisor in a long division is 0, *ldiv* throws an
Exception   ArithmeticException.

lload   *lload*

Operation   Load long from local variable

Format

lload
index

Forms   *lload* = 22 (0x16)

Operand   ... $\Rightarrow$
Stack   ..., *value*

Description   The *index* is an unsigned byte. Both *index* and *index* + 1 must be indices into the local variable array of the current frame (§3.6). The local variable at *index* must contain a long. The *value* of the local variable at *index* is pushed onto the operand stack.

Notes   The *lload* opcode can be used in conjunction with the *wide* instruction to access a local variable using a two-byte unsigned index.

lload_<n>   *lload_<n>*

Operation   Load long from local variable

Format

lload_<n>

Forms   *lload_0* = 30 (0x1e)
                lload_1 = 31 (0x1f)
                lload_2 = 32 (0x20)
                lload_3 = 33 (0x21)

Operand   ... ⇒
Stack   ..., *value*

Description Both *<n>* and *<n> + 1* must be indices into the local variable array
                of the current frame (§3.6). The local variable at *<n>* must contain
                a long. The *value* of the local variable at *<n>* is pushed onto the
                operand stack.

Notes   Each of the *lload_<n>* instructions is the same as *lload* with an
                index of *<n>*, except that the operand *<n>* is implicit.

lmul *lmul*

Operation   Multiply `long`

Format

lmul

Forms   *lmul* = 105 (0x69)

Operand   ..., *value1*, *value2* $\Rightarrow$
Stack   ..., *result*

Description   Both *value1* and *value2* must be of type `long`. The values are popped from the operand stack. The `long` *result* is *value1* * *value2*. The *result* is pushed onto the operand stack.

The result is the 64 low-order bits of the true mathematical result in a sufficiently wide two's-complement format, represented as a value of type `long`. If overflow occurs, the sign of the result may not be the same as the sign of the mathematical sum of the two values.

Despite the fact that overflow may occur, execution of an *lmul* instruction never throws a runtime exception.

lneg   *lneg*

Operation   Negate long

Format

lneg

Forms   *lneg* = 117 (0x75)

Operand   ..., *value* $\Rightarrow$
Stack   ..., *result*

Description   The *value* must be of type long. It is popped from the operand
stack. The long *result* is the arithmetic negation of *value*, *−value*.
The *result* is pushed onto the operand stack.

For long values, negation is the same as subtraction from zero.
Because the Java virtual machine uses two's-complement representation for integers and the range of two's-complement values is not
symmetric, the negation of the maximum negative long results in
that same maximum negative number. Despite the fact that overflow has occurred, no exception is thrown.

For all long values x, −x equals (~x) + 1.

lookupswitch *lookupswitch*

Operation   Access jump table by key match and jump

Format

lookupswitch
<0-3 byte pad>
defaultbyte1
defaultbyte2
defaultbyte3
defaultbyte4
npairs1
npairs2
npairs3
npairs4
match-offset pairs...

Forms   *lookupswitch* = 171 (0xab)

Operand   ..., *key* ⇒
Stack   ...

Description   A *lookupswitch* is a variable-length instruction. Immediately after the *lookupswitch* opcode, between zero and three null bytes (zeroed bytes, not the null object) are inserted as padding. The number of null bytes is chosen so that the *defaultbyte1* begins at an address that is a multiple of four bytes from the start of the current method (the opcode of its first instruction). Immediately after the padding follow a series of signed 32-bit values: *default*, *npairs*, and then *npairs* pairs of signed 32-bit values. The *npairs* must be greater than or equal to 0. Each of the *npairs* pairs consists of an int *match* and a signed 32-bit *offset*. Each of these signed 32-bit values is constructed from four unsigned bytes as (*byte1* << 24) | (*byte2* << 16) | (*byte3* << 8) | *byte4*.

lookupswitch (*cont.*)   *lookupswitch* (*cont.*)

The table *match-offset* pairs of the *lookupswitch* instruction must be sorted in increasing numerical order by *match*.

The *key* must be of type `int` and is popped from the operand stack. The *key* is compared against the *match* values. If it is equal to one of them, then a target address is calculated by adding the corresponding *offset* to the address of the opcode of this *lookupswitch* instruction. If the *key* does not match any of the *match* values, the target address is calculated by adding *default* to the address of the opcode of this *lookupswitch* instruction. Execution then continues at the target address.

The target address that can be calculated from the offset of each *match-offset* pair, as well as the one calculated from *default*, must be the address of an opcode of an instruction within the method that contains this *lookupswitch* instruction.

Notes   The alignment required of the 4-byte operands of the *lookupswitch* instruction guarantees 4-byte alignment of those operands if and only if the method that contains the *lookupswitch* is positioned on a 4-byte boundary.

The *match-offset* pairs are sorted to support lookup routines that are quicker than linear search.

lor *lor*

Operation   Boolean OR long

Format

lor

Forms   *lor* = 129 (0x81)

Operand   ..., *value1*, *value2* $\Rightarrow$
Stack   ..., *result*

Description   Both *value1* and *value2* must be of type long. They are popped from the operand stack. A long *result* is calculated by taking the bitwise inclusive OR of *value1* and *value2*. The *result* is pushed onto the operand stack.

lrem   *lrem*

Operation   Remainder long

Format

lrem

Forms   *lrem* = 113 (0x71)

Operand   ..., *value1*, *value2* $\Rightarrow$
Stack   ..., *result*

Description   Both *value1* and *value2* must be of type long. The values are popped from the operand stack. The long *result* is *value1* − (*value1* / *value2*) ∗ *value2*. The *result* is pushed onto the operand stack.

The result of the *lrem* instruction is such that (a/b)∗b + (a%b) is equal to a. This identity holds even in the special case in which the dividend is the negative long of largest possible magnitude for its type and the divisor is −1 (the remainder is 0). It follows from this rule that the result of the remainder operation can be negative only if the dividend is negative and can be positive only if the dividend is positive; moreover, the magnitude of the result is always less than the magnitude of the divisor.

Runtime   If the value of the divisor for a long remainder operator is 0, *lrem*
Exception   throws an ArithmeticException.

lreturn   *lreturn*

Operation   Return long from method

Format

lreturn

Forms   *lreturn* = 173 (0xad)

Operand   ..., *value* ⇒
Stack   [empty]

Description   The current method must have return type long. The *value* must be of type long. If the current method is a synchronized method, the monitor acquired or reentered on invocation of the method is released or exited (respectively) as if by execution of a *monitorexit* instruction. If no exception is thrown, *value* is popped from the operand stack of the current frame (§3.6) and pushed onto the operand stack of the frame of the invoker. Any other values on the operand stack of the current method are discarded.

The interpreter then returns control to the invoker of the method, reinstating the frame of the invoker.

Runtime   If the current method is a synchronized method and the current
Exceptions   thread is not the owner of the monitor acquired or reentered on invocation of the method, *lreturn* throws an IllegalMonitorStateException. This can happen, for example, if a synchronized method contains a *monitorexit* instruction, but no *monitorenter* instruction, on the object on which the method is synchronized.

Otherwise, if the virtual machine implementation enforces the rules on structured use of locks described in Section 8.13 and if the first of those rules is violated during invocation of the current method, then *lreturn* throws an IllegalMonitorStateException.

lshl   *lshl*

Operation   Shift left long

Format

lshl

Forms   *lshl* = 121 (0x79)

Operand   ..., *value1*, *value2* $\Rightarrow$
Stack   ..., *result*

Description The *value1* must be of type long, and *value2* must be of type int. The values are popped from the operand stack. A long *result* is calculated by shifting *value1* left by *s* bit positions, where *s* is the low 6 bits of *value2*. The *result* is pushed onto the operand stack.

Notes   This is equivalent (even if overflow occurs) to multiplication by 2 to the power *s*. The shift distance actually used is therefore always in the range 0 to 63, inclusive, as if *value2* were subjected to a bitwise logical AND with the mask value 0x3f.

lshr *lshr*

Operation   Arithmetic shift right `long`

Format

lshr

Forms   *lshr* = 123 (0x7b)

Operand   ..., *value1*, *value2* $\Rightarrow$
Stack   ..., *result*

Description   The *value1* must be of type `long`, and *value2* must be of type `int`. The values are popped from the operand stack. A `long` *result* is calculated by shifting *value1* right by *s* bit positions, with sign extension, where *s* is the value of the low 6 bits of *value2*. The *result* is pushed onto the operand stack.

Notes   The resulting value is $\lfloor value1 / 2^s \rfloor$, where *s* is *value2* & 0x3f. For nonnegative *value1*, this is equivalent to truncating `long` division by 2 to the power `s`. The shift distance actually used is therefore always in the range 0 to 63, inclusive, as if *value2* were subjected to a bitwise logical AND with the mask value 0x3f.

lstore   *lstore*

Operation   Store long into local variable

Format

lstore
index

Forms   *lstore* = 55 (0x37)

Operand   ..., *value* $\Rightarrow$
Stack   ...

Description   The *index* is an unsigned byte. Both *index* and *index* + 1 must be indices into the local variable array of the current frame (§3.6). The *value* on the top of the operand stack must be of type long. It is popped from the operand stack, and the local variables at *index* and *index* + 1 are set to *value*.

Notes   The *lstore* opcode can be used in conjunction with the *wide* instruction to access a local variable using a two-byte unsigned index.

lstore_<n> *lstore_<n>*

Operation   Store long into local variable

Format

lstore_<n>

Forms   *lstore_0* = 63 (0x3f)
lstore_1 = 64 (0x40)
lstore_2 = 65 (0x41)
lstore_3 = 66 (0x42)

Operand   ..., *value* $\Rightarrow$
Stack   ...

Description   Both *<n>* and *<n> + 1* must be indices into the local variable array of the current frame (§3.6). The *value* on the top of the operand stack must be of type long. It is popped from the operand stack, and the local variables at *<n>* and *<n> + 1* are set to *value*.

Notes   Each of the *lstore_<n>* instructions is the same as *lstore* with an *index* of *<n>*, except that the operand *<n>* is implicit.

lsub   *lsub*

Operation   Subtract long

Format

lsub

Forms   *lsub* = 101 (0x65)

Operand   ..., *value1*, *value2* $\Rightarrow$
Stack   ..., *result*

Description   Both *value1* and *value2* must be of type long. The values are
                  popped from the operand stack. The long *result* is *value1* − *value2*.
                  The *result* is pushed onto the operand stack.

                  For long subtraction, a−b produces the same result as a+(−b). For
                  long values, subtraction from zero is the same as negation.

                  The result is the 64 low-order bits of the true mathematical result in
                  a sufficiently wide two's-complement format, represented as a
                  value of type long. If overflow occurs, then the sign of the result
                  may not be the same as the sign of the mathematical sum of the two
                  values.

                  Despite the fact that overflow may occur, execution of an *lsub*
                  instruction never throws a runtime exception.

lushr *lushr*

Operation   Logical shift right `long`

Format

lushr

Forms   *lushr* = 125 (0x7d)

Operand   ..., *value1*, *value2* $\Rightarrow$
Stack   ..., *result*

Description   The *value1* must be of type `long`, and *value2* must be of type `int`. The values are popped from the operand stack. A `long` *result* is calculated by shifting *value1* right logically (with zero extension) by the amount indicated by the low 6 bits of *value2*. The *result* is pushed onto the operand stack.

Notes   If *value1* is positive and *s* is *value2* & 0x3f, the result is the same as that of *value1* >> *s*; if *value1* is negative, the result is equal to the value of the expression (*value1* >> *s*) + (2L << ~*s*). The addition of the (2L << ~*s*) term cancels out the propagated sign bit. The shift distance actually used is always in the range 0 to 63, inclusive.

lxor   *lxor*

Operation   Boolean XOR long

Format | *lxor* |

Forms   *lxor* = 131 (0x83)

Operand   ..., *value1*, *value2* $\Rightarrow$
Stack   ..., *result*

Description   Both *value1* and *value2* must be of type long. They are popped from the operand stack. A long *result* is calculated by taking the bitwise exclusive OR of *value1* and *value2*. The *result* is pushed onto the operand stack.

monitorenter *monitorenter*

Operation Enter monitor for object

Format

monitorenter

Forms *monitorenter* = 194 (0xc2)

Operand Stack ..., *objectref* ⇒

...

Description The *objectref* must be of type `reference`.

Each object has a monitor associated with it. The thread that executes *monitorenter* gains ownership of the monitor associated with *objectref*. If another thread already owns the monitor associated with *objectref*, the current thread waits until the object is unlocked, then tries again to gain ownership. If the current thread already owns the monitor associated with *objectref*, it increments a counter in the monitor indicating the number of times this thread has entered the monitor. If the monitor associated with *objectref* is not owned by any thread, the current thread becomes the owner of the monitor, setting the entry count of this monitor to 1.

Runtime Exception If *objectref* is `null`, *monitorenter* throws a `NullPointerException`.

Notes For detailed information about threads and monitors in the Java virtual machine, see Chapter 8, "Threads and Locks."

monitorenter (*cont.*)   *monitorenter* (*cont.*)
monitorenter (*cont.*)

A *monitorenter* instruction may be used with one or more *monitorexit* instructions to implement a `synchronized` statement in the Java programming language. The *monitorenter* and *monitorexit* instructions are not used in the implementation of `synchronized` methods, although they can be used to provide equivalent locking semantics; however, monitor entry on invocation of a `synchronized` method is handled implicitly by the Java virtual machine's method invocation instructions. See Section 7.14 for more information on the use of the *monitorenter* and *monitorexit* instructions.

The association of a monitor with an object may be managed in various ways that are beyond the scope of this specification. For instance, the monitor may be allocated and deallocated at the same time as the object. Alternatively, it may be dynamically allocated at the time when a thread attempts to gain exclusive access to the object and freed at some later time when no thread remains in the monitor for the object.

The synchronization constructs of the Java programming language require support for operations on monitors besides entry and exit. These include waiting on a monitor (`Object.wait`) and notifying other threads waiting on a monitor (`Object.notifyAll` and `Object.notify`). These operations are supported in the standard package `java.lang` supplied with the Java virtual machine. No explicit support for these operations appears in the instruction set of the Java virtual machine.

monitorexit *monitorexit*

Operation   Exit monitor for object

Format

```
monitorexit
```

Forms   *monitorexit* = 195 (0xc3)

Operand   ..., *objectref* ⇒
Stack   ...

Description   The *objectref* must be of type `reference`.

The current thread should be the owner of the monitor associated with the instance referenced by *objectref*. The thread decrements the counter indicating the number of times it has entered this monitor. If as a result the value of the counter becomes zero, the current thread releases the monitor. If the monitor associated with *objectref* becomes free, other threads that are waiting to acquire that monitor are allowed to attempt to do so.

Runtime Exceptions   If *objectref* is `null`, *monitorexit* throws a `NullPointerException`.

Otherwise, if the current thread is not the owner of the monitor, *monitorexit* throws an `IllegalMonitorStateException`.

Otherwise, if the virtual machine implementation enforces the rules on structured use of locks described in Section 8.13 and if the second of those rules is violated by the execution of this *monitorexit* instruction, then *monitorexit* throws an `IllegalMonitorState-Exception`.

Notes   For detailed information about threads and monitors in the Java virtual machine, see Chapter 8, "Threads and Locks."

monitorexit (*cont.*)   *monitorexit* (*cont.*)

One or more *monitorexit* instructions may be used with a *monitorenter* instruction to implement a `synchronized` statement in the Java programming language. The *monitorenter* and *monitorexit* instructions are not used in the implementation of `synchronized` methods, although they can be used to provide equivalent locking semantics.

The Java virtual machine supports exceptions thrown within `synchronized` methods and `synchronized` statements differently. Monitor exit on normal `synchronized` method completion is handled by the Java virtual machine's return instructions. Monitor exit on abrupt `synchronized` method completion is handled implicitly by the Java virtual machine's *athrow* instruction. When an exception is thrown from within a `synchronized` statement, exit from the monitor entered prior to the execution of the `synchronized` statement is achieved using the Java virtual machine's exception handling mechanism. See Section 7.14 for more information on the use of the *monitorenter* and *monitorexit* instructions.

multianewarray   *multianewarray*

Operation   Create new multidimensional array

Format

multianewarray
indexbyte1
indexbyte2
dimensions

Forms   *multianewarray* = 197 (0xc5)

Operand   ..., *count1*, [*count2*, ...] $\Rightarrow$
Stack   ..., *arrayref*

Description   The *dimensions* operand is an unsigned byte that must be greater than or equal to 1. It represents the number of dimensions of the array to be created. The operand stack must contain *dimensions* values. Each such value represents the number of components in a dimension of the array to be created, must be of type int, and must be nonnegative. The *count1* is the desired length in the first dimension, *count2* in the second, etc.

All of the *count* values are popped off the operand stack. The unsigned *indexbyte1* and *indexbyte2* are used to construct an index into the runtime constant pool of the current class (§3.6), where the value of the index is (*indexbyte1* << 8) | *indexbyte2*. The runtime constant pool item at the index must be a symbolic reference to a class, array, or interface type. The named class, array, or interface type is resolved (§5.4.3.1). The resulting entry must be an array class type of dimensionality greater than or equal to *dimensions*.

multianewarray (*cont.*)   *multianewarray* (*cont.*)
multianewarray (*cont.*)

A new multidimensional array of the array type is allocated from the garbage-collected heap. If any *count* value is zero, no subsequent dimensions are allocated. The components of the array in the first dimension are initialized to subarrays of the type of the second dimension, and so on. The components of the last allocated dimension of the array are initialized to the default initial value for the type of the components (§2.5.1). A `reference` *arrayref* to the new array is pushed onto the operand stack.

Linking Exceptions

During resolution of the symbolic reference to the class, array, or interface type, any of the exceptions documented in Section 5.4.3.1 can be thrown.

Otherwise, if the current class does not have permission to access the element type of the resolved array class, *multianewarray* throws an `IllegalAccessError`.

Runtime Exception

Otherwise, if any of the *dimensions* values on the operand stack are less than zero, the *multianewarray* instruction throws a `Negative-ArraySizeException`.

Notes

It may be more efficient to use *newarray* or *anewarray* when creating an array of a single dimension.

The array class referenced via the runtime constant pool may have more dimensions than the *dimensions* operand of the *multianewarray* instruction. In that case, only the first *dimensions* of the dimensions of the array are created.

new   *new*

Operation   Create new object

Format

new
indexbyte1
indexbyte2

Forms   *new* = 187 (0xbb)

Operand   … ⇒
Stack   …, *objectref*

Description   The unsigned *indexbyte1* and *indexbyte2* are used to construct an index into the runtime constant pool of the current class (§3.6), where the value of the index is (*indexbyte1* << 8) | *indexbyte2*. The runtime constant pool item at the index must be a symbolic reference to a class, array, or interface type. The named class, array, or interface type is resolved (§5.4.3.1) and should result in a class type (it should not result in an array or interface type). Memory for a new instance of that class is allocated from the garbage-collected heap, and the instance variables of the new object are initialized to their default initial values (§2.5.1). The *objectref*, a `reference` to the instance, is pushed onto the operand stack.

On successful resolution of the class, it is initialized (§5.5) if it has not already been initialized.

Linking   During resolution of the symbolic reference to the class, array, or
Exceptions   interface type, any of the exceptions documented in Section 5.4.3.1 can be thrown.

Otherwise, if the symbolic reference to the class, array, or interface type resolves to an interface or is an `abstract` class, *new* throws an `InstantiationError`.

new (*cont.*)   *new* (*cont.*)

Runtime   Otherwise, if execution of this *new* instruction causes initialization
Exception   of the referenced class, *new* may throw an `Error` as detailed in
                   Section 2.17.5.

Note   The *new* instruction does not completely create a new instance;
                   instance creation is not completed until an instance initialization
                   method has been invoked on the uninitialized instance.

newarray *newarray*

Operation Create new array

Format

newarray
atype

Forms *newarray* = 188 (0xbc)

Operand ..., *count* $\Rightarrow$
Stack ..., *arrayref*

Description The *count* must be of type int. It is popped off the operand stack. The *count* represents the number of elements in the array to be created.

The *atype* is a code that indicates the type of array to create. It must take one of the following values:

Array Type	*atype*
T_BOOLEAN	4
T_CHAR	5
T_FLOAT	6
T_DOUBLE	7
T_BYTE	8
T_SHORT	9
T_INT	10
T_LONG	11

A new array whose components are of type *atype* and of length *count* is allocated from the garbage-collected heap. A reference *arrayref* to this new array object is pushed into the operand stack. Each of the elements of the new array is initialized to the default initial value for the type of the array (§2.5.1).

newarray (*cont.*)   *newarray* (*cont.*)

Runtime   If *count* is less than zero, *newarray* throws a NegativeArray-
Exception   SizeException.

Notes   In Sun's implementation of the Java virtual machine, arrays of type
                   boolean (*atype* is T_BOOLEAN) are stored as arrays of 8-bit values
                   and are manipulated using the *baload* and *bastore* instructions,
                   instructions that also access arrays of type byte. Other implemen-
                   tations may implement packed boolean arrays; the *baload* and
                   bastore instructions must still be used to access those arrays.

nop   *nop*

Operation   Do nothing

Format
nop

Forms   *nop* = 0 (0x0)

**Operand
Stack**   No change

Description   Do nothing.

pop   *pop*

Operation   Pop the top operand stack value

Format

pop

Forms   *pop* = 87 (0x57)

Operand   ..., *value* ⇒
Stack   ...

Description Pop the top value from the operand stack.

The *pop* instruction must not be used unless *value* is a value of a category 1 computational type (§3.11.1).

pop2 *pop2*

Operation   Pop the top one or two operand stack values

Format

pop2

Forms   *pop2* = 88 (0x58)

Operand   Form 1:
Stack
..., *value2*, *value1* $\Rightarrow$

...

where each of *value1* and *value2* is a value of a category 1 computational type (§3.11.1).

Form 2:

..., *value* $\Rightarrow$

...

where *value* is a value of a category 2 computational type (§3.11.1).

Description   Pop the top one or two values from the operand stack.

putfield   *putfield*

Operation   Set field in object

Format

putfield
indexbyte1
indexbyte2

Forms   *putfield* = 181 (0xb5)

Operand   ..., *objectref*, *value* ⇒
Stack   ...

Description   The unsigned *indexbyte1* and *indexbyte2* are used to construct an
index into the runtime constant pool of the current class (§3.6),
where the value of the index is (*indexbyte1* << 8) | *indexbyte2*. The
runtime constant pool item at that index must be a symbolic reference to a field (§5.1), which gives the name and descriptor of the
field as well as a symbolic reference to the class in which the field
is to be found. The class of *objectref* must not be an array. If the
field is protected (§4.6), and it is either a member of the current
class or a member of a superclass of the current class, then the class
of *objectref* must be either the current class or a subclass of the current class.

The referenced field is resolved (§5.4.3.2). The type of a *value*
stored by a *putfield* instruction must be compatible with the
descriptor of the referenced field (§4.3.2). If the field descriptor
type is boolean, byte, char, short, or int, then the *value* must be
an int. If the field descriptor type is float, long, or double, then
the *value* must be a float, long, or double, respectively. If the
field descriptor type is a reference type, then the *value* must be of a
type that is assignment compatible (§2.6.7) with the field descriptor
type. If the field is final, it should be declared in the current class.
Otherwise, an IllegalAccessError is thrown.

putfield (*cont.*)   *putfield* (*cont.*)

The *value* and *objectref* are popped from the operand stack. The *objectref* must be of type `reference`. The *value* undergoes value set conversion (§3.8.3), resulting in *value'*, and the referenced field in *objectref* is set to *value'*.

Linking Exceptions

During resolution of the symbolic reference to the field, any of the exceptions pertaining to field resolution documented in Section 5.4.3.2 can be thrown.

Otherwise, if the resolved field is a `static` field, *putfield* throws an `IncompatibleClassChangeError`.

Otherwise, if the field is `final`, it must be declared in the current class. Otherwise, an `IllegalAccessError` is thrown.

Runtime Exception

Otherwise, if *objectref* is `null`, the *putfield* instruction throws a `NullPointerException`.

putstatic   *putstatic*

Operation   Set `static` field in class

Format

putstatic
indexbyte1
indexbyte2

Forms   *putstatic* = 179 (0xb3)

Operand   ..., *value* ⇒
Stack   ...

Description   The unsigned *indexbyte1* and *indexbyte2* are used to construct an
index into the runtime constant pool of the current class (§3.6),
where the value of the index is (*indexbyte1* << 8) | *indexbyte2*. The
runtime constant pool item at that index must be a symbolic reference to a field (§5.1), which gives the name and descriptor of the
field as well as a symbolic reference to the class or interface in
which the field is to be found. The referenced field is resolved
(§5.4.3.2).

On successful resolution of the field the class or interface that
declared the resolved field is initialized (§5.5) if that class or interface has not already been initialized.

The type of a *value* stored by a *putstatic* instruction must be compatible with the descriptor of the referenced field (§4.3.2). If the
field descriptor type is `boolean`, `byte`, `char`, `short`, or `int`, then
the *value* must be an `int`. If the field descriptor type is `float`,
`long`, or `double`, then the *value* must be a `float`, `long`, or `double`,
respectively. If the field descriptor type is a reference type, then the
value must be of a type that is assignment compatible (§2.6.7) with
the field descriptor type. If the field is `final`, it should be declared
in the current class. Otherwise, an `IllegalAccessError` is
thrown.

putstatic (*cont.*)   *putstatic* (*cont.*)

The *value* is popped from the operand stack and undergoes value set conversion (§3.8.3), resulting in *value'*. The class field is set to *value'*.

Linking Exceptions

During resolution of the symbolic reference to the class or interface field, any of the exceptions pertaining to field resolution documented in Section 5.4.3.2 can be thrown.

Otherwise, if the resolved field is not a `static` (class) field or an interface field, *putstatic* throws an `IncompatibleClassChangeError`.

Otherwise, if the field is `final`, it must be declared in the current class. Otherwise, an `IllegalAccessError` is thrown.

Runtime Exception

Otherwise, if execution of this *putstatic* instruction causes initialization of the referenced class or interface, *putstatic* may throw an `Error` as detailed in Section 2.17.5.

Notes

A *putstatic* instruction may be used only to set the value of an interface field on the initialization of that field. Interface fields may be assigned to only once, on execution of an interface variable initialization expression when the interface is initialized (§2.17.4).

ret   *ret*

Operation   Return from subroutine

Format

ret
index

Forms   *ret* = 169 (0xa9)

Operand   No change
Stack

Description   The *index* is an unsigned byte between 0 and 255, inclusive. The
                   local variable at *index* in the current frame (§3.6) must contain a
                   value of type `returnAddress`. The contents of the local variable
                   are written into the Java virtual machine's `pc` register, and execu-
                   tion continues there.

Notes   The *ret* instruction is used with *jsr* or *jsr_w* instructions in the
                   implementation of the `finally` clauses of the Java programming
                   language (see Section 7.13, "Compiling `finally`"). Note that *jsr*
                   pushes the address onto the operand stack and *ret* gets it out of a
                   local variable. This asymmetry is intentional.

                   The *ret* instruction should not be confused with the *return* instruc-
                   tion. A *return* instruction returns control from a method to its
                   invoker, without passing any value back to the invoker.

                   The *ret* opcode can be used in conjunction with the *wide* instruction
                   to access a local variable using a two-byte unsigned index.

return   *return*

Operation   Return void from method

Format

return

Forms   *return* = 177 (0xb1)

Operand   … ⇒
Stack   [empty]

Description   The current method must have return type void. If the current
                  method is a synchronized method, the monitor acquired or reen-
                  tered on invocation of the method is released or exited (respec-
                  tively) as if by execution of a *monitorexit* instruction. If no
                  exception is thrown, any values on the operand stack of the current
                  frame (§3.6) are discarded.

                  The interpreter then returns control to the invoker of the method,
                  reinstating the frame of the invoker.

Runtime   If the current method is a synchronized method and the current
Exceptions   thread is not the owner of the monitor acquired or reentered on
                  invocation of the method, *return* throws an IllegalMonitor-
                  StateException. This can happen, for example, if a synchro-
                  nized method contains a *monitorexit* instruction, but no
                  monitorenter instruction, on the object on which the method is syn-
                  chronized.

                  Otherwise, if the virtual machine implementation enforces the rules
                  on structured use of locks described in Section 8.13 and if the first
                  of those rules is violated during invocation of the current method,
                  then *return* throws an IllegalMonitorStateException.

saload   *saload*

Operation   Load short from array

Format

saload

Forms   *saload* = 53 (0x35)

Operand   ..., *arrayref, index* ⇒
Stack   ..., *value*

Description   The *arrayref* must be of type reference and must refer to an array whose components are of type short. The *index* must be of type int. Both *arrayref* and *index* are popped from the operand stack. The component of the array at *index* is retrieved and sign-extended to an int *value*. That *value* is pushed onto the operand stack.

Runtime   If *arrayref* is null, *saload* throws a NullPointerException.
Exceptions
                  Otherwise, if *index* is not within the bounds of the array referenced by *arrayref*, the *saload* instruction throws an ArrayIndexOutOf-BoundsException.

sastore *sastore*

Operation   Store into short array

Format

sastore

Forms   *sastore* = 86 (0x56)

Operand Stack   ..., *array, index, value* $\Rightarrow$

...

Description   The *arrayref* must be of type reference and must refer to an array whose components are of type short. Both *index* and *value* must be of type int. The *arrayref*, *index*, and *value* are popped from the operand stack. The int *value* is truncated to a short and stored as the component of the array indexed by *index*.

Runtime Exceptions   If *arrayref* is null, *sastore* throws a NullPointerException.

Otherwise, if *index* is not within the bounds of the array referenced by *arrayref*, the *sastore* instruction throws an ArrayIndexOutOf-BoundsException.

sipush   *sipush*

Operation   Push short

Format
sipush
byte1
byte2

Forms   *sipush* = 17 (0x11)

Operand   ... $\Rightarrow$
Stack   ..., *value*

Description The immediate unsigned *byte1* and *byte2* values are assembled into
                 an intermediate short where the value of the short is (*byte1* << 8) |
                 byte2. The intermediate value is then sign-extended to an int
                 value. That *value* is pushed onto the operand stack.

swap   *swap*

Operation   Swap the top two operand stack values

Format

swap

Forms   *swap* = 95 (0x5f)

Operand   ..., *value2*, *value1* $\Rightarrow$
Stack   ..., *value1*, *value2*

Description   Swap the top two values on the operand stack.

The *swap* instruction must not be used unless *value1* and *value2* are both values of a category 1 computational type (§3.11.1).

Notes   The Java virtual machine does not provide an instruction implementing a swap on operands of category 2 computational types.

tableswitch   *tableswitch*

Operation   Access jump table by index and jump

Format

tableswitch
<0-3 byte pad>
defaultbyte1
defaultbyte2
defaultbyte3
defaultbyte4
lowbyte1
lowbyte2
lowbyte3
lowbyte4
highbyte1
highbyte2
highbyte3
highbyte4
jump offsets…

Forms   *tableswitch* = 170 (0xaa)

Operand   *…, index* $\Rightarrow$
Stack   *…*

Description   A *tableswitch* is a variable-length instruction. Immediately after the
                   tableswitch opcode, between 0 and 3 null bytes (zeroed bytes, not
                   the null object) are inserted as padding. The number of null bytes is
                   chosen so that the following byte begins at an address that is a mul-
                   tiple of 4 bytes from the start of the current method (the opcode of
                   its first instruction). Immediately after the padding follow bytes
                   constituting three signed 32-bit values: *default*, *low*, and *high*.
                   Immediately following those bytes are bytes constituting a series of
                   high − *low* + 1 signed 32-bit offsets. The value *low* must be less
                   than or equal to *high*. The *high* − *low* + 1 signed 32-bit offsets are
                   treated as a 0-based jump table. Each of these signed 32-bit values
                   is constructed as (*byte1* << 24) | (*byte2* << 16) | (*byte3* << 8) | *byte4*.

tableswitch (*cont.*)   *tableswitch* (*cont.*)

The *index* must be of type `int` and is popped from the operand stack. If *index* is less than *low* or *index* is greater than *high*, then a target address is calculated by adding *default* to the address of the opcode of this *tableswitch* instruction. Otherwise, the offset at position *index − low* of the jump table is extracted. The target address is calculated by adding that offset to the address of the opcode of this *tableswitch* instruction. Execution then continues at the target address.

The target address that can be calculated from each jump table offset, as well as the ones that can be calculated from *default*, must be the address of an opcode of an instruction within the method that contains this *tableswitch* instruction.

Notes   The alignment required of the 4-byte operands of the *tableswitch* instruction guarantees 4-byte alignment of those operands if and only if the method that contains the *tableswitch* starts on a 4-byte boundary.

wide   *wide*

Operation   Extend local variable index by additional bytes

Format 1:

wide
<opcode>
indexbyte1
indexbyte2

where *<opcode>* is one of *iload*, *fload*, *aload*, *lload*, *dload*, *istore*, *fstore*, *astore*, *lstore*, *dstore*, or *ret*

Format 2:

wide
iinc
indexbyte1
indexbyte2
constbyte1
constbyte2

Forms   *wide* = 196 (0xc4)

Operand Stack Same as modified instruction

Description   The *wide* instruction modifies the behavior of another instruction. It takes one of two formats, depending on the instruction being modified. The first form of the *wide* instruction modifies one of the instructions *iload*, *fload*, *aload*, *lload*, *dload*, *istore*, *fstore*, *astore*, *lstore*, *dstore*, or *ret*. The second form applies only to the *iinc* instruction.

In either case, the *wide* opcode itself is followed in the compiled code by the opcode of the instruction *wide* modifies. In either form, two unsigned bytes *indexbyte1* and *indexbyte2* follow the modified opcode and are assembled into a 16-bit unsigned index to a local variable in the current frame (§3.6), where the value of the index is *wide* (*cont.*)   *wide* (*cont.*)

(*indexbyte1* << 8) | *indexbyte2*. The calculated index must be an index into the local variable array of the current frame. Where the *wide* instruction modifies an *lload*, *dload*, *lstore*, or *dstore* instruction, the index following the calculated index (index + 1) must also be an index into the local variable array. In the second form, two immediate unsigned bytes *constbyte1* and *constbyte2* follow *indexbyte1* and *indexbyte2* in the code stream. Those bytes are also assembled into a signed 16-bit constant, where the constant is (*constbyte1* << 8) | *constbyte2*.

The widened bytecode operates as normal, except for the use of the wider index and, in the case of the second form, the larger increment range.

Notes   Although we say that *wide* "modifies the behavior of another instruction," the *wide* instruction effectively treats the bytes constituting the modified instruction as operands, denaturing the embedded instruction in the process. In the case of a modified *iinc* instruction, one of the logical operands of the *iinc* is not even at the normal offset from the opcode. The embedded instruction must never be executed directly; its opcode must never be the target of any control transfer instruction.

CHAPTER 7

Compiling for the
Java Virtual Machine

T HE Java virtual machine is designed to support the Java programming language. Sun's JDK releases and Java 2 SDK contain both a compiler from source code written in the Java programming language to the instruction set of the Java virtual machine, and a runtime system that implements the Java virtual machine itself. Understanding how one compiler utilizes the Java virtual machine is useful to the prospective compiler writer, as well as to one trying to understand the Java virtual machine itself.

Although this chapter concentrates on compiling source code written in the Java programming language, the Java virtual machine does not assume that the instructions it executes were generated from such code. While there have been a number of efforts aimed at compiling other languages to the Java virtual machine, the current version of the Java virtual machine was not designed to support a wide range of languages. Some languages may be hosted fairly directly by the Java virtual machine. Other languages may be implemented only inefficiently.

Note that the term "compiler" is sometimes used when referring to a translator from the instruction set of a Java virtual machine to the instruction set of a specific CPU. One example of such a translator is a just-in-time (JIT) code generator, which generates platform-specific instructions only after Java virtual machine code has been loaded. This chapter does not address issues associated with code generation, only those associated with compiling source code written in the Java programming language to Java virtual machine instructions.

7.1 Format of Examples

This chapter consists mainly of examples of source code together with annotated listings of the Java virtual machine code that the `javac` compiler in Sun's JDK release 1.0.2 generates for the examples. The Java virtual machine code is written in the informal "virtual machine assembly language" output by Sun's `javap` utility, distributed with the JDK software and the Java 2 SDK. You can use `javap` to generate additional examples of compiled methods.

The format of the examples should be familiar to anyone who has read assembly code. Each instruction takes the form

$$<index> <opcode> [<operand1> [<operand2>...]] [<comment>]$$

The *<index>* is the index of the opcode of the instruction in the array that contains the bytes of Java virtual machine code for this method. Alternatively, the *<index>* may be thought of as a byte offset from the beginning of the method. The *<opcode>* is the mnemonic for the instruction's opcode, and the zero or more *<operandN>* are the operands of the instruction. The optional *<comment>* is given in end-of-line comment syntax:

       8   bipush 100   // Push `int` *constant* `100`

Some of the material in the comments is emitted by `javap`; the rest is supplied by the authors. The *<index>* prefacing each instruction may be used as the target of a control transfer instruction. For instance, a *goto 8* instruction transfers control to the instruction at index 8. Note that the actual operands of Java virtual machine control transfer instructions are offsets from the addresses of the opcodes of those instructions; these operands are displayed by `javap` (and are shown in this chapter) as more easily read offsets into their methods.

We preface an operand representing a runtime constant pool index with a hash sign and follow the instruction by a comment identifying the runtime constant pool item referenced, as in

      10   ldc #1   // Push `float` *constant* `100.0`

or

      9   invokevirtual #4   // Method `Example.addTwo(II)I`

For the purposes of this chapter, we do not worry about specifying details such as operand sizes.

7.2 Use of Constants, Local Variables, and Control Constructs

Java virtual machine code exhibits a set of general characteristics imposed by the Java virtual machine's design and use of types. In the first example we encounter many of these, and we consider them in some detail.

The `spin` method simply spins around an empty `for` loop 100 times:

```
void spin() {
    int i;
      for (i = 0; i < 100; i++) {
        ;              // Loop body is empty
    }
}
```

A compiler might compile `spin` to

```
Method void spin()
    0   iconst_0        // Push int constant 0
    1   istore_1        // Store into local variable 1 (i=0)
    2   goto 8          // First time through don't increment
    5   iinc 1 1        // Increment local variable 1 by 1 (i++)
    8   iload_1         // Push local variable 1 (i)
    9   bipush 100      // Push int constant 100
   11   if_icmplt 5     // Compare and loop if less than (i < 100)
   14   return          // Return void when done
```

The Java virtual machine is stack-oriented, with most operations taking one or more operands from the operand stack of the Java virtual machine's current frame or pushing results back onto the operand stack. A new frame is created each time a method is invoked, and with it is created a new operand stack and set of local variables for use by that method (see Section 3.6, "Frames"). At any one point of the computation, there are thus likely to be many frames and equally many operand stacks per thread of control, corresponding to many nested method invocations. Only the operand stack in the current frame is active.

The instruction set of the Java virtual machine distinguishes operand types by using distinct bytecodes for operations on its various data types. The method `spin` operates only on values of type `int`. The instructions in its compiled code chosen to operate on typed data (*iconst_0, istore_1, iinc, iload_1, if_icmplt*) are all specialized for type `int`.

The two constants in spin, 0 and 100, are pushed onto the operand stack using two different instructions. The 0 is pushed using an *iconst_0* instruction, one of the family of *iconst_<i>* instructions. The 100 is pushed using a *bipush* instruction, which fetches the value it pushes as an immediate operand.

The Java virtual machine frequently takes advantage of the likelihood of certain operands (int constants *−1, 0, 1, 2, 3, 4* and *5* in the case of the *iconst_<i>* instructions) by making those operands implicit in the opcode. Because the *iconst_0* instruction knows it is going to push an int 0, *iconst_0* does not need to store an operand to tell it what value to push, nor does it need to fetch or decode an operand. Compiling the push of 0 as *bipush 0* would have been correct, but would have made the compiled code for spin one byte longer. A simple virtual machine would have also spent additional time fetching and decoding the explicit operand each time around the loop. Use of implicit operands makes compiled code more compact and efficient.

The int i in spin is stored as Java virtual machine local variable *1*. Because most Java virtual machine instructions operate on values popped from the operand stack rather than directly on local variables, instructions that transfer values between local variables and the operand stack are common in code compiled for the Java virtual machine. These operations also have special support in the instruction set. In spin, values are transferred to and from local variables using the *istore_1* and *iload_1* instructions, each of which implicitly operates on local variable *1*. The *istore_1* instruction pops an int from the operand stack and stores it in local variable *1*. The *iload_1* instruction pushes the value in local variable *1* onto the operand stack.

The use (and reuse) of local variables is the responsibility of the compiler writer. The specialized load and store instructions should encourage the compiler writer to reuse local variables as much as is feasible. The resulting code is faster, more compact, and uses less space in the frame.

Certain very frequent operations on local variables are catered to specially by the Java virtual machine. The *iinc* instruction increments the contents of a local variable by a one-byte signed value. The *iinc* instruction in spin increments the first local variable (its first operand) by *1* (its second operand). The *iinc* instruction is very handy when implementing looping constructs.

The for loop of spin is accomplished mainly by these instructions:

```
 5   iinc 1 1        // Increment local 1 by 1 (i++)
 8   iload_1         // Push local variable 1 (i)
 9   bipush 100      // Push int constant 100
11   if_icmplt 5     // Compare and loop if less than (i < 100)
```

The *bipush* instruction pushes the value *100* onto the operand stack as an `int`, then the *if_icmplt* instruction pops that value off the operand stack and compares it against *i*. If the comparison succeeds (the variable i is less than `100`), control is transferred to index *5* and the next iteration of the `for` loop begins. Otherwise, control passes to the instruction following the *if_icmplt*.

If the `spin` example had used a data type other than `int` for the loop counter, the compiled code would necessarily change to reflect the different data type. For instance, if instead of an `int` the `spin` example uses a `double`, as shown,

```
void dspin() {
    double i;
        for (i = 0.0; i < 100.0; i++) {
        ;              // Loop body is empty
    }
}
```

the compiled code is

Method `void dspin()`

0	*dconst_0*	// *Push* `double` *constant* `0.0`
1	*dstore_1*	// *Store into local variables 1 and 2*
2	*goto 9*	// *First time through don't increment*
5	*dload_1*	// *Push local variables 1 and 2*
6	*dconst_1*	// *Push* `double` *constant* `1.0`
7	*dadd*	// *Add; there is no dinc instruction*
8	*dstore_1*	// *Store result in local variables 1 and 2*
9	*dload_1*	// *Push local variables 1 and 2*
10	*ldc2_w #4*	// *Push* `double` *constant* `100.0`
13	*dcmpg*	// *There is no if_dcmplt instruction*
14	*iflt 5*	// *Compare and loop if less than* (i < `100.0`)
17	*return*	// *Return* `void` *when done*

The instructions that operate on typed data are now specialized for type `double`. (The *ldc2_w* instruction will be discussed later in this chapter.)

Recall that `double` values occupy two local variables, although they are only accessed using the lesser index of the two local variables. This is also the case for values of type `long`. Again for example,

```
double doubleLocals(double d1, double d2) {
    return d1 + d2;
}
```

becomes

> *Method* `double doubleLocals(double,double)`
>   *0   dload_1*   *// First argument in local variables 1 and 2*
>   *1   dload_3*   *// Second argument in local variables 3 and 4*
>   *2   dadd*
>   *3   dreturn*

Note that local variables of the local variable pairs used to store `double` values in `doubleLocals` must never be manipulated individually.

The Java virtual machine's opcode size of 1 byte results in its compiled code being very compact. However, 1-byte opcodes also mean that the Java virtual machine instruction set must stay small. As a compromise, the Java virtual machine does not provide equal support for all data types: it is not completely orthogonal (see Table 3.2, "Type support in the Java virtual machine instruction set").

For example, the comparison of values of type `int` in the `for` statement of example `spin` can be implemented using a single *if_icmplt* instruction; however, there is no single instruction in the Java virtual machine instruction set that performs a conditional branch on values of type `double`. Thus, `dspin` must implement its comparison of values of type `double` using a *dcmpg* instruction followed by an *iflt* instruction.

The Java virtual machine provides the most direct support for data of type `int`. This is partly in anticipation of efficient implementations of the Java virtual machine's operand stacks and local variable arrays. It is also motivated by the frequency of `int` data in typical programs. Other integral types have less direct support. There are no `byte`, `char`, or `short` versions of the store, load, or add instructions, for instance. Here is the `spin` example written using a `short`:

```
void sspin() {
    short i;
     for (i = 0; i < 100; i++) {
        ;   // Loop body is empty
     }
}
```

It must be compiled for the Java virtual machine, as follows, using instructions operating on another type, most likely `int`, converting between `short` and `int` values as necessary to ensure that the results of operations on `short` data stay within the appropriate range:

Method void sspin()

```
 0   iconst_0
 1   istore_1
 2   goto 10
 5   iload_1          // The short is treated as though an int
 6   iconst_1
 7   iadd
 8   i2s              // Truncate int to short
 9   istore_1
10   iload_1
11   bipush 100
13   if_icmplt 5
16   return
```

The lack of direct support for byte, char, and short types in the Java virtual machine is not particularly painful, because values of those types are internally promoted to int (byte and short are sign-extended to int, char is zero-extended). Operations on byte, char, and short data can thus be done using int instructions. The only additional cost is that of truncating the values of int operations to valid ranges.

The long and floating-point types have an intermediate level of support in the Java virtual machine, lacking only the full complement of conditional control transfer instructions.

7.3 Arithmetic

The Java virtual machine generally does arithmetic on its operand stack. (The exception is the *iinc* instruction, which directly increments the value of a local variable.) For instance, the align2grain method aligns an int value to a given power of 2:

```
int align2grain(int i, int grain) {
    return ((i + grain-1) & ~(grain-1));
}
```

Operands for arithmetic operations are popped from the operand stack, and the results of operations are pushed back onto the operand stack. Results of arithmetic subcomputations can thus be made available as operands of their nesting computation. For instance, the calculation of ~(grain–1) is handled by these instructions:

```
5   iload_2      // Push grain
6   iconst_1     // Push int constant 1
7   isub         // Subtract; push result
8   iconst_m1    // Push int constant −1
9   ixor         // Do XOR; push result
```

First grain − 1 is calculated using the contents of local variable 2 and an immediate int value 1. These operands are popped from the operand stack and their difference pushed back onto the operand stack. The difference is thus immediately available for use as one operand of the *ixor* instruction. (Recall that ~x == −1^x.) Similarly, the result of the *ixor* instruction becomes an operand for the subsequent *iand* instruction.

The code for the entire method follows:

```
Method int align2grain(int,int)
 0   iload_1
 1   iload_2
 2   iadd
 3   iconst_1
 4   isub
 5   iload_2
 6   iconst_1
 7   isub
 8   iconst_m1
 9   ixor
10   iand
11   ireturn
```

7.4 Accessing the Runtime Constant Pool

Many numeric constants, as well as objects, fields, and methods, are accessed via the runtime constant pool of the current class. Object access is considered later (§7.8). Data of types int, long, float, and double, as well as references to instances of class String, are managed using the *ldc*, *ldc_w*, and *ldc2_w* instructions.

The *ldc* and *ldc_w* instructions are used to access values in the runtime constant pool (including instances of class String) of types other than double and long. The *ldc_w* instruction is used in place of *ldc* only when there is a large number of runtime constant pool items and a larger index is needed to access an item. The *ldc2_w* instruction is used to access all values of types double and long; there is no non-wide variant.

Integral constants of types byte, char, or short, as well as small int values, may be compiled using the *bipush*, *sipush*, or *iconst_<i>* instructions, as seen earlier (§7.2). Certain small floating-point constants may be compiled using the *fconst_<f>* and *dconst_<d>* instructions.

In all of these cases, compilation is straightforward. For instance, the constants for

```
void useManyNumeric() {
    int i = 100;
    int j = 1000000;
    long l1 = 1;
    long l2 = 0xffffffff;
    double d = 2.2;
    ...do some calculations...
}
```

are set up as follows:

Method void useManyNumeric()

0	*bipush 100*	// *Push a small* int *with bipush*
2	*istore_1*	
3	*ldc #1*	// *Push* int *constant* 1000000; *a larger* int // *value uses ldc*
5	*istore_2*	
6	*lconst_1*	// *A tiny* long *value uses short, fast lconst_1*
7	*lstore_3*	
8	*ldc2_w #6*	// *Push* long 0xffffffff *(that is, an* int −1*); any* // long *constant value can be pushed using ldc2_w*
11	*lstore 5*	
13	*ldc2_w #8*	// *Push* double *constant* 2.200000; *uncommon* // double *values are also pushed using ldc2_w*
16	*dstore 7*	

...do those calculations...

7.5 More Control Examples

Compilation of for statements was shown in an earlier section (§7.2). Most of the Java programming language's other control constructs (if-then-else, do, while, break, and continue) are also compiled in the obvious ways. The compilation of switch statements is handled in a separate section (Section 7.10, "Compiling Switches"), as are the compilation of exceptions (Section 7.12, "Throwing and Handling Exceptions") and the compilation of finally clauses (Section 7.13, "Compiling finally").

As a further example, a while loop is compiled in an obvious way, although the specific control transfer instructions made available by the Java virtual machine vary by data type. As usual, there is more support for data of type int, for example:

```
void whileInt() {
    int i = 0;
    while (i < 100) {
        i++;
    }
}
```

is compiled to

```
Method void whileInt()
   0   iconst_0
   1   istore_1
   2   goto 8
   5   iinc 1 1
   8   iload_1
   9   bipush 100
  11   if_icmplt 5
  14   return
```

Note that the test of the while statement (implemented using the *if_icmplt* instruction) is at the bottom of the Java virtual machine code for the loop. (This was also the case in the spin examples earlier.) The test being at the bottom of the loop forces the use of a *goto* instruction to get to the test prior to the first iteration of the loop. If that test fails, and the loop body is never entered, this extra instruction is wasted. However, while loops are typically used when their body is expected to be run, often for many iterations. For subsequent iterations, putting the test at the bottom of the loop saves a Java virtual machine instruction each time around the loop: if the test were at the top of the loop, the loop body would need a trailing *goto* instruction to get back to the top.

Control constructs involving other data types are compiled in similar ways, but must use the instructions available for those data types. This leads to somewhat less efficient code because more Java virtual machine instructions are needed, for example:

```
void whileDouble() {
    double i = 0.0;
      while (i < 100.1) {
        i++;
    }
}
```

is compiled to

```
Method void whileDouble()
   0   dconst_0
   1   dstore_1
   2   goto 9
   5   dload_1
   6   dconst_1
   7   dadd
   8   dstore_1
   9   dload_1
  10   ldc2_w #4      // Push double constant 100.1
  13   dcmpg          // To do the compare and branch we have to use...
  14   iflt 5         // ...two instructions
  17   return
```

Each floating-point type has two comparison instructions: *fcmpl* and *fcmpg* for type `float`, and *dcmpl* and *dcmpg* for type `double`. The variants differ only in their treatment of NaN. NaN is unordered, so all floating-point comparisons fail if either of their operands is NaN. The compiler chooses the variant of the comparison instruction for the appropriate type that produces the same result whether the comparison fails on non-NaN values or encounters a NaN.

For instance:

```
int lessThan100(double d) {
    if (d < 100.0) {
        return 1;
    } else {
        return -1;
    }
}
```

compiles to

Method `int lessThan100(double)`
```
  0  dload_1
  1  ldc2_w #4        // Push double constant 100.0
  4  dcmpg            // Push 1 if d is NaN or d > 100.0;
                      // push 0 if d == 100.0
  5  ifge 10          // Branch on 0 or 1
  8  iconst_1
  9  ireturn
 10  iconst_m1
 11  ireturn
```

If d is not NaN and is less than `100.0`, the *dcmpg* instruction pushes an `int` *–1* onto the operand stack, and the *ifge* instruction does not branch. Whether d is greater than `100.0` or is NaN, the *dcmpg* instruction pushes an `int` *1* onto the operand stack, and the *ifge* branches. If d is equal to `100.0`, the *dcmpg* instruction pushes an `int` *0* onto the operand stack, and the *ifge* branches.

The *dcmpl* instruction achieves the same effect if the comparison is reversed:

```
int greaterThan100(double d) {
    if (d > 100.0) {
        return 1;
    } else {
        return -1;
    }
}
```

becomes

    Method `int greaterThan100(double)`

   0 *dload_1*
   1 *ldc2_w #4*   // *Push* `double` *constant* `100.0`
   4 *dcmpl*   // *Push −1 if* d *is Nan or* d < `100.0`*;*
                       // *push 0 if* d == `100.0`
   5 *ifle 10*   // *Branch on 0 or −1*
   8 *iconst_1*
   9 *ireturn*
  10 *iconst_m1*
  11 *ireturn*

Once again, whether the comparison fails on a non-NaN value or because it is passed a NaN, the *dcmpl* instruction pushes an `int` value onto the operand stack that causes the *ifle* to branch. If both of the *dcmp* instructions did not exist, one of the example methods would have had to do more work to detect NaN.

7.6 Receiving Arguments

If *n* arguments are passed to an instance method, they are received, by convention, in the local variables numbered *1* through *n* of the frame created for the new method invocation. The arguments are received in the order they were passed. For example:

```
int addTwo(int i, int j) {
    return i + j;
}
```

compiles to

    Method `int addTwo(int,int)`

   0 *iload_1*   // *Push value of local variable 1 (*i*)*
   1 *iload_2*   // *Push value of local variable 2 (*j*)*
   2 *iadd*   // *Add; leave* `int` *result on operand stack*
   3 *ireturn*   // *Return* `int` *result*

By convention, an instance method is passed a `reference` to its instance in local variable *0*. In the Java programming language the instance is accessible via the `this` keyword.

Class (`static`) methods do not have an instance, so for them this use of local variable zero is unnecessary. A class method starts using local variables at index zero. If the addTwo method were a class method, its arguments would be passed in a similar way to the first version:

```
static int addTwoStatic(int i, int j) {
    return i + j;
}
```

compiles to

Method `int addTwoStatic(int,int)`
  0 iload_0
  1 iload_1
  2 iadd
  3 ireturn

The only difference is that the method arguments appear starting in local variable *0* rather than *1*.

7.7 Invoking Methods

The normal method invocation for a instance method dispatches on the runtime type of the object. (They are virtual, in C++ terms.) Such an invocation is implemented using the *invokevirtual* instruction, which takes as its argument an index to a runtime constant pool entry giving the fully qualified name of the class type of the object, the name of the method to invoke, and that method's descriptor (§4.3.3). To invoke the addTwo method, defined earlier as an instance method, we might write

```
int add12and13() {
    return addTwo(12, 13);
}
```

This compiles to

Method `int add12and13()`
  0 aload_0   *// Push local variable 0 (*`this`*)*
  1 bipush 12   *// Push* `int` *constant* `12`
  3 bipush 13   *// Push* `int` *constant* `13`
  5 invokevirtual #4   *// Method* `Example.addtwo(II)I`
  8 ireturn   *// Return* `int` *on top of operand stack; it is*
                             // the `int` *result of* `addTwo()`

The invocation is set up by first pushing a `reference` to the current instance, `this`, onto the operand stack. The method invocation's arguments, `int` values 12 and 13, are then pushed. When the frame for the `addTwo` method is created, the arguments passed to the method become the initial values of the new frame's local variables. That is, the `reference` for `this` and the two arguments, pushed onto the operand stack by the invoker, will become the initial values of local variables *0*, *1*, and *2* of the invoked method.

Finally, `addTwo` is invoked. When it returns, its `int` return value is pushed onto the operand stack of the frame of the invoker, the `add12and13` method. The return value is thus put in place to be immediately returned to the invoker of `add12and13`.

The return from `add12and13` is handled by the *ireturn* instruction of `add12and13`. The *ireturn* instruction takes the `int` value returned by `addTwo`, on the operand stack of the current frame, and pushes it onto the operand stack of the frame of the invoker. It then returns control to the invoker, making the invoker's frame current. The Java virtual machine provides distinct return instructions for many of its numeric and `reference` data types, as well as a *return* instruction for methods with no return value. The same set of return instructions is used for all varieties of method invocations.

The operand of the *invokevirtual* instruction (in the example, the runtime constant pool index #4) is not the offset of the method in the class instance. The compiler does not know the internal layout of a class instance. Instead, it generates symbolic references to the methods of an instance, which are stored in the runtime constant pool. Those runtime constant pool items are resolved at run time to determine the actual method location. The same is true for all other Java virtual machine instructions that access class instances.

Invoking `addTwoStatic`, a class (`static`) variant of `addTwo`, is similar, as shown:

```
int add12and13() {
    return addTwoStatic(12, 13);
}
```

although a different Java virtual machine method invocation instruction is used:

Method `int add12and13()`
   0 bipush 12
   2 bipush 13
   4 invokestatic #3   // *Method* `Example.addTwoStatic(II)I`
   7 ireturn

Compiling an invocation of a class (static) method is very much like compiling an invocation of an instance method, except this is not passed by the invoker. The method arguments will thus be received beginning with local variable *0* (see Section 7.6, "Receiving Arguments"). The *invokestatic* instruction is always used to invoke class methods.

The *invokespecial* instruction must be used to invoke instance initialization methods (see Section 7.8, "Working with Class Instances"). It is also used when invoking methods in the superclass (super) and when invoking private methods. For instance, given classes Near and Far declared as

```
class Near {
    int it;
    public int getItNear() {
        return getIt();
    }
    private int getIt() {
        return it;
    }
}
class Far extends Near {
    int getItFar() {
        return super.getItNear();
    }
}
```

the method Near.getItNear (which invokes a private method) becomes

> *Method* int getItNear()
> 0 *aload_0*
> 1 *invokespecial #5*   // *Method* Near.getIt()I
> 4 *ireturn*

The method Far.getItFar (which invokes a superclass method) becomes

> *Method* int getItFar()
> 0 *aload_0*
> 1 *invokespecial #4*   // *Method* Near.getItNear()I
> 4 *ireturn*

Note that methods called using the *invokespecial* instruction always pass this to the invoked method as its first argument. As usual, it is received in local variable *0*.

7.8 Working with Class Instances

Java virtual machine class instances are created using the Java virtual machine's *new* instruction. Recall that at the level of the Java virtual machine, a constructor appears as a method with the compiler-supplied name <init>. This specially named method is known as the instance initialization method (§3.9). Multiple instance initialization methods, corresponding to multiple constructors, may exist for a given class. Once the class instance has been created and its instance variables, including those of the class and all of its superclasses, have been initialized to their default values, an instance initialization method of the new class instance is invoked. For example:

```
Object create() {
    return new Object();
}
```

compiles to

```
Method java.lang.Object create()
  0  new #1              // Class java.lang.Object
  3  dup
  4  invokespecial #4    // Method java.lang.Object.<init>()V
  7  areturn
```

Class instances are passed and returned (as reference types) very much like numeric values, although type reference has its own complement of instructions, for example:

```
int i;                  // An instance variable
MyObj example() {
    MyObj o = new MyObj();
    return silly(o);
}
```

```
MyObj silly(MyObj o) {
    if (o != null) {
        return o;
    } else {
        return o;
    }
}
```

becomes

Method `MyObj example()`
0	*new #2*	*// Class* `MyObj`
3	*dup*	
4	*invokespecial #5*	*// Method* `MyObj.<init>()V`
7	*astore_1*	
8	*aload_0*	
9	*aload_1*	
10	*invokevirtual #4*	

           // Method `Example.silly(LMyObj;)LMyObj;`

13	*areturn*	

Method `MyObj silly(MyObj)`
0	*aload_1*
1	*ifnull 6*
4	*aload_1*
5	*areturn*
6	*aload_1*
7	*areturn*

The fields of a class instance (instance variables) are accessed using the *getfield* and *putfield* instructions. If `i` is an instance variable of type `int`, the methods `setIt` and `getIt`, defined as

```
void setIt(int value) {
    i = value;
}
int getIt() {
    return i;
}
```

become

```
Method void setIt(int)
   0   aload_0
   1   iload_1
   2   putfield #4      // Field Example.i I
   5   return

Method int getIt()
   0   aload_0
   1   getfield #4      // Field Example.i I
   4   ireturn
```

As with the operands of method invocation instructions, the operands of the *putfield* and *getfield* instructions (the runtime constant pool index #4) are not the offsets of the fields in the class instance. The compiler generates symbolic references to the fields of an instance, which are stored in the runtime constant pool. Those runtime constant pool items are resolved at run time to determine the location of the field within the referenced object.

7.9 Arrays

Java virtual machine arrays are also objects. Arrays are created and manipulated using a distinct set of instructions. The *newarray* instruction is used to create an array of a numeric type. The code

```
void createBuffer() {
    int buffer[];
    int bufsz = 100;
    int value = 12;
    buffer = new int[bufsz];
    buffer[10] = value;
    value = buffer[11];
}
```

might be compiled to

Method `void createBuffer()`

```
 0  bipush 100     // Push int constant 100 (bufsz)
 2  istore_2       // Store bufsz in local variable 2
 3  bipush 12      // Push int constant 12 (value)
 5  istore_3       // Store value in local variable 3
 6  iload_2        // Push bufsz...
 7  newarray int   // ...and create new array of int of that length
 9  astore_1       // Store new array in buffer
10  aload_1        // Push buffer
11  bipush 10      // Push int constant 10
13  iload_3        // Push value
14  iastore        // Store value at buffer[10]
15  aload_1        // Push buffer
16  bipush 11      // Push int constant 11
18  iaload         // Push value at buffer[11]...
19  istore_3       // ...and store it in value
20  return
```

The *anewarray* instruction is used to create a one-dimensional array of object references, for example:

```
void createThreadArray() {
    Thread threads[];
    int count = 10;
    threads = new Thread[count];
    threads[0] = new Thread();
}
```

becomes

Method `void createThreadArray()`

```
 0  bipush 10           // Push int constant 10
 2  istore_2            // Initialize count to that
 3  iload_2             // Push count, used by anewarray
 4  anewarray class #1  // Create new array of class Thread
 7  astore_1            // Store new array in threads
 8  aload_1             // Push value of threads
 9  iconst_0            // Push int constant 0
10  new #1              // Create instance of class Thread
```

```
13  dup                    // Make duplicate reference...
14  invokespecial #5       // ...to pass to instance initialization method
                           // Method java.lang.Thread.<init>()V
17  aastore                // Store new Thread in array at 0
18  return
```

The *anewarray* instruction can also be used to create the first dimension of a multi-dimensional array. Alternatively, the *multianewarray* instruction can be used to create several dimensions at once. For example, the three-dimensional array:

```
int[][][] create3DArray() {
    int grid[][][];
    grid = new int[10][5][];
    return grid;
}
```

is created by

```
Method int create3DArray()[][][]
    0  bipush 10               // Push int 10 (dimension one)
    2  iconst_5                // Push int 5 (dimension two)
    3  multianewarray #1 dim #2  // Class [[[I, a three
                               // dimensional int array;
                               // only create first two
                               // dimensions
    7  astore_1                // Store new array...
    8  aload_1                 // ...then prepare to return it
    9  areturn
```

The first operand of the *multianewarray* instruction is the runtime constant pool index to the array class type to be created. The second is the number of dimensions of that array type to actually create. The *multianewarray* instruction can be used to create all the dimensions of the type, as the code for create3DArray shows. Note that the multi-dimensional array is just an object and so is loaded and returned by an *aload_1* and *areturn* instruction, respectively. For information about array class names, see Section 4.4.1.

All arrays have associated lengths, which are accessed via the *arraylength* instruction.

7.10 Compiling Switches

Compilation of switch statements uses the *tableswitch* and *lookupswitch* instructions. The *tableswitch* instruction is used when the cases of the switch can be efficiently represented as indices into a table of target offsets. The default target of the switch is used if the value of the expression of the switch falls outside the range of valid indices. For instance,

```
int chooseNear(int i) {
    switch (i) {
        case 0:  return 0;
        case 1:  return 1;
        case 2:  return 2;
        default: return -1;
    }
}
```

compiles to

```
Method int chooseNear(int)
  0   iload_1                // Push local variable 1 (argument i)
  1   tableswitch 0 to 2:    // Valid indices are 0 through 2
          0: 28              // If i is 0, continue at 28
          1: 30              // If i is 1, continue at 30
          2: 32              // If i is 2, continue at 32
          default:34         // Otherwise, continue at 34
 28   iconst_0               // i was 0; push int constant 0...
 29   ireturn                // ...and return it
 30   iconst_1               // i was 1; push int constant 1...
 31   ireturn                // ...and return it
 32   iconst_2               // i was 2; push int constant 2...
 33   ireturn                // ...and return it
 34   iconst_m1              // otherwise push int constant −1...
 35   ireturn                // ...and return it
```

The Java virtual machine's *tableswitch* and *lookupswitch* instructions operate only on int data. Because operations on byte, char, or short values are internally promoted to int, a switch whose expression evaluates to one of those types is compiled as though it evaluated to type int. If the chooseNear method had been written using type short, the same Java virtual machine instructions would have been generated as when using type `int`. Other numeric types must be narrowed to type `int` for use in a `switch`.

Where the cases of the `switch` are sparse, the table representation of the *tableswitch* instruction becomes inefficient in terms of space. The *lookupswitch* instruction may be used instead. The *lookupswitch* instruction pairs `int` keys (the values of the `case` labels) with target offsets in a table. When a *lookupswitch* instruction is executed, the value of the expression of the `switch` is compared against the keys in the table. If one of the keys matches the value of the expression, execution continues at the associated target offset. If no key matches, execution continues at the `default` target. For instance, the compiled code for

```
int chooseFar(int i) {
    switch (i) {
        case -100:    return -1;
        case 0:       return 0;
        case 100:     return 1;
        default:      return -1;
    }
}
```

looks just like the code for `chooseNear`, except for the use of the *lookupswitch* instruction:

> *Method* `int chooseFar(int)`
> 0   *iload_1*
> 1   *lookupswitch 3:*
>   *−100: 36*
>   *0: 38*
>   *100: 40*
>   *default:42*
> 36   *iconst_m1*
> 37   *ireturn*
> 38   *iconst_0*
> 39   *ireturn*
> 40   *iconst_1*
> 41   *ireturn*
> 42   *iconst_m1*
> 43   *ireturn*

The Java virtual machine specifies that the table of the *lookupswitch* instruction must be sorted by key so that implementations may use searches more efficient than a linear scan. Even so, the *lookupswitch* instruction must search its keys for a match rather than simply perform a bounds check and index into a table like *tableswitch*. Thus, a *tableswitch* instruction is probably more efficient than a *lookupswitch* where space considerations permit a choice.

7.11 Operations on the Operand Stack

The Java virtual machine has a large complement of instructions that manipulate the contents of the operand stack as untyped values. These are useful because of the Java virtual machine's reliance on deft manipulation of its operand stack. For instance,

```
public long nextIndex() {
    return index++;
}

private long index = 0;
```

is compiled to

```
Method long nextIndex()
   0   aload_0        // Push this
   1   dup            // Make a copy of it
   2   getfield #4    // One of the copies of this is consumed
                      // pushing long field index,
                      // above the original this
   5   dup2_x1        // The long on top of the operand stack is
                      // inserted into the operand stack below the
                      // original this
   6   lconst_1       // Push long constant 1
   7   ladd           // The index value is incremented...
   8   putfield #4    // ...and the result stored back in the field
  11   lreturn        // The original value of index is left on
                      // top of the operand stack, ready to be returned
```

Note that the Java virtual machine never allows its operand stack manipulation instructions to modify or break up individual values on the operand stack.

7.12 Throwing and Handling Exceptions

Exceptions are thrown from programs using the `throw` keyword. Its compilation is simple:

```
void cantBeZero(int i) throws TestExc {
    if (i == 0) {
        throw new TestExc();
    }
}
```

becomes

Method `void cantBeZero(int)`

0	*iload_1*	*// Push argument 1 (*`i`*)*
1	*ifne 12*	*// If* `i==0`*, allocate instance and throw*
4	*new #1*	*// Create instance of* `TestExc`
7	*dup*	*// One reference goes to the constructor*
8	*invokespecial #7*	*// Method* `TestExc.<init>()V`
11	*athrow*	*// Second reference is thrown*
12	*return*	*// Never get here if we threw* `TestExc`

Compilation of `try-catch` constructs is straightforward. For example,

```
void catchOne() {
    try {
        tryItOut();
    } catch (TestExc e) {
        handleExc(e);
    }
}
```

is compiled as

Method `void catchOne()`

0	*aload_0*	*// Beginning of* `try` *block*
1	*invokevirtual #6*	*// Method* `Example.tryItOut()V`
4	*return*	*// End of* `try` *block; normal return*
5	*astore_1*	*// Store thrown value in local variable 1*
6	*aload_0*	*// Push* `this`
7	*aload_1*	*// Push thrown value*

	8	*invokevirtual #5*	// *Invoke handler method:*
			// `Example.handleExc(LTestExc;)V`
	11	*return*	// *Return after handling* `TestExc`

Exception table:

From	To	Target	Type
0	4	5	*Class* `TestExc`

Looking more closely, the `try` block is compiled just as it would be if the `try` were not present:

Method `void catchOne()`

	0	*aload_0*	// *Beginning of* `try` *block*
	1	*invokevirtual #4*	// *Method* `Example.tryItOut()V`
	4	*return*	// *End of* `try` *block; normal return*

If no exception is thrown during the execution of the `try` block, it behaves as though the `try` were not there: `tryItOut` is invoked and `catchOne` returns.

Following the `try` block is the Java virtual machine code that implements the single `catch` clause:

	5	*astore_1*	// *Store thrown value in local variable 1*
	6	*aload_0*	// *Push* `this`
	7	*aload_1*	// *Push thrown value*
	8	*invokevirtual #5*	// *Invoke handler method:*
			// `Example.handleExc(LTestExc;)V`
	11	*return*	// *Return after handling* `TestExc`

Exception table:

From	To	Target	Type
0	4	5	*Class* `TestExc`

The invocation of `handleExc`, the contents of the `catch` clause, is also compiled like a normal method invocation. However, the presence of a `catch` clause causes the compiler to generate an exception table entry. The exception table for the `catchOne` method has one entry corresponding to the one argument (an instance of class `TestExc`) that the `catch` clause of `catchOne` can handle. If some value that is an instance of `TestExc` is thrown during execution of the instructions between indices 0 and 4 in `catchOne`, control is transferred to the Java virtual machine code at index 5, which implements the block of the `catch` clause. If the value that is thrown is not an instance of `TestExc`, the `catch` clause of `catchOne` cannot handle it. Instead, the value is rethrown to the invoker of `catchOne`.

A `try` may have multiple `catch` clauses:

```
void catchTwo() {
    try {
        tryItOut();
    } catch (TestExc1 e) {
        handleExc(e);
    } catch (TestExc2 e) {
        handleExc(e);
    }
}
```

Multiple `catch` clauses of a given `try` statement are compiled by simply appending the Java virtual machine code for each `catch` clause one after the other and adding entries to the exception table, as shown:

Method `void catchTwo()`		
0	*aload_0*	*// Begin* `try` *block*
1	*invokevirtual #5*	*// Method* `Example.tryItOut()V`
4	*return*	*// End of* `try` *block; normal return*
5	*astore_1*	*// Beginning of handler for* `TestExc1`;
		// Store thrown value in local variable 1
6	*aload_0*	*// Push* `this`
7	*aload_1*	*// Push thrown value*
8	*invokevirtual #7*	*// Invoke handler method:*
		// `Example.handleExc(LTestExc1;)V`
11	*return*	*// Return after handling* `TestExc1`
12	*astore_1*	*// Beginning of handler for* `TestExc2`;
		// Store thrown value in local variable 1
13	*aload_0*	*// Push* `this`
14	*aload_1*	*// Push thrown value*
15	*invokevirtual #7*	*// Invoke handler method:*
		// `Example.handleExc(LTestExc2;)V`
18	*return*	*// Return after handling* `TestExc2`

Exception table:

From	To	Target	Type
0	*4*	*5*	*Class* `TestExc1`
0	*4*	*12*	*Class* `TestExc2`

If during the execution of the `try` clause (between indices *0* and *4*) a value is thrown that matches the parameter of one or more of the `catch` clauses (the value is an instance of one or more of the parameters), the first (innermost) such `catch` clause is selected. Control is transferred to the Java virtual machine code for the block of that `catch` clause. If the value thrown does not match the parameter of any of the `catch` clauses of catchTwo, the Java virtual machine rethrows the value without invoking code in any `catch` clause of catchTwo.

Nested `try-catch` statements are compiled very much like a `try` statement with multiple `catch` clauses:

```
void nestedCatch() {
    try {
        try {
            tryItOut();
        } catch (TestExc1 e) {
            handleExc1(e);
        }
    } catch (TestExc2 e) {
        handleExc2(e);
    }
}
```

becomes

```
Method void nestedCatch()
   0   aload_0            // Begin try block
   1   invokevirtual #8   // Method Example.tryItOut()V
   4   return             // End of try block; normal return
   5   astore_1           // Beginning of handler for TestExc1;
                          // Store thrown value in local variable 1
   6   aload_0            // Push this
   7   aload_1            // Push thrown value
   8   invokevirtual #7   // Invoke handler method:
                          // Example.handleExc1(LTestExc1;)V
  11   return             // Return after handling TestExc1
  12   astore_1           // Beginning of handler for TestExc2;
                          // Store thrown value in local variable 1
  13   aload_0            // Push this
  14   aload_1            // Push thrown value
```

	15 *invokevirtual #6*	*// Invoke handler method:*
		// `Example.handleExc2(LTestExc2;)V`
	18 *return*	*// Return after handling* `TestExc2`

Exception table:

From	To	Target	Type
0	*4*	*5*	*Class* `TestExc1`
0	*12*	*12*	*Class* `TestExc2`

The nesting of `catch` clauses is represented only in the exception table. When an exception is thrown, the first (innermost) catch clause that contains the site of the exception and with a matching parameter is selected to handle it. For instance, if the invocation of `tryItOut` (at index *1*) threw an instance of `TestExc1`, it would be handled by the `catch` clause that invokes `handleExc1`. This is so even though the exception occurs within the bounds of the outer `catch` clause (catching `TestExc2`) and even though that outer `catch` clause might otherwise have been able to handle the thrown value.

As a subtle point, note that the range of a `catch` clause is inclusive on the "from" end and exclusive on the "to" end (§4.7.3). Thus, the exception table entry for the `catch` clause catching `TestExc1` does not cover the *return* instruction at offset *4*. However, the exception table entry for the `catch` clause catching `TestExc2` does cover the *return* instruction at offset *11*. Return instructions within nested `catch` clauses are included in the range of instructions covered by nesting `catch` clauses.

7.13 Compiling `finally`

Compilation of a `try-finally` statement is similar to that of `try-catch`. Prior to transferring control outside the `try` statement, whether that transfer is normal or abrupt, because an exception has been thrown, the `finally` clause must first be executed. For this simple example

```
void tryFinally() {
    try {
        tryItOut();
    } finally {
        wrapItUp();
    }
}
```

the compiled code is

```
Method void tryFinally()
    0  aload_0              // Beginning of try block
    1  invokevirtual #6     // Method Example.tryItOut()V
    4  jsr 14               // Call finally block
    7  return               // End of try block
    8  astore_1             // Beginning of handler for any throw
    9  jsr 14               // Call finally block
   12  aload_1              // Push thrown value
   13  athrow               // ...and rethrow the value to the invoker
   14  astore_2             // Beginning of finally block
   15  aload_0              // Push this
   16  invokevirtual #5     // Method Example.wrapItUp()V
   19  ret 2                // Return from finally block
Exception table:
    From To  Target   Type
     0   4    8       any
```

There are four ways for control to pass outside of the try statement: by falling through the bottom of that block, by returning, by executing a break or continue statement, or by raising an exception. If tryItOut returns without raising an exception, control is transferred to the finally block using a *jsr* instruction. The *jsr 14* instruction at index *4* makes a "subroutine call" to the code for the finally block at index *14* (the finally block is compiled as an embedded subroutine). When the finally block completes, the *ret 2* instruction returns control to the instruction following the *jsr* instruction at index *4*.

In more detail, the subroutine call works as follows: The *jsr* instruction pushes the address of the following instruction (*return* at index *7*) onto the operand stack before jumping. The *astore_2* instruction that is the jump target stores the address on the operand stack into local variable 2. The code for the finally block (in this case the *aload_0* and *invokevirtual* instructions) is run. Assuming execution of that code completes normally, the *ret* instruction retrieves the address from local variable 2 and resumes execution at that address. The *return* instruction is executed, and tryFinally returns normally.

A try statement with a finally clause is compiled to have a special exception handler, one that can handle any exception thrown within the try statement. If tryItOut throws an exception, the exception table for tryFinally is searched for an appropriate exception handler. The special handler is found, causing execution to continue at index *8*. The *astore_1* instruction at index *8* stores the thrown value into local variable *1*. The following *jsr* instruction does a subroutine call to the code for the `finally` block. Assuming that code returns normally, the *aload_1* instruction at index *12* pushes the thrown value back onto the operand stack, and the following *athrow* instruction rethrows the value.

Compiling a `try` statement with both a `catch` clause and a `finally` clause is more complex:

```
void tryCatchFinally() {
    try {
        tryItOut();
    } catch (TestExc e) {
        handleExc(e);
    } finally {
        wrapItUp();
    }
}
```

becomes

Method `void tryCatchFinally()`

0	*aload_0*	// *Beginning of* `try` *block*
1	*invokevirtual #4*	// *Method* `Example.tryItOut()V`
4	*goto 16*	// *Jump to* `finally` *block*
7	*astore_3*	// *Beginning of handler for* `TestExc`;
		// *Store thrown value in local variable 3*
8	*aload_0*	// *Push* `this`
9	*aload_3*	// *Push thrown value*
10	*invokevirtual #6*	// *Invoke handler method:*
		// `Example.handleExc(LTestExc;)V`
13	*goto 16*	// *Huh???*[1]
16	*jsr 26*	// *Call* `finally` *block*
19	*return*	// *Return after handling* `TestExc`
20	*astore_1*	// *Beginning of handler for exceptions*
		// *other than* `TestExc`, *or exceptions*
		// *thrown while handling* `TestExc`

---

[1] This *goto* instruction is strictly unnecessary, but is generated by the `javac` compiler of Sun's JDK release 1.0.2.

```
21  jsr 26              // Call finally block
24  aload_1            // Push thrown value...
25  athrow             // ...and rethrow the value to the invoker
26  astore_2           // Beginning of finally block
27  aload_0            // Push this
28  invokevirtual #5   // Method Example.wrapItUp()V
31  ret 2              // Return from finally block
Exception table:
    From To  Target   Type
     0    4    7      Class TestExc
     0   16   20      any
```

If the try statement completes normally, the *goto* instruction at index *4* jumps
to the subroutine call for the finally block at index *16*. The finally block at
index *26* is executed, control returns to the *return* instruction at index *19*, and
tryCatchFinally returns normally.

If tryItOut throws an instance of TestExc, the first (innermost) applicable
exception handler in the exception table is chosen to handle the exception. The
code for that exception handler, beginning at index 7, passes the thrown value to
handleExc and on its return makes the same subroutine call to the finally block
at index *26* as in the normal case. If an exception is not thrown by handleExc,
tryCatchFinally returns normally.

If tryItOut throws a value that is not an instance of TestExc or if handle-
Exc itself throws an exception, the condition is handled by the second entry in the
exception table, which handles any value thrown between indices *0* and *16*. That
exception handler transfers control to index *20*, where the thrown value is first
stored in local variable *1*. The code for the finally block at index *26* is called as
a subroutine. If it returns, the thrown value is retrieved from local variable *1* and
rethrown using the *athrow* instruction. If a new value is thrown during execution
of the finally clause, the finally clause aborts, and tryCatchFinally returns
abruptly, throwing the new value to its invoker.

7.14 Synchronization

The Java virtual machine provides explicit support for synchronization through its
monitorenter and *monitorexit* instructions. For code written in the Java programming language, however, perhaps the most common form of synchronization is the
synchronized method.

A synchronized method is not normally implemented using *monitorenter* and *monitorexit*. Rather, it is simply distinguished in the runtime constant pool by the ACC_SYNCHRONIZED flag, which is checked by the method invocation instructions. When invoking a method for which ACC_SYNCHRONIZED is set, the current thread acquires a monitor, invokes the method itself, and releases the monitor whether the method invocation completes normally or abruptly. During the time the executing thread owns the monitor, no other thread may acquire it. If an exception is thrown during invocation of the synchronized method and the synchronized method does not handle the exception, the monitor for the method is automatically released before the exception is rethrown out of the synchronized method.

The *monitorenter* and *monitorexit* instructions exist to support synchronized statements. For example:

```
void onlyMe(Foo f) {
    synchronized(f) {
        doSomething();
    }
}
```

is compiled to

```
Method void onlyMe(Foo)
   0  aload_1            // Push f
   1  astore_2           // Store it in local variable 2
   2  aload_2            // Push local variable 2 (f)
   3  monitorenter       // Enter the monitor associated with f
   4  aload_0            // Holding the monitor, pass this and...
   5  invokevirtual #5   // ...call Example.doSomething()V
   8  aload_2            // Push local variable 2 (f)
   9  monitorexit        // Exit the monitor associated with f
  10  return             // Return normally
  11  aload_2            // In case of any throw, end up here
  12  monitorexit        // Be sure to exit monitor...
  13  athrow             // ...then rethrow the value to the invoker
Exception table:
     From To   Target  Type
       4   8    11     any
```

7.15 Compiling Nested Classes and Interfaces

JDK release 1.1 added *nested classes and interfaces* to the Java programming language. Nested classes and interfaces are sometimes referred to as *inner classes and interfaces*, which are one sort of nested classes and interfaces. However, nested classes and interfaces also encompass nested top-level classes and interfaces, which are not inner classes or interfaces.

A full treatment of the compilation of nested classes and interfaces is outside the scope of this chapter. However, interested readers can refer to the Inner Classes Specification at `http://java.sun.com/products/jdk/1.1/docs/guide/innerclasses/spec/innerclasses.doc.html`.

CHAPTER 8

Threads and Locks

THIS chapter details the low-level actions that may be used to explain the interaction of Java virtual machine threads with a shared main memory. It has been adapted with minimal changes from Chapter 17 of the first edition of *The Java*™ *Language Specification*, by James Gosling, Bill Joy, and Guy Steele.

8.1 Terminology and Framework

A *variable* is any location within a program that may be stored into. This includes not only class variables and instance variables, but also components of arrays. Variables are kept in a *main memory* that is shared by all threads. Because it is impossible for one thread to access parameters or local variables of another thread, it does not matter whether parameters and local variables are thought of as residing in the shared main memory or in the working memory of the thread that owns them.

Every thread has a *working memory* in which it keeps its own *working copy* of variables that it must use or assign. As the thread executes a program, it operates on these working copies. The main memory contains the *master copy* of every variable. There are rules about when a thread is permitted or required to transfer the contents of its working copy of a variable into the master copy or vice versa.

The main memory also contains *locks*; there is one lock associated with each object. Threads may compete to acquire a lock.

For the purposes of this chapter, the verbs *use, assign, load, store, lock,* and *unlock* name actions that a thread can perform. The verbs *read, write, lock,* and *unlock* name actions that the main memory subsystem can perform. Each of these operations is atomic (indivisible).

A *use* or *assign* operation is a tightly coupled interaction between a thread's execution engine and the thread's working memory. A *lock* or *unlock* operation is a tightly coupled interaction between a thread's execution engine and the main memory. But the transfer of data between the main memory and a thread's working memory is loosely coupled. When data is copied from the main memory to a working memory, two actions must occur: a *read* operation performed by the main memory, followed some time later by a corresponding *load* operation performed by the working memory. When data is copied from a working memory to the main memory, two actions must occur: a *store* operation performed by the working memory, followed some time later by a corresponding *write* operation performed by the main memory. There may be some transit time between main memory and a working memory, and the transit time may be different for each transaction; thus, operations initiated by a thread on different variables may be viewed by another thread as occurring in a different order. For each variable, however, the operations in main memory on behalf of any one thread are performed in the same order as the corresponding operations by that thread. (This is explained in greater detail later.)

A single thread issues a stream of *use*, *assign*, *lock*, and *unlock* operations as dictated by the semantics of the program it is executing. The underlying Java virtual machine implementation is then required additionally to perform appropriate *load*, *store*, *read*, and *write* operations so as to obey a certain set of constraints, explained later. If the implementation correctly follows these rules and the programmer follows certain other rules of programming, then data can be reliably transferred between threads through shared variables. The rules are designed to be "tight" enough to make this possible, but "loose" enough to allow hardware and software designers considerable freedom to improve speed and throughput through such mechanisms as registers, queues, and caches.

Here are the detailed definitions of each of the operations:

- A *use* action (by a thread) transfers the contents of the thread's working copy of a variable to the thread's execution engine. This action is performed whenever a thread executes a virtual machine instruction that uses the value of a variable.

- An *assign* action (by a thread) transfers a value from the thread's execution engine into the thread's working copy of a variable. This action is performed whenever a thread executes a virtual machine instruction that assigns to a variable.

- A *read* action (by the main memory) transmits the contents of the master copy of a variable to a thread's working memory for use by a later *load* operation.

- A *load* action (by a thread) puts a value transmitted from main memory by a *read* action into the thread's working copy of a variable.

- A *store* action (by a thread) transmits the contents of the thread's working copy of a variable to main memory for use by a later *write* operation.

- A *write* action (by the main memory) puts a value transmitted from the thread's working memory by a *store* action into the master copy of a variable in main memory.

- A *lock* action (by a thread tightly synchronized with main memory) causes a thread to acquire one claim on a particular lock.

- An *unlock* action (by a thread tightly synchronized with main memory) causes a thread to release one claim on a particular lock.

Thus, the interaction of a thread with a variable over time consists of a sequence of *use, assign, load,* and *store* operations. Main memory performs a *read* operation for every *load* and a *write* operation for every *store*. A thread's interactions with a lock over time consist of a sequence of *lock* and *unlock* operations. All the globally visible behavior of a thread thus comprises all the thread's operations on variables and locks.

8.2 Execution Order and Consistency

The rules of execution order constrain the order in which certain events may occur. There are four general constraints on the relationships among actions:

- The actions performed by any one thread are totally ordered; that is, for any two actions performed by a thread, one action precedes the other.

- The actions performed by the main memory for any one variable are totally ordered; that is, for any two actions performed by the main memory on the same variable, one action precedes the other.

- The actions performed by the main memory for any one lock are totally ordered; that is, for any two actions performed by the main memory on the same lock, one action precedes the other.

- It is not permitted for an action to follow itself.

The last rule may seem trivial, but it does need to be stated separately and explicitly for completeness. Without the rule, it would be possible to propose a set of actions by two or more threads and precedence relationships among the actions that would satisfy all the other rules but would require an action to follow itself.

Threads do not interact directly; they communicate only through the shared main memory. The relationships between the actions of a thread and the actions of main memory are constrained in three ways:

- Each *lock* or *unlock* action is performed jointly by some thread and the main memory.

- Each *load* action by a thread is uniquely paired with a *read* action by the main memory such that the *load* action follows the *read* action.

- Each *store* action by a thread is uniquely paired with a *write* action by the main memory such that the *write* action follows the *store* action.

Most of the rules in the following sections further constrain the order in which certain actions take place. A rule may state that one action must precede or follow some other action. Note that this relationship is transitive: if action *A* must precede action *B*, and *B* must precede *C*, then *A* must precede *C*. The programmer must remember that these rules are the *only* constraints on the ordering of actions; if no rule or combination of rules implies that action *A* must precede action *B*, then a Java virtual machine implementation is free to perform action *B* before action *A*, or to perform action *B* concurrently with action *A*. This freedom can be the key to good performance. Conversely, an implementation is not required to take advantage of all the freedoms given it.

In the rules that follow, the phrasing "*B* must intervene between *A* and *C*" means that action *B* must follow action *A* and precede action *C*.

8.3 Rules About Variables

Let *T* be a thread and *V* be a variable. There are certain constraints on the operations performed by *T* with respect to *V*:

- A *use* or *assign* by *T* of *V* is permitted only when dictated by execution by *T* of the program according to the standard execution model. For example, an occurrence of *V* as an operand of the + operator requires that a single *use* operation occur on *V*; an occurrence of *V* as the left-hand operand of the assignment operator = requires that a single *assign* operation occur. All *use* and *assign* actions by a given thread must occur in the order specified by the program being executed by the thread. If the following rules forbid *T* to perform a required *use* as its next action, it may be necessary for *T* to perform a *load* first in order to make progress.

- A *store* operation by *T* on *V* must intervene between an *assign* by *T* of *V* and a subsequent *load* by *T* of *V*. (Less formally: a thread is not permitted to lose the most recent assign.)

- An *assign* operation by *T* on *V* must intervene between a *load* or *store* by *T* of *V* and a subsequent *store* by *T* of *V*. (Less formally: a thread is not permitted to write data from its working memory back to main memory for no reason.)

- After a thread is created, it must perform an *assign* or *load* operation on a variable before performing a *use* or *store* operation on that variable. (Less formally: a new thread starts with an empty working memory.)

- After a variable is created, every thread must perform an *assign* or *load* operation on that variable before performing a *use* or *store* operation on that variable. (Less formally: a new variable is created only in main memory and is not initially in any thread's working memory.)

Provided that all the constraints in Sections 8.3, 8.6, and 8.7 are obeyed, a *load* or *store* operation may be issued at any time by any thread on any variable, at the whim of the implementation.

There are also certain constraints on the *read* and *write* operations performed by main memory:

- For every *load* operation performed by any thread *T* on its working copy of a variable *V*, there must be a corresponding preceding *read* operation by the main memory on the master copy of *V*, and the *load* operation must put into the working copy the data transmitted by the corresponding *read* operation.

- For every *store* operation performed by any thread *T* on its working copy of a variable *V*, there must follow a corresponding *write* operation by the main memory on the master copy of *V*, and the *write* operation must put into the master copy the data transmitted by the corresponding *store* operation.

- Let action *A* be a *load* or *store* by thread *T* on variable *V*, and let action *P* be the corresponding *read* or *write* by the main memory on variable *V*. Similarly, let action *B* be some other *load* or *store* by thread *T* on that same variable *V*, and let action *Q* be the corresponding *read* or *write* by the main memory on variable *V*. If *A* precedes *B*, then *P* must precede *Q*. (Less formally: operations on the master copy of any given variable on behalf of a thread are performed by the main memory in exactly the order that the thread requested.)

Note that this last rule applies *only* to actions by a thread on the *same* variable. However, there is a more stringent rule for volatile variables (§8.7).

8.4   Nonatomic Treatment of double and long Variables

If a double or long variable is not declared volatile, then for the purposes of *load*, *store*, *read*, and *write* operations it is treated as if it were two variables of 32 bits each; wherever the rules require one of these operations, two such operations are performed, one for each 32-bit half. The manner in which the 64 bits of a double or long variable are encoded into two 32-bit quantities and the order of the operations on the halves of the variables are not defined by *The Java*™ *Language Specification*.

This matters only because a *read* or *write* of a double or long variable may be handled by an actual main memory as two 32-bit *read* or *write* operations that may be separated in time, with other operations coming between them. Consequently, if two threads concurrently assign distinct values to the same shared nonvolatile double or long variable, a subsequent use of that variable may obtain a value that is not equal to either of the assigned values, but rather some implementation-dependent mixture of the two values.

An implementation is free to implement *load*, *store*, *read*, and *write* operations for double and long values as atomic 64-bit operations; in fact, this is strongly encouraged. The model divides them into 32-bit halves for the sake of currently popular microprocessors that fail to provide efficient atomic memory transactions on 64-bit quantities. It would have been simpler for the Java virtual machine to define all memory transactions on single variables as atomic; this more complex definition is a pragmatic concession to current hardware practice. In the future this concession may be eliminated. Meanwhile, programmers are cautioned to explicitly synchronize access to shared double and long variables.

8.5   Rules About Locks

Let *T* be a thread and *L* be a lock. There are certain constraints on the operations performed by *T* with respect to *L*:

- A *lock* operation by T on L may occur only if, for every thread S other than T, the number of preceding *unlock* operations by S on L equals the number of preceding *lock* operations by S on L. (Less formally: only one thread at a time is permitted to lay claim to a lock; moreover, a thread may acquire the same lock multiple times and does not relinquish ownership of it until a matching number of *unlock* operations have been performed.)

- An *unlock* operation by thread T on lock L may occur only if the number of preceding *unlock* operations by T on L is strictly less than the number of preceding *lock* operations by T on L. (Less formally: a thread is not permitted to unlock a lock it does not own.)

With respect to a lock, the *lock* and *unlock* operations performed by all the threads are performed in some total sequential order. This total order must be consistent with the total order on the operations of each thread.

8.6 Rules About the Interaction of Locks and Variables

Let T be any thread, let V be any variable, and let L be any lock. There are certain constraints on the operations performed by T with respect to V and L:

- Between an *assign* operation by T on V and a subsequent *unlock* operation by T on L, a *store* operation by T on V must intervene; moreover, the *write* operation corresponding to that *store* must precede the *unlock* operation, as seen by main memory. (Less formally: if a thread is to perform an *unlock* operation on *any* lock, it must first copy *all* assigned values in its working memory back out to main memory.)

- Between a *lock* operation by T on L and a subsequent *use* or *store* operation by T on a variable V, an *assign* or *load* operation on V must intervene; moreover, if it is a *load* operation, then the *read* operation corresponding to that *load* must follow the *lock* operation, as seen by main memory. (Less formally: a *lock* operation behaves as if it flushes *all* variables from the thread's working memory, after which the thread must either assign them itself or load copies anew from main memory.)

8.7 Rules for `volatile` Variables

If a variable is declared volatile, then additional constraints apply to the operations of each thread. Let *T* be a thread and let *V* and *W* be volatile variables.

- A *use* operation by *T* on *V* is permitted only if the previous operation by *T* on *V* was *load*, and a *load* operation by *T* on *V* is permitted only if the next operation by *T* on *V* is *use*. The *use* operation is said to be "associated" with the *read* operation that corresponds to the *load*.

- A *store* operation by *T* on *V* is permitted only if the previous operation by *T* on *V* was *assign*, and an *assign* operation by *T* on *V* is permitted only if the next operation by *T* on *V* is *store*. The *assign* operation is said to be "associated" with the *write* operation that corresponds to the *store*.

- Let action *A* be a *use* or *assign* by thread *T* on variable *V*, let action *F* be the *load* or *store* associated with *A*, and let action *P* be the *read* or *write* of *V* that corresponds to *F*. Similarly, let action *B* be a *use* or *assign* by thread *T* on variable *W*, let action *G* be the *load* or *store* associated with *B*, and let action *Q* be the *read* or *write* of *W* that corresponds to *G*. If *A* precedes *B*, then *P* must precede *Q*. (Less formally: operations on the master copies of volatile variables on behalf of a thread are performed by the main memory in exactly the order that the thread requested.)

8.8 Prescient Store Operations

If a variable is not declared `volatile`, then the rules in the previous sections are relaxed slightly to allow *store* operations to occur earlier than would otherwise be permitted. The purpose of this relaxation is to allow optimizing compilers to perform certain kinds of code rearrangement that preserve the semantics of properly synchronized programs, but might be caught in the act of performing memory operations out of order by programs that are not properly synchronized.

Suppose that a *store* by *T* of *V* would follow a particular *assign* by *T* of *V* according to the rules of the previous sections, with no intervening *load* or *assign* by *T* of *V*. Then that *store* operation would send to the main memory the value that the *assign* operation put into the working memory of thread *T*. The special rule allows the *store* operation actually to occur before the *assign* operation instead, if the following restrictions are obeyed:

- If the *store* operation occurs, the *assign* is bound to occur. (Remember, these are restrictions on what actually happens, not on what a thread plans to do. No fair performing a *store* and then throwing an exception before the *assign* occurs!)

- No *lock* operation intervenes between the relocated *store* and the *assign*.

- No *load* of *V* intervenes between the relocated *store* and the *assign*.

- No other *store* of *V* intervenes between the relocated *store* and the *assign*.

- The *store* operation sends to the main memory the value that the *assign* operation will put into the working memory of thread *T*.

This last property inspires us to call such an early *store* operation *prescient*: it has to know ahead of time, somehow, what value will be stored by the *assign* that it should have followed. In practice, optimized compiled code will compute such values early (which is permitted if, for example, the computation has no side effects and throws no exceptions), store them early (before entering a loop, for example), and keep them in working registers for later use within the loop.

8.9 Discussion

Any association between locks and variables is purely conventional. Locking any lock conceptually flushes *all* variables from a thread's working memory, and unlocking any lock forces the writing out to main memory of *all* variables that the thread has assigned. That a lock may be associated with a particular object or a class is purely a convention. For example, in some applications it may be appropriate always to lock an object before accessing any of its instance variables; `synchronized` methods are a convenient way to follow this convention. In other applications, it may suffice to use a single lock to synchronize access to a large collection of objects.

   If a thread uses a particular shared variable only after locking a particular lock and before the corresponding unlocking of that same lock, then the thread will read the shared value of that variable from main memory after the *lock* operation, if necessary, and will copy back to main memory the value most recently assigned to that variable before the *unlock* operation. This, in conjunction with the mutual exclusion rules for locks, suffices to guarantee that values are correctly transmitted from one thread to another through shared variables.

The rules for volatile variables effectively require that main memory be touched exactly once for each *use* or *assign* of a volatile variable by a thread, and that main memory be touched in exactly the order dictated by the thread execution semantics. However, such memory operations are not ordered with respect to *read* and *write* operations on nonvolatile variables.

8.10 Example: Possible Swap

Consider a class that has class variables a and b and methods hither and yon:

```
class Sample {
    int a = 1, b = 2;
    void hither() {
        a = b;
    }
    void yon()
        b = a;
    }
}
```

Now suppose that two threads are created and that one thread calls hither while the other thread calls yon. What is the required set of actions and what are the ordering constraints?

Let us consider the thread that calls hither. According to the rules, this thread must perform a *use* of b followed by an *assign* of a. That is the bare minimum required to execute a call to the method hither.

Now, the first operation on variable b by the thread cannot be *use*. But it may be *assign* or *load*. An *assign* to b cannot occur because the program text does not call for such an *assign* operation, so a *load* of b is required. This *load* operation by the thread in turn requires a preceding *read* operation for b by the main memory.

The thread may optionally *store* the value of a after the *assign* has occurred. If it does, then the *store* operation in turn requires a following *write* operation for a by the main memory.

The situation for the thread that calls yon is similar, but with the roles of a and b exchanged.

The total set of operations may be pictured as follows:

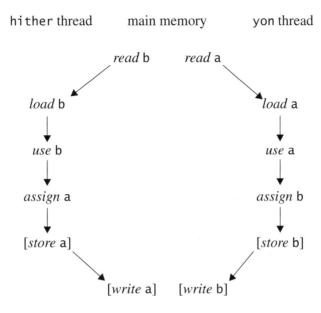

Here an arrow from action *A* to action *B* indicates that *A* must precede *B*.

In what order may the operations by the main memory occur? The only constraint is that it is not possible both for the *write* of a to precede the *read* of a and for the *write* of b to precede the *read* of b, because the causality arrows in the diagram would form a loop so that an action would have to precede itself, which is not allowed. Assuming that the optional *store* and *write* operations are to occur, there are three possible orderings in which the main memory might legitimately perform its operations. Let ha and hb be the working copies of a and b for the hither thread, let ya and yb be the working copies for the yon thread, and let ma and mb be the master copies in main memory. Initially ma=1 and mb=2. Then the three possible orderings of operations and the resulting states are as follows:

- *write* a→*read* a, *read* b→*write* b (then ha=2, hb=2, ma=2, mb=2, ya=2, yb=2)

- *read* a→*write* a, *write* b→*read* b (then ha=1, hb=1, ma=1, mb=1, ya=1, yb=1)

- *read* a→*write* a, *read* b→*write* b (then ha=2, hb=2, ma=2, mb=1, ya=1, yb=1)

Thus, the net result might be that, in main memory, b is copied into a, a is copied into b, or the values of a and b are swapped; moreover, the working copies of the variables might or might not agree. It would be incorrect, of course, to assume that any one of these outcomes is more likely than another. This is one place in which the behavior of a program is necessarily timing-dependent.

Of course, an implementation might also choose not to perform the *store* and *write* operations, or only one of the two pairs, leading to yet other possible results.

Now suppose that we modify the example to use `synchronized` methods:

```
class SynchSample {
    int a = 1, b = 2;
    synchronized void hither() {
        a = b;
    }
    synchronized void yon()
        b = a;
    }
}
```

Let us again consider the thread that calls `hither`. According to the rules, this thread must perform a *lock* operation (on the instance of class `SynchSample` on which the `hither` method is being called) before the body of method `hither` is executed. This is followed by a *use* of b and then an *assign* of a. Finally, an *unlock* operation on that same instance of `SynchSample` must be performed after the body of method `hither` completes. That is the bare minimum required to execute a call to the method `hither`.

As before, a *load* of b is required, which in turn requires a preceding *read* operation for b by the main memory. Because the *load* follows the *lock* operation, the corresponding *read* must also follow the *lock* operation.

Because an *unlock* operation follows the *assign* of a, a *store* operation on a is mandatory, which in turn requires a following *write* operation for a by the main memory. The *write* must precede the *unlock* operation.

The situation for the thread that calls yon is similar, but with the roles of a and b exchanged.

The total set of operations may be pictured as follows:

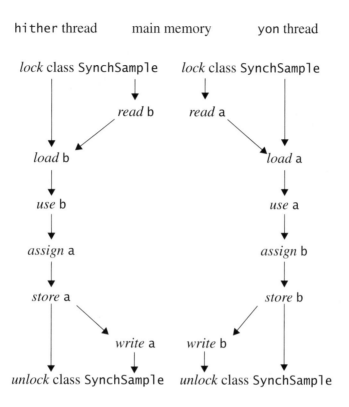

The *lock* and *unlock* operations provide further constraints on the order of operations by the main memory; the *lock* operation by one thread cannot occur between the *lock* and *unlock* operations of the other thread. Moreover, the *unlock* operations require that the *store* and *write* operations occur. It follows that only two sequences are possible:

- *write* a→*read* a, *read* b→*write* b (then ha=2, hb=2, ma=2, mb=2, ya=2, yb=2)

- *read* a→*write* a, *write* b→*read* b (then ha=1, hb=1, ma=1, mb=1, ya=1, yb=1)

While the resulting state is timing-dependent, it can be seen that the two threads will necessarily agree on the values of a and b.

8.11 Example: Out-of-Order Writes

This example is similar to that in the preceding section, except that one method assigns to both variables and the other method reads both variables. Consider a class that has class variables a and b and methods to and fro:

```
class Simple {
    int a = 1, b = 2;
    void to() {
        a = 3;
        b = 4;
    }
    void fro()
        System.out.println("a= " + a + ", b=" + b);
    }
}
```

Now suppose that two threads are created and that one thread calls to while the other thread calls fro. What is the required set of actions and what are the ordering constraints?

Let us consider the thread that calls to. According to the rules, this thread must perform an *assign* of a followed by an *assign* of b. That is the bare minimum required to execute a call to the method to. Because there is no synchronization, it is at the option of the implementation whether or not to *store* the assigned values back to main memory! Therefore, the thread that calls fro may obtain either 1 or 3 for the value of a and independently may obtain either 2 or 4 for the value of b.

Now suppose that to is synchronized but fro is not:

```
class SynchSimple {
    int a = 1, b = 2;
    synchronized void to() {
        a = 3;
        b = 4;
    }
    void fro()
        System.out.println("a= " + a + ", b=" + b);
    }
}
```

In this case the method to will be forced to *store* the assigned values back to main memory before the *unlock* operation at the end of the method. The method fro must, of course, use a and b (in that order) and so must *load* values for a and b from main memory.

The total set of operations may be pictured as follows:

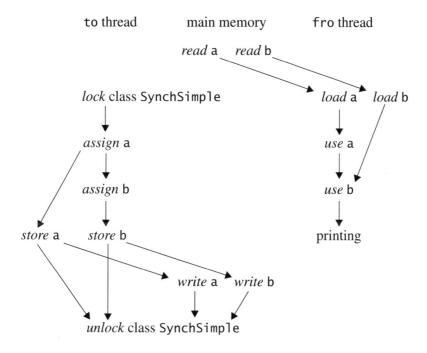

Here an arrow from action *A* to action *B* indicates that *A* must precede *B*.

In what order may the operations by the main memory occur? Note that the rules do not require that *write* a occur before *write* b; neither do they require that *read* a occur before *read* b. Also, even though method to is synchronized, method fro is not synchronized, so there is nothing to prevent the *read* operations from occurring between the *lock* and *unlock* operations. (The point is that declaring one method synchronized does not of itself make that method behave as if it were atomic.)

As a result, the method fro could still obtain either 1 or 3 for the value of a and independently could obtain either 2 or 4 for the value of b. In particular, fro might observe the value 1 for a and 4 for b. Thus, even though to does an *assign* to a and then an *assign* to b, the *write* operations to main memory may be observed by another thread to occur as if in the opposite order.

Finally, suppose that to and fro are both synchronized:

```
class SynchSynchSimple {
    int a = 1, b = 2;
    synchronized void to() {
        a = 3;
        b = 4;
    }
    synchronized void fro()
        System.out.println("a= " + a + ", b=" + b);
    }
}
```

In this case, the actions of method `fro` cannot be interleaved with the actions of method `to`, and so `fro` will print either "a=1, b=2" or "a=3, b=4".

8.12 Threads

Threads are created and managed by the classes `Thread` and `ThreadGroup`. Creating a `Thread` object creates a thread, and that is the only way to create a thread. When the thread is created, it is not yet active; it begins to run when its `start` method is called.

8.13 Locks and Synchronization

There is a lock associated with every object. The Java programming language does not provide a way to perform separate *lock* and *unlock* operations; instead, they are implicitly performed by high-level constructs that always arrange to pair such operations correctly. (The Java virtual machine, however, provides separate *monitorenter* and *monitorexit* instructions that implement the *lock* and *unlock* operations.)

The `synchronized` statement computes a reference to an object; it then attempts to perform a *lock* operation on that object and does not proceed further until the *lock* operation has successfully completed. (A *lock* operation may be delayed because the rules about locks can prevent the main memory from participating until some other thread is ready to perform one or more *unlock* operations.) After the lock operation has been performed, the body of the `synchronized` statement is executed. Normally, a compiler for the Java programming language ensures that the *lock* operation implemented by a *monitorenter* instruction executed prior to the execution of the body of the `synchronized` statement is matched by an unlock operation implemented by a *monitorexit* instruction whenever the `synchronized` statement completes, whether completion is normal or abrupt.

A `synchronized` method automatically performs a *lock* operation when it is invoked; its body is not executed until the *lock* operation has successfully completed. If the method is an instance method, it locks the lock associated with the instance for which it was invoked (that is, the object that will be known as `this` during execution of the method's body). If the method is `static`, it locks the lock associated with the `Class` object that represents the class in which the method is defined. If execution of the method's body is ever completed, either normally or abruptly, an *unlock* operation is automatically performed on that same lock.

Best practice is that if a variable is ever to be assigned by one thread and used or assigned by another, then all accesses to that variable should be enclosed in `synchronized` methods or `synchronized` statements.

Although a compiler for the Java programming language normally guarantees structured use of locks (see Section 7.14, "Synchronization"), there is no assurance that all code submitted to the Java virtual machine will obey this property. Implementations of the Java virtual machine are permitted but not required to enforce both of the following two rules guaranteeing structured locking.

Let T be a thread and L be a lock. Then:

1. The number of *lock* operations performed by T on L during a method invocation must equal the number of *unlock* operations performed by T on L during the method invocation whether the method invocation completes normally or abruptly.

2. At no point during a method invocation may the number of *unlock* operations performed by T on L since the method invocation exceed the number of *lock* operations performed by T on L since the method invocation.

In less formal terms, during a method invocation every *unlock* operation on L must match some preceding *lock* operation on L.

Note that the locking and unlocking automatically performed by the Java virtual machine when invoking a synchronized method are considered to occur during the calling method's invocation.

8.14 Wait Sets and Notification

Every object, in addition to having an associated lock, has an associated wait set, which is a set of threads. When an object is first created, its wait set is empty.

Wait sets are used by the methods `wait`, `notify`, and `notifyAll` of class `Object`. These methods also interact with the scheduling mechanism for threads.

The method `wait` should be invoked for an object only when the current thread (call it *T*) has already locked the object's lock. Suppose that thread *T* has in fact performed *N* *lock* operations on the object that have not been matched by *unlock* operations on that same object. The `wait` method then adds the current thread to the wait set for the object, disables the current thread for thread scheduling purposes, and performs *N* *unlock* operations on the object to relinquish the lock on it. Locks having been locked by thread *T* on objects other than the one *T* is to wait on are not relinquished. The thread *T* then lies dormant until one of three things happens:

- Some other thread invokes the `notify` method for that object, and thread *T* happens to be the one arbitrarily chosen as the one to notify.

- Some other thread invokes the `notifyAll` method for that object.

- If the call by thread *T* to the `wait` method specified a time-out interval, then the specified amount of real time elapses.

The thread *T* is then removed from the wait set and reenabled for thread scheduling. It then locks the object again (which may involve competing in the usual manner with other threads); once it has gained control of the lock, it performs *N* − *1* additional *lock* operations on that same object and then returns from the invocation of the `wait` method. Thus, on return from the `wait` method, the state of the object's lock is exactly as it was when the `wait` method was invoked.

The `notify` method should be invoked for an object only when the current thread has already locked the object's lock, or an `IllegalMonitorState-Exception` will be thrown. If the wait set for the object is not empty, then some arbitrarily chosen thread is removed from the wait set and reenabled for thread scheduling. (Of course, that thread will not be able to proceed until the current thread relinquishes the object's lock.)

The `notifyAll` method should be invoked for an object only when the current thread has already locked the object's lock, or an `IllegalMonitorState-Exception` will be thrown. Every thread in the wait set for the object is removed from the wait set and reenabled for thread scheduling. (Those threads will not be able to proceed until the current thread relinquishes the object's lock.)

Opcode Mnemonics by Opcode

THIS chapter gives the mapping from Java virtual machine instruction opcodes, including the reserved opcodes (§6.2), to the mnemonics for the instructions represented by those opcodes.

0 (0x00).................................... *nop*	24 (0x18)................................... *dload*
1 (0x01)...................... *aconst_null*	25 (0x19)................................... *aload*
2 (0x02)........................... *iconst_m1*	26 (0x1a) .... *iload_0*
3 (0x03)............................ *iconst_0*	27 (0x1b)............................... *iload_1*
4 (0x04)............................ *iconst_1*	28 (0x1c) .... *iload_2*
5 (0x05)............................ *iconst_2*	29 (0x1d).............................. *iload_3*
6 (0x06)............................ *iconst_3*	30 (0x1e) .... *lload_0*
7 (0x07)............................ *iconst_4*	31 (0x1f)............................... *lload_1*
8 (0x08)............................ *iconst_5*	32 (0x20)............................... *lload_2*
9 (0x09)............................ *lconst_0*	33 (0x21)............................... *lload_3*
10 (0x0a)............................ *lconst_1*	34 (0x22)............................... *fload_0*
11 (0x0b)............................ *fconst_0*	35 (0x23)............................... *fload_1*
12 (0x0c)............................ *fconst_1*	36 (0x24)............................... *fload_2*
13 (0x0d)............................ *fconst_2*	37 (0x25)............................... *fload_3*
14 (0x0e)........................... *dconst_0*	38 (0x26)............................ *dload_0*
15 (0x0f) .... *dconst_1*	39 (0x27)............................*dload_1*
16 (0x10)............................... *bipush*	40 (0x28)............................ *dload_2*
17 (0x11)............................... *sipush*	41 (0x29)............................ *dload_3*
18 (0x12)...................................... *ldc*	42 (0x2a)............................ *aload_0*
19 (0x13)................................ *ldc_w*	43 (0x2b)............................ *aload_1*
20 (0x14)................................ *ldc2_w*	44 (0x2c) .... *aload_2*
21 (0x15)................................. *iload*	45 (0x2d) .... *aload_3*
22 (0x16)................................. *lload*	46 (0x2e) .... *iaload*
23 (0x17)................................. *fload*	47 (0x2f)............................... *laload*

48 (0x30)	*faload*
49 (0x31)	*daload*
50 (0x32)	*aaload*
51 (0x33)	*baload*
52 (0x34)	*caload*
53 (0x35)	*saload*
54 (0x36)	*istore*
55 (0x37)	*lstore*
56 (0x38)	*fstore*
57 (0x39)	*dstore*
58 (0x3a)	*astore*
59 (0x3b)	*istore_0*
60 (0x3c)	*istore_1*
61 (0x3d)	*istore_2*
62 (0x3e)	*istore_3*
63 (0x3f)	*lstore_0*
64 (0x40)	*lstore_1*
65 (0x41)	*lstore_2*
66 (0x42)	*lstore_3*
67 (0x43)	*fstore_0*
68 (0x44)	*fstore_1*
69 (0x45)	*fstore_2*
70 (0x46)	*fstore_3*
71 (0x47)	*dstore_0*
72 (0x48)	*dstore_1*
73 (0x49)	*dstore_2*
74 (0x4a)	*dstore_3*
75 (0x4b)	*astore_0*
76 (0x4c)	*astore_1*
77 (0x4d)	*astore_2*
78 (0x4e)	*astore_3*
79 (0x4f)	*iastore*
80 (0x50)	*lastore*
81 (0x51)	*fastore*
82 (0x52)	*dastore*
83 (0x53)	*aastore*
84 (0x54)	*bastore*
85 (0x55)	*castore*
86 (0x56)	*sastore*
87 (0x57)	*pop*
88 (0x58)	*pop2*

89 (0x59)	*dup*
90 (0x5a)	*dup_x1*
91 (0x5b)	*dup_x2*
92 (0x5c)	*dup2*
93 (0x5d)	*dup2_x1*
94 (0x5e)	*dup2_x2*
95 (0x5f)	*swap*
96 (0x60)	*iadd*
97 (0x61)	*ladd*
98 (0x62)	*fadd*
99 (0x63)	*dadd*
100 (0x64)	*isub*
101 (0x65)	*lsub*
102 (0x66)	*fsub*
103 (0x67)	*dsub*
104 (0x68)	*imul*
105 (0x69)	*lmul*
106 (0x6a)	*fmul*
107 (0x6b)	*dmul*
108 (0x6c)	*idiv*
109 (0x6d)	*ldiv*
110 (0x6e)	*fdiv*
111 (0x6f)	*ddiv*
112 (0x70)	*irem*
113 (0x71)	*lrem*
114 (0x72)	*frem*
115 (0x73)	*drem*
116 (0x74)	*ineg*
117 (0x75)	*lneg*
118 (0x76)	*fneg*
119 (0x77)	*dneg*
120 (0x78)	*ishl*
121 (0x79)	*lshl*
122 (0x7a)	*ishr*
123 (0x7b)	*lshr*
124 (0x7c)	*iushr*
125 (0x7d)	*lushr*
126 (0x7e)	*iand*
127 (0x7f)	*land*
128 (0x80)	*ior*
129 (0x81)	*lor*

130 (0x82)..................................... *ixor*	168 (0xa8) .... *jsr*
131 (0x83)..................................... *lxor*	169 (0xa9) .... *ret*
132 (0x84)..................................... *iinc*	170 (0xaa) .... *tableswitch*
133 (0x85)...................................... *i2l*	171 (0xab) .... *lookupswitch*
134 (0x86)..................................... *i2f*	172 (0xac) .... *ireturn*
135 (0x87)..................................... *i2d*	173 (0xad) .... *lreturn*
136 (0x88)...................................... *l2i*	174 (0xae) .... *freturn*
137 (0x89)..................................... *l2f*	175 (0xaf)............................. *dreturn*
138 (0x8a)..................................... *l2d*	176 (0xb0) .... *areturn*
139 (0x8b)..................................... *f2i*	177 (0xb1) .... *return*
140 (0x8c)..................................... *f2l*	178 (0xb2) .... *getstatic*
141 (0x8d)..................................... *f2d*	179 (0xb3) .... *putstatic*
142 (0x8e)..................................... *d2i*	180 (0xb4) .... *getfield*
143 (0x8f)..................................... *d2l*	181 (0xb5) .... *putfield*
144 (0x90)..................................... *d2f*	182 (0xb6)....................... *invokevirtual*
145 (0x91)..................................... *i2b*	183 (0xb7) .... *invokespecial*
146 (0x92)..................................... *i2c*	184 (0xb8) .... *invokestatic*
147 (0x93)..................................... *i2s*	185 (0xb9) .... *invokeinterface*
148 (0x94)................................... *lcmp*	186 (0xba) .... *xxxunusedxxx*[1]
149 (0x95).................................... *fcmpl*	187 (0xbb)................................. *new*
150 (0x96).................................. *fcmpg*	188 (0xbc) .... *newarray*
151 (0x97)................................. *dcmpl*	189 (0xbd) .... *anewarray*
152 (0x98)................................ *dcmpg*	190 (0xbe) .... *arraylength*
153 (0x99).................................... *ifeq*	191 (0xbf)............................... *athrow*
154 (0x9a) .... *ifne*	192 (0xc0) .... *checkcast*
155 (0x9b) .... *iflt*	193 (0xc1) .... *instanceof*
156 (0x9c).................................... *ifge*	194 (0xc2) .... *monitorenter*
157 (0x9d).................................... *ifgt*	195 (0xc3) .... *monitorexit*
158 (0x9e) .... *ifle*	196 (0xc4) .... *wide*
159 (0x9f) .... *if_icmpeq*	197 (0xc5) .... *multianewarray*
160 (0xa0)......................... *if_icmpne*	198 (0xc6) .... *ifnull*
161 (0xa1) .... *if_icmplt*	199 (0xc7) .... *ifnonnull*
162 (0xa2) .... *if_icmpge*	200 (0xc8) .... *goto_w*
163 (0xa3) .... *if_icmpgt*	201 (0xc9) .... *jsr_w*
164 (0xa4)......................... *if_icmple*	Reserved opcodes:
165 (0xa5) .... *if_acmpeq*	202 (0xca) .... *breakpoint*
166 (0xa6)......................... *if_acmpne*	254 (0xfe)........................... *impdep1*
167 (0xa7).................................... *goto*	255 (0xff) *impdep2*

---

[1] For historical reasons, opcode value 186 is not used.

Appendix

Summary of Clarifications and Amendments

THIS appendix discusses the differences between the original version of *The Java*[TM] *Virtual Machine Specification* and the present revision. Its purpose is twofold: to summarize what changes have been made and to explain why they were made.

Throughout this appendix, we refer to the original version of *The Java*[TM] *Virtual Machine Specification* (that is, the first published version of this book) as the *original specification* or *the original specification of the Java virtual machine*. We refer to the current book as the *revised specification*. We denote the first edition of *The Java*[TM] *Language Specification* as simply *The Java*[TM] *Language Specification*.

The revised specification seeks to clarify points that gave rise to misunderstanding and to correct ambiguities, errors, and omissions in the original specification.

Except for the treatment of floating-point computation, the differences between the revised specification and its predecessor have no effect on valid programs written in the Java programming language. The revisions influence only how the virtual machine handles incorrect programs. In many of these instances, most implementations did not implement the original specification. The revised specification documents the intended behavior.

The most obvious changes are in the specification of floating-point types and operations; `class` file verification; initialization, loading, and linking; and the method invocation instructions. In addition, several other important corrections have been made.

The revised specification also fixes errors or clarifies issues that were brought to our attention by readers of the original specification.

While we have made every effort to correct as many problems as possible, we recognize that additional improvements would benefit this specification. In particular, we believe that the description of class file verification should be further refined, ideally to the point of constituting a formal specification. We anticipate that future revisions will address remaining weaknesses and correct any newly reported bugs, while retaining unchanged the semantics of the Java programming language.

The following sections discuss the changes to the original specification in greater detail and explain why the changes were necessary.

Floating-Point Types and Operations

The original specification required that all single- and double-precision floating-point calculations round their results to the IEEE 754 single- and double-precision formats, respectively. The revised specification permits additional floating-point calculations to be done using IEEE 754 extended precision formats.

As a result of this change, implementations on processors that more naturally and efficiently support extended precision formats and floating-point operations on extended precision formats can deliver better performance for floating-point calculations. Implementations on processors that naturally and efficiently implement IEEE 754 single- and double-precision operations as mandated by the original specification may continue to do so. The floating-point behavior of any Java virtual machine implementation that conforms to the original specification also conforms to the revised specification.

Changes to class File Verification

The most important clarification on the topic of class file verification is that every Java virtual machine implementation must in fact perform verification. This is stated unambiguously in the *The Java™ Language Specification*. The original specification of the Java virtual machine contained several misleading sentences that led some readers to conclude that verification was optional.

The discussion of the class file format in Chapter 4 also corrects a number of small errors in the original specification. The most significant of these corrections are:

- Interfaces can contain methods other than class or interface initialization methods (`<clinit>` methods).

- The class reference in a `CONSTANT_Fieldref_info` can be an interface type since interfaces can contain `static` fields.

- Methods that are `native` or `abstract` cannot have a `Code` attribute.

- Multiple declarations of a field or method with the same name and descriptor are illegal.

All of the preceding changes correct misstatements in the original specification that were obviously untrue. In addition, `class` file verification no longer bans attempts to invoke `abstract` methods; see a complete discussion of this issue later in this appendix.

Initialization

The Java[TM] *Language Specification* and the original specification of the Java virtual machine contradict each other on the question of whether the element type of an array type must be initialized when an instance of the array type is created. *The Java*[TM] *Language Specification* specifies that the element type should be initialized in this case, whereas the original specification of the Java virtual machine states that it should not. We have resolved this contradiction in favor of the original Java virtual machine specification. *The Java*[TM] *Language Specification* is thus in error, and will be corrected in its next edition.

The evident confusion over the circumstances triggering initialization led us to reword the specification of when initialization occurs (§2.17.4). However, this reworded specification is equivalent to the original.

One of the original requirements was that a class would be initialized the first time one of its constructors is invoked. In the Java programming language, constructor invocation constitutes instance creation. Furthermore, since no instance method can be invoked if no instances exist, it is clear that the requirement that a class be initialized the first time one of its methods is invoked is relevant only for `static` methods. By similar reasoning, the requirement that a class be initialized if any of its fields is accessed applies only to `static` fields.

The original specification did not accurately describe the circumstances that would trigger initialization at the Java virtual machine level (see discussion later in this appendix). Section 5.5 now gives a simple and precise definition in terms of Java virtual machine instructions.

Loading and Linking

Chapter 5, "Loading, Linking, and Initializing," has been completely rewritten (and retitled). Chapter 5 of the original specification was erroneous in several important respects. The new chapter corrects these errors and tries to be both clearer and more precise. The organization of the revised chapter closely follows the structure of the corresponding sections in Chapter 12 of *The Java™ Language Specification*.

The key changes include the following:

- *Clarifying that loading a class causes its superinterfaces to be resolved.*

  The description of class loading in the original specification did not state that resolving a class required its superinterfaces to be resolved. This was an error in early Java virtual machine implementations that has been corrected.

- *Clarifying that resolution does not necessarily imply further linking.*

  The description of CONSTANT_Class_info resolution in Section 5.1.1 of the original specification implied that resolution of a reference to a class causes it to be linked. While this was true of Sun's Java virtual machine implementation, the description was more restrictive than *The Java™ Language Specification*, which clearly states that Java virtual machine implementations have flexibility in the timing of linking activities. The revised specification of the Java virtual machine agrees with *The Java™ Language Specification* on this issue.

- *Clarifying that resolution does not imply initialization.*

  The description of CONSTANT_Class_info resolution in Section 5.1.1 of the original specification implied that resolution of a class causes it to be initialized. However, the original specification also included the contradictory statement that initialization should occur only on the first active use of a class. In a Java virtual machine implementation that performs lazy resolution, the distinction is subtle. In other implementations the distinction is much clearer. For example, eager resolution is explicitly allowed by *The Java™ Language Specification*. If resolution always provoked initialization, such an implementation would be forced to perform eager initialization, in clear contradiction to *The Java™ Language Specification*. The contradiction is resolved by decoupling resolution from initialization.

A closely related problem is the statement in Section 5.1.2 of the original specification that the `loadClass` method of class `ClassLoader` can cause initialization to occur if its second argument is `true`. This contradicts *The Java™ Language Specification*, which states that only loading and linking occur in this case. Again, the contradiction has been resolved to conform to *The Java™ Language Specification*, for essentially the same reasons.

- *Clarifying that class loading uses `ClassLoader.loadClass(String)`.*

The original specification stated that when loading a class or interface using a user-defined class loader the Java virtual machine invokes the two-argument method `ClassLoader.loadClass(String, boolean)`. The purpose of the `boolean` argument was to indicate whether linking should take place. However, it was noted on page 144 of the original specification that this interface was likely to change. It was recognized that placing responsibility for linking on the class loader was both inappropriate and unreliable.

Beginning with JDK release 1.1, linking is handled directly by the Java virtual machine. An additional method `loadClass(String)` has also been added to class `ClassLoader`. This method may similarly be invoked by the Java virtual machine. The revised specification defines class loading in terms of the new method. The two argument version is still retained in the Java 2 platform v1.2 in the interests of compatibility, but plays no role in the revised specification.

- *Making explicit requirements for type safe class loading.*

The subtleties of type safe linkage in the presence of multiple, user-defined class loaders were not sufficiently appreciated when the original specification was written. It has subsequently become clear that a detailed description of loading constraints on runtime types is warranted. Of course, the presence of loading constraints is observable only by invalid programs.

- *Specifying explicitly the rules for access control.*

These rules follow from *The Java™ Language Specification*, but were left implicit in the original specification. The rules correspond to the behavior of existing implementations.

- *Indicating that more appropriate exceptions are thrown when a class or interface is invalid.*

Section 5.1.1 of the original specification states that a `NoClassDefFound-Error` should be thrown if the representation of a class or interface is invalid. However, both *The Java™ Language Specification* and Section 2.16.2 of the original specification state that a `ClassFormatError` is thrown in this case. Clearly, a `ClassFormatError` is more appropriate.

- *Clarifying that the class hierarchy is searched when resolving fields and methods.*

The original specification was unclear as to whether, during method or field resolution, the referenced field had to be declared in the exact class referenced or could be inherited. This led to variations among Java virtual machine implementations and inconsistency between *The Java*™ *Virtual Machine Specification* and *The Java*™ *Language Specification*. The revised specification gives a more precise description that agrees with the behavior of most implementations, but not with *The Java*™ *Language Specification*. *The Java*™ *Language Specification* will be corrected in its next edition.

 This choice gives programmers the flexibility of moving methods and fields in the class hierarchy while retaining binary compatibility with previous implementations of their programs.

- *Clarifying that an `AbstractMethodError` may not be raised during preparation.*

The Java™ *Language Specification* requires that adding a method to an interface be a binary compatible change. However, Sections 5.1.1 and 2.16.3 of the original specification require that preparation reject a class that has an `abstract` method unless that class is itself `abstract`. The latter requirement contradicts the former.

 Consider the case of an interface *I* implemented by a class *C* that is not `abstract`. If a new method is added to *I*, *C* must implement it. However, if an old version of *C* is used together with the new version of *I* at run time, *C* will indeed have an `abstract` method. If preparation were to raise an `AbstractMethodError` in this case, adding a method to *I* would not have been a binary compatible change, since it would have resulted in a link-time failure. Consequently, the check at preparation time has been dropped. This change has implications for method invocation, as discussed below.

- *Clarifying that interface method resolution may raise exceptions.*

The description in Section 5.3 of the original specification omitted the checks required during interface method resolution. These checks (that the referenced interface exists and that the referenced method exists in that interface) are required by *The Java*™ *Language Specification* and are performed by most widely used implementations of the Java virtual machine. The checks are documented in Section 5.4.3.4 of the revised specification.

- *Specifying events triggering class or interface initialization.*

  As a consequence of the decoupling of class and interface initialization from resolution, it became necessary to specify when the Java virtual machine triggers initialization. This specification is given in Section 5.5 of the revised specification. As noted earlier, this description agrees with the specification of the events at the Java programming language level triggering initialization, given in Section 2.17.4 of the revised specification.

Changes to Method Invocation

The following changes have been made to the specification of the method invocation instructions. Many of these are direct consequences of the changes described in the previous section; others are designed merely to clarify the presentation.

- *Reliance on method tables, which was merely illustrative, has been removed.*

  The descriptions of the method invocation instructions made use of the well-known concept of a method dispatch table. The method tables were used as expository devices, but unfortunately many readers mistakenly thought that the use of such tables was a requirement of the specification. To clarify this point, a lookup algorithm is given instead.

- *Link-time and runtime exceptions are used consistently.*

  The original specification sometimes listed exceptions that could be raised by an instruction according to their position in the exception hierarchy, rather than by when they might occur. This usage was inconsistent and sometimes erroneous.

  The intent of the categories Linking Exceptions and Runtime Exceptions at the end of each instruction description is to describe at what phase of execution an error will be thrown. An important example of this is the treatment of `UnsatisfiedLinkError`. The descriptions of all method invocation instructions specify that `native` methods are bound at run time if they have not been bound already. If the binding fails, an `UnsatisfiedLinkError` is thrown. However, `UnsatisfiedLinkError` is consistently listed in the instruction descriptions of the original specification as a Linking Exception. To make it clear that the exception is actually thrown at run time, the revised specification lists `UnsatisfiedLinkError` as a Runtime Exception in the descriptions of all the method invocation instructions.

Another instance of this problem was in the description of the *invoke-interface* instruction. Most of the exceptions listed in the original specification of *invokeinterface* as Linking Exceptions actually occurred at run time. They are listed in the revised specification as Runtime Exceptions.

- *It is possible to attempt to invoke* `abstract` *methods at run time.*

  This is a direct result of the elimination of the `abstract` method check during class or interface preparation, as discussed earlier. While in many cases the use of an `abstract` method on a class that is not `abstract` will still result in a link-time error, it is possible to construct cases where the error will not occur until run time.

  Consider an `abstract` class *A* with `abstract` method `foo` and concrete subclass *B*. If *B* neglects to implement `foo`, then a method

  ```
  void bar(A a) {a.foo();}
  ```

  will fail if invoked upon an instance of *B*. This will not be detected at link time, but at run time. As a result, *invokeinterface* and *invokevirtual* may raise an `AbstractMethodError` at run time.

- *The invokeinterface instruction specification has changed.*

  The description of the *invokeinterface* instruction now states that the target of the method invocation must support the referenced interface. This is required by *The Java*™ *Language Specification* and has been a property of all major Java virtual machine implementations for some time.

- *The description of the invokespecial instruction has been clarified.*

  The second bullet on page 261 of the original specification was redundant and has been removed. The other bullets have been reordered, and the fact that ordinarily the resolved method is selected for execution has been asserted explicitly. These changes do not alter the specification in any way, but serve only to make the text more understandable.

Nested Classes

Nested classes were introduced into the Java programming language after the original specification of the Java virtual machine and the first edition of *The Java*™ *Language Specification* were printed. The `Innerclasses` and `Synthetic` attributes, described in the revised specification in Section 4.7.5 and Section 4.7.6, respectively, were added in JDK release 1.1 in order to support nested classes.

Unfortunately, we have not been able to include a description of nested classes in the Java programming language overview given in Chapter 2. A complete description will be included in the next edition of the *The Java*™ *Language Specification*. Until then, refer to the documentation on the World Wide Web at `http://java.sun.com/products/jdk/1.1/docs/guide/innerclasses`.

Chapter 9 of Original Specification Deleted

Chapter 9, "An Optimization," of the original specification documented an optimization technique used in Sun's contemporary Java virtual machine implementation. The original specification was clear that this chapter and the technique it described were not part of the Java virtual machine specification. However, the chapter provided an example of the flexibility that the Java virtual machine specification intends to give implementors. This information about Sun's implementation was also considered possibly useful to writers of tools such as debuggers.

The chapter has been removed from the revised specification. The optimization technique it described is now well understood. More important, the technique exactly as described is not used by many of the Java virtual machine implementations, including some of Sun's, developed since the original specification was published. The value of the chapter to tool writers has diminished for the same reason. Thus, the chapter is now best seen as documentation for a specific Java virtual machine implementation, making it inappropriate for the Java virtual machine specification.

Other Issues

- In light of our experience with several releases of the Java platform, the interpretation of the version numbers defined as part of the `class` file format has changed. The major version number is now intended to correspond to new platform major releases (for instance, the Java 2 platform, Standard Edition, v1.2), while the minor version number may be used to represent release levels of platform implementations (for instance, the Java 2 SDK, Standard Edition, v1.2.1). Since the first public release of the Java platform, all `class` files have been generated using major version number 45 and minor version number 3. Hence, no existing well-formed `class` file is affected by this change in interpretation.

- Corresponding to the change in version number interpretation, the actual version numbers accepted by new implementations of the Java virtual machine have changed. Existing binaries are not affected by this change because these new virtual machine implementations will continue to accept `class` files with the historically used version numbers.

- It is now clear that reflective operations can cause class initialization. The original specification did not discuss the topic of reflection at all, since reflection did not yet exist in the Java programming language. Many subsequently added reflective operations correspond to language-level constructs that do require initialization and similarly must cause initialization. This is documented in the revised specification.

- Class finalization has been removed from the Java programming language and, consequently, from the revised specification as well. Class finalization had never been implemented, so the change had no effect on existing programs. The effects of class finalization are obtainable via instance finalization.

- The rules for class unloading have been clarified. The description of class unloading in the original specification gave, by way of illustration, certain necessary conditions for unloading a class. These conditions were misinterpreted as being sufficient conditions. This led to implementations that unloaded classes usable by a running program. The revised specification describes the precise circumstances under which classes may be unloaded.

- The instructions *aastore, checkcast*, and *instanceof* contain a subtyping algorithm. The original version of this algorithm was flawed in that it did not cover the case where two arrays whose component types were interfaces were being compared. The revised specification corrects this.

- The descriptions of the *getfield* and *putfield* instructions have been made less implementation specific. In particular, the revised specification eliminates the notion of particular field widths and offsets.

- The descriptions of the instructions *putfield* and *putstatic* now include a specification of their behavior when a field is `final`. This documents the behavior of existing implementations.

- The description of the process of throwing an exception in Section 3.10 has been made clearer and more precise.

- The descriptions of the various return instructions and *athrow* failed to note that these instructions could raise an `IllegalMonitorStateException`. The original specification implicitly allowed for the raising of such an exception as a consequence of Section 8.5:

> An *unlock* operation by thread T on lock L may occur only if the number of preceding *unlock* operations by T on L is strictly less than the number of preceding *lock* operations by T on L.

and Section 8.13:

> If execution of the method's body is ever completed, either normally or abruptly, an *unlock* operation is automatically performed on that same lock.

However, this had not been stated clearly and explicitly.

- Structured use of locks may now be enforced. The description of locking in `synchronized` statements given in Section 8.13 of the original specification was erroneous. It stated the following:

  > If execution of the body is ever completed, either normally or abruptly, an *unlock* operation is automatically performed on that same lock.

  This is a property of programs written in the Java programming language, guaranteed by correct compilers for the Java programming language; it is not guaranteed by the Java virtual machine. However, programs do indeed make structured use of locking, and Java virtual machine implementations may rely on and enforce this property. The appropriate rules are given in the revised version of Section 8.13. As a consequence of those rules, `IllegalMonitor-StateException` exceptions may be raised by the return instructions and *athrow*, and by the method invocation instructions when invoking `native` methods.

- The `Deprecated` attribute, an attribute introduced in JDK release 1.1 to support the `@deprecated` tag in documentation comments, has been specified. The presence of a `Deprecated` attribute does not alter the semantics of a class or interface.

Index

threads (*continued*)
  shared (*continued*)
    variables, mechanisms for handling, 31
  synchronization issues during
    initialization, 52
Throwable class
  exceptions as instances or
    subclasses of, 40
throwing
  exceptions, athrow, 186
  throw statement, as exception cause, 41
  Throwable as exception hierarchy
    root, 43
  Throwable exceptions as instances
    or subclasses, 40
timing
  dependencies, in concurrent
    programming, 59
transient modifier
  See also ACC_TRANSIENT flag
  definition, 30
try-catch-finally statement
  See also exceptions
  as exception handling statement, 79
  exception handling use of, 42
try-finally statement
  See also exceptions
  exception handling use of, 42
  Sun's Java compiler output
    characteristics, 149

U

u1
  as class file data type, 93
u2
  as class file data type, 93
u4
  as class file data type, 93
underflow
  floating-point, Java virtual machine
    handling, 85
  integer data types, not signaled by Java
    virtual machine, 85
Unicode
  bibliographic reference, 5
  characteristics, 5

UnknownError
  as Java virtual machine error, 46
unloading
  class or interface, 57
UnsatisfiedLinkError
  See also binding; LinkageError;
    native method
  definition, 45
  thrown by
    invokeinterface, 282
    invokespecial, 287
    invokestatic, 290
    invokevirtual, 293
UnsupportedClassVersionError
  definition, 49
UTF-8 format
  See also CONSTANT_Utf8_info structure
  bibliographic reference, 111
  standard, differences between Java virtual
    machine UTF-8 strings and, 111

V

V character
  meaning in method descriptor, 102
value set conversion
  definition, 77
values
  concrete, mapping symbolic references
    to, as part of resolution, 165
  default, 14
  floating-point, 7
  primitive, 7
  return, frame use for, 72
variables
  See also constants; literals
  array type, 38
  definition, 13
  double nonatomic treatment of,
    memory operations on, 402
  initial values of, 14
  interaction with locks, rules about, 403
  kinds of, 13
  local
    accessing, structural constraints on
      instructions, 137

Z

Mr. Lindholm's mother surely has many wonderful qualities, but we doubt anyone would consider her a public interface to the Java Runtime Interpreter.

Sun Microsystems, Inc.'s Reply in Support of Its Motion for Preliminary Injunction Under 17 U.S.C. § 502

The Addison-Wesley Java™ Series

Ken Arnold · James Gosling

The Java™ Programming Language
Second Edition

ISBN 0-201-31006-6

Mary Campione · Kathy Walrath

The Java™ Tutorial
Second Edition
Object-Oriented Programming
for the Internet

ISBN 0-201-31007-4

Campione · Walrath · Huml · Tutorial Team

The Java™ Tutorial
Continued
The Rest of the JDK™

ISBN 0-201-48558-3

Patrick Chan

The Java™ Developers ALMANAC 1999

ISBN 0-201-43298-6

Patrick Chan · Rosanna Lee

The Java™ Class Libraries
Second Edition, Volume 2
java.applet java.awt java.beans

ISBN 0-201-31003-1

Patrick Chan · Rosanna Lee · Douglas Kramer

The Java™ Class Libraries
Second Edition, Volume 1
java.io java.lang java.math
java.net java.text java.util

ISBN 0-201-31002-3

Patrick Chan · Rosanna Lee · Douglas Kramer

The Java™ Class Libraries
Second Edition, Volume 1
1.2 Supplement

ISBN 0-201-48552-4

James Gosling · Bill Joy · Guy Steele

The Java™ Language Specification

ISBN 0-201-63451-1

James Gosling · Frank Yellin · The Java Team

The Java™ Application Programming Interface, Volume 1
Core Packages

ISBN 0-201-63453-8

James Gosling · Frank Yellin · The Java Team

The Java™ Application Programming Interface, Volume 2
Window Toolkit and Applets

ISBN 0-201-63459-7

Graham Hamilton · Rick Cattell · Maydene Fisher

JDBC™ Database Access with Java™
A Tutorial and Annotated Reference

ISBN 0-201-30995-5

Jonni Kanerva

The Java™ FAQ

ISBN 0-201-63456-2

Doug Lea

Concurrent Programming in Java™
Design Principles and Patterns

ISBN 0-201-69581-2

Tim Lindholm · Frank Yellin

The Java™ Virtual Machine Specification

ISBN 0-201-63452-X

Henry Sowizral · Kevin Rushforth · Michael Deering

The Java™ 3D API Specification

ISBN 0-201-32576-4

Please see our web site (http://www.awl.com/cseng/javaseries)
for more information on these titles.

Addison-Wesley Computer and Engineering Publishing Group

How to Interact with Us

1. Visit our Web site

http://www.awl.com/cseng

When you think you've read enough, there's always more content for you at Addison-Wesley's web site. Our web site contains a directory of complete product information including:

- Chapters
- Exclusive author interviews
- Links to authors' pages
- Tables of contents
- Source code

You can also discover what tradeshows and conferences Addison-Wesley will be attending, read what others are saying about our titles, and find out where and when you can meet our authors and have them sign your book.

2. Subscribe to Our Email Mailing Lists

Subscribe to our electronic mailing lists and be the first to know when new books are publishing. Here's how it works: Sign up for our electronic mailing at **http://www.awl.com/cseng/mailinglists.html**. Just select the subject areas that interest you and you will receive notification via email when we publish a book in that area.

3. Contact Us via Email

cepubprof@awl.com
Ask general questions about our books.
Sign up for our electronic mailing lists.
Submit corrections for our web site.

bexpress@awl.com
Request an Addison-Wesley catalog.
Get answers to questions regarding your order or our products.

innovations@awl.com
Request a current Innovations Newsletter.

webmaster@awl.com
Send comments about our web site.

mikeh@awl.com
Submit a book proposal.
Send errata for an Addison-Wesley book.

cepubpublicity@awl.com
Request a review copy for a member of the media interested in reviewing new Addison-Wesley titles.

We encourage you to patronize the many fine retailers who stock Addison-Wesley titles. Visit our online directory and stores near you or visit our online store: //store.awl.com/ or call 800-824-7799.

son Wesley Longman
ter and Engineering Publishing Group
ob Way, Reading, Massachusetts 01867 USA
944-3700 • FAX 781-942-3076